...rth of England and has b...
Hebrides. In the early 1970s he edite...
Out before joining the radical weekly ...t *Highland Free Press*, for which newspaper he is still a columnist. His book *The Soap Man* was shortlisted for the Saltire Book of the Year award, and *Calum's Road* was shortlisted for the Royal Society of Literature's Ondaatje Prize.

'A warm-hearted book about a uniquely British triumph, a resource of a depth unrivalled anywhere in the world ... His achievement, beneath the joy of the detail, teeming with Dickensian energy, is to suggest that the census is also a story of enterprise, vision, trust and reliability – a force of enlightenment. This is not a dense book. Rather it is light, wry and compassionate' *The Times*

'Compelling ... Hutchinson's book is a sobering reminder of how often we have ignored facts and listened to panic merchants' *Sunday Telegraph*

'Using the census records as the basis for a history of Britain is clearly an excellent idea for a book. Even so, Roger Hutchinson has carried it out particularly well ... Happily, too, he manages to do this without the result ever becoming merely a blizzard of statistics. Admittedly, if you have ever wondered how many Brits made artificial flowers for a living in 1851, then here's where you'll find out. (Spoiler alert: it was 3,510.) Yet Hutchinson's sharp eye for the telling detail, his deft use of individual stories to illustrate the wider trends and his willingness to throw in any vaguely related facts that he (rightly) thinks we might find interesting make this a book to read with much pleasure' *Spectator*

'Filled with interesting titbits, the book burrows into the official records to present a story that is sometimes

THE BUTCHER THE BAKER THE CANDLESTICK MAKER

The Story of Britain through
its Census, since 1801

ROGER HUTCHINSON

ABACUS

ABACUS

First published in Great Britain in 2017 by Little, Brown
This paperback edition published in 2017 by Abacus

1 3 5 7 9 10 8 6 4 2

A CIP catalogue record for this book
is available from the British Library.

ISBN 978-0-349-14122-0

Typeset in Bembo by M Rules
Printed and bound in Great Britain by
Clays Ltd, St Ives plc

Papers used by Abacus are from well-managed forests
and other responsible sources.

MIX
Paper from
responsible sources
FSC® C104740

Abacus
An imprint of
Little, Brown Book Group
Carmelite House
50 Victoria Embankment
London EC4Y 0DZ

An Hachette UK Company
www.hachette.co.uk

www.littlebrown.co.uk

To Nan Hutchinson
who has appeared in a few of them

Contents

Preface

If the national census is a snapshot of the British Isles taken every ten years, it proves that cameras sometimes lie. The lens is not always in focus and the photographer's hand occasionally shakes.

That should not surprise us. A survey which since the beginning of the nineteenth century has attempted to offer basic biographies of tens of millions of people cannot be expected to achieve total accuracy. As those biographies are based on autobiographies, on individuals' accounts of their own and their families' and their lodgers' life stories, the potential for distortion is amplified.

Not everybody is who they claim to be. People forget. People also fib about their job, their marital status and their age. Some people – not many, but some – evade offering their autobiographies to the authorities. Some people are ignored. In 1851, for instance, was every urchin in every East End rookery counted? In 2011, was every person trying to catch some hungry sleep in a London shop doorway recorded by a census enumerator?

The surprise is more that the British census has, over its 210 years, managed to document what can best be called the nature of the population of the United Kingdom with a remarkably high level of accuracy. Its success can be understated; its achievements taken for granted. That success is due largely to its honest and reasonable subjects who, by and large, have been given no overwhelming reasons to mistrust or conceal themselves from their governments.

It is also thanks to a certain national genius for imaginative organisation. The British are fond of presenting themselves as muddling amateurishly along while such people as the Germans are contrarily obsessed by neatness, clarity and order. Much, although not all, of British history suggests that the opposite is true. Those consummate, dedicated and insatiably curious social statisticians and national census-takers John Rickman, William Donnelly, George Graham, William Farr and William Dunbar were from the British Isles, not Bavaria.

One result has been a series of decennial surveys which are a uniquely dependable historical source: possibly the most reliable such resource in the world. That was once a guarded secret of professional and academic historians. In the age of the internet, when virtually every surviving and permissible census return and report is accessible online, it has become a popular delight.

This book is the result of a realisation that if the census first taken in 1801 can be trusted to trace the histories of families, as presently occurs daily in households throughout the land, it can also trace a history of the nation.

The term 'a history' is considered and advised. Apart from the fact that there can be no such definite article as 'the history' of anything, the only certain way of offering in print the national census's history of the United Kingdom since 1801 would be to republish every single one of several million pages of documents. A commercial publisher would not do that, because – trust me – you would not buy or read it. You would not be able to carry it home.

A great deal of filtering and the exercise of personal preference and prejudice, of the kind which actual census takers only occasionally permit themselves, has therefore been involved in researching and then writing *The Butcher, the Baker, the Candlestick Maker.* I have tried to work chiefly on the premise that as the national census is by definition a gazetteer of individual citizens, it can best offer an auto-biography of my country, the United Kingdom, through examples of those citizens' own lives.

That has led to my frequent intrusion into the affairs of ordinary families I have never personally encountered, people who have never previously appeared in published history and whose descendants are probably still alive. In at least a couple of cases my revelations might cause dismay. For what it's worth, with the possible exception of William Calcraft, who may have enjoyed his profession of public executioner a little too much for comfort, I am opposed to making judgements on the lives and careers of those of our ancestors who appear in this book. At this point in time we should be quicker to understand than condemn.

Without the financial and moral support of Creative Scotland in my own country, this book would never have been conceived. I hope that I have repaid their faith.

I owe many thanks to the staff, past and present, of institutions such as the various General Register Offices and their modern equivalents, to Cambridge University Library, and to every single commissioner or clerk who has laboured with a quill pen or a computer to compile the British censuses.

I am also in debt to several other people who are, at the time of writing, still alive. My agent Stan is one of them.

Richard Beswick of Little, Brown is another. I am, finally, luckier than I have known to have such an enviable family and such valuable friends, particularly in Cambridge and London and in my lifelong homes of Skye and Raasay.

Roger Hutchinson, Raasay, 2017

1

A Perfect Man

In 1800 the poet Charles Lamb acquired a new home and a new neighbour. Lamb had moved into an 'airy' attic apartment in Mitre Court Buildings, an Elizabethan tenement in the City of London from which he could sit up in bed and watch the white sails of trading ships glide down the River Thames.

The 25-year-old Lamb was in poor physical and mental health, and despite the view from his bed he was not enamoured of the draughty and damp upper storeys of Mitre Court Buildings. A genial older friend named George Dyer realised that he knew another resident of the quadrangle and introduced his two associates – 'George brings all sorts of people together.'

John Rickman consequently erupted into the life of Charles Lamb, who wrote delightedly to yet another friend:

> This Rickman lives in our buildings, immediately opposite our house; the finest fellow to drop in a' nights, about nine or ten o'clock – cold bread and cheese time – just in the wishing time of the night, when you wish for

somebody to come in, without a distinct idea of a probable anybody. Just in the nick, neither too early to be tedious nor too late to sit a reasonable time.

He is a most pleasant hand; a fine, rattling fellow; has gone through life laughing at solemn apes; himself hugely literate, oppressively full of information in all stuff of conversation, from matter of fact to Xenophon and Plato; can talk Greek with Porson, politics with Thelwall, conjecture with George Dyer, nonsense with me, and anything with anybody; a great farmer, somewhat concerned in an agricultural magazine; reads no poetry but Shakspeare, very intimate with Southey; loves George Dyer; thoroughly penetrates into the ridiculous, wherever found; understands the first time (a great desideratum in common minds), you need never twice speak to him; does not want explanations, translations, limitations, as Professor Godwin does when you make an assertion; up to anything; down to everything; whatever sapit hominem.

A perfect man. All this farrago, which must perplex you to read, and has put me to a little trouble to select! only proves how impossible it is to describe a pleasant hand. You must see Rickman to know him, for he is a species in one. A new class. An exotic, any slip of which I am proud to put in my garden-pot. The clearestheaded fellow. Fullest of matter, with least verbosity. If there be any alloy in my fortune to have met with such a man, it is that he commonly divides his time between town and country, having some foolish family ties at Christchurch, by which means he can only gladden our London hemisphere with returns of light.

Porson, Thelwall, Dyer, Southey . . . that was an interesting assembly. Richard Porson was the Regius Professor of Greek at Cambridge University, John Thelwall a radical journalist and orator who six years earlier, following a period of incarceration in the Tower of London, had been tried and acquitted of treason. George Dyer was both an eminent classicist and an early socialist who in 1793 had written *Complaints of the Poor People of England*, while Robert Southey was a romantic poet who had been close to Rickman since they had first met in Hampshire in 1797.

The 'clearestheaded fellow' John Rickman was twenty-nine years old when he was introduced to Charles Lamb at Mitre Court Buildings in 1800. Within less than a year he would have established the decennial survey for which he would always be remembered: the national census of the British Isles.

Rickman was born in the village of Newburn in Northumberland on 22 August 1771, a son of the Reverend Thomas Rickman, a Hampshire man who had served as a Church of England pastor in the Upper Tyne Valley since 1766. When it was first properly enumerated in his 1821 census John Rickman may have been interested to note that the parish of Newburn, which consisted of fourteen villages from Black-Callerton to tiny Woolsington, had a population of 4080, almost a thousand of whom lived in Newburn itself.

Outside the largest settlement of Newburn the great majority of parishioners still worked in agriculture, as had been the case when John Rickman was a boy and the area was noted as a supplier of vegetables to Newcastle upon Tyne. But by 1821 increasing quantities of coal were being mined in Newburn village and a large steelworks was about to be established. The industrial revolution remodelled the place and its people. Fifty years after John Rickman's birth 272 families in Newburn were employed in trade, manufacture or handicrafts; only twenty-five still grew vegetables for the Newcastle markets.

By 1821 the Rickman family was long gone from Newburn. In 1776 the Reverend Thomas returned with his family to the south of England, first to Compton in his native Hampshire and then in 1780 to the village of Ash, just across the Hampshire border in western Surrey. The county town of Ash was Guildford and so in 1781, at the age of ten, having spent his first decade in three different English counties, John Rickman was sent to Guildford Royal Grammar School.

Seven years later, in 1788, John went up to Oxford University. He applied himself more diligently than his friend Robert Southey, who later said that all he had learned at Oxford was 'a little swimming . . . and a little boating'.

After four years Rickman left Oxford with his degree and returned to a society at war and in convulsion. The French Revolution of 1789 inspired men and women, particularly the young, throughout the rest of Europe to espouse such radical beliefs as had caused John Thelwall to be imprisoned in the Tower of London on a charge of treason, had led George Dyer to revive the cause of the English poor and had provoked Robert Southey to write his famous anti-war poem 'After Blenheim', as well as a lengthy homage to the medieval peasant insurrectionist Wat Tyler: 'On, on to Freedom; feel but your own strength, / Be but resolved, and these destructive tyrants / Shall shrink before your vengeance.' Rickman himself would recall in middle age that 'I was such an Oliverian' – a Cromwellian republican – 'in my time at Oxford as to have obtained the agnomen of Old

Nol . . . ' Many of those young radicals, including Rickman, would later turn to the political right, but in the 1790s an anti-royalist and anti-clerical revolutionary virus had drifted across the Channel and was in the British air.

That contagion dissuaded the young John Rickman from following his father into the Church. He would later write that he had '(somewhat to my cost) declined telling lies once a week for hire'. In the absence of another vocation, he resorted to his ancestral home at Christchurch, which was then in the New Forest region of the County of Southampton, as Hampshire was officially known until 1959. He immersed himself in his grandfather's large library, worked as a private tutor to the sons of the local plutocracy and, despite a lifelong aversion to writing, laboured on several essays, one of which would shortly change the history of Great Britain. He was joined in Christchurch in 1796 by his retired father, who would remain there until his death in 1809. Those were years of frustration and 'reasonable misery' for John Rickman. They would soon be over.

In the summer of 1797 Robert Southey went to live in the village of Burton, two miles from Christchurch. Rickman's 1821 census would assess the borough of Christchurch, of which Burton was a part, as having a total population of 4644 agriculturalists and tradespeople. It would have been no larger and not much different twenty years earlier. It was all but inevitable that Robert Southey and John Rickman would meet.

When they did, each impressed the other. Southey found Rickman to be 'a sensible young man, of rough but mild manners, and very seditious'. The seditious Rickman was in his turn delighted to befriend the author of 'After Blenheim' – the man who had, with his fellow poet Samuel Taylor Coleridge, three years earlier developed the egalitarian social concept they christened pantisocracy. Southey and Rickman would be kindred spirits until death divided them.

In 1800 Southey left England for Portugal. In April of the same year, armed with a newfound confidence and a list of Southey's contacts, Rickman left Christchurch for London. One of his first calls was upon the good-natured classicist and social facilitator George Dyer. Within a few days, Dyer had found Rickman a job.

The Commercial and Agricultural Magazine was launched in August 1799 by a Paternoster Row printer named Vaughan Griffiths. Its founding principles were sound: the magazine was intended to keep its readers abreast of rapid innovations in agriculture, industry and trade. By April 1800 Griffiths had turned out eight issues containing articles on such subjects as the fertilising action of manures, the economy of the sugar trade, cowpox inoculations and the chemical ratio of bleaches. He claimed some success and a promising future for his publication, despite having just lost his first editorial 'conductor', who had placed too much of his own writing in its pages, 'thereby . . . disgusting the best correspondents'.

'[George Dyer] has been very attentive to my interest,' Rickman wrote to Southey on 18 April 1800, 'as he has offered to my acceptance, the task of conducting a Magazine. As its proprietor Griffiths seems no haughty bookseller, and is in much present distress, I shall do what I can for him for this month or two; and afterwards consider more maturely about the business.

> The circumstances of this publication stand thus: the title is promising The Commercial and Agricultural Magazine. It has reached No. 8 with tolerable, not splendid success.

Indeed it has not deserved much, and the bundle of papers the Editor has sent me for selection are very pitiful. It is printed with about the same letterpress as a Review. He offers 2 1/2 guineas p. sheet [for written contributions], and 2 guineas p. month for arrangement and correction. The last sum seems very low. He excuses the offer by the infant state and small returns of the Magazine.

I suppose it may be possible for me to manage this concern with success; as the usual subjects are things on which I have been accustomed to think often. Luckily I have some short essays (which you have not seen) which may help out the present dearth of matter, and the editor [Griffiths] seems rather fearfull that I should chuse to contribute too much than too little for the future. He seems to have been ill-used in this respect by his last conductor . . .

In my opinion to write anonymously is small trouble, because it requires no fastidious correction; and I am persuaded I write better speedily, than maturely. But the conduct of a publication infers a kind of conscious, irksome responsibility, which I do not like so well: and I should not meddle with this, but from a sincere wish to save a publication from sinking, whose future repute may possibly collect a useful body of information. I am also somewhat biassed towards an acceptance of the task that I may not seem to undervalue the efforts of so good a man as G.D.

Despite his misgivings, Rickman took on *The Commercial and Agricultural Magazine*, which soon became *The Commercial, Agricultural and Manufacturers Magazine*. In its issue of June 1800 he published one of the 'short essays' he had shyly kept secret from Southey. It had first been written in 1796 during his dog days in Christchurch, and he made amendments for the printed version of 1800. Its title was 'Thoughts on the Utility and Facility of Ascertaining the Population of England'.

2

Censuses, Taxation and War

In 1800, nobody knew the population of England or any of the other nations of the British Isles. That was not unusual. In 1800 few countries on earth had even an approximate headcount of their citizens. To complicate matters in Britain, the nation was going through serious internal changes, it was involved in an apparently interminable war with France, and a controversy raged between those amateur demographers who argued that the kingdom was growing at an unsustainable pace and those who maintained that it was in terminal decline.

The world's first recorded censuses were probably those conducted by the Israelites at the beginning of the second millennium before Christ. The Old Testament book of Exodus tells of the Lord instructing Moses to take 'the sum of the children of Israel after their number ... Every one that passeth among them that are numbered, from twenty years old and above, shall give an offering unto the Lord.'

Shortly afterwards, in the Sinai desert, according to the eponymous book of Numbers, 'in the second year after they were come out of the land of Egypt' Moses once again assessed 'the sum of all the congregation of the children of Israel, after their families, by the house of their fathers, with the number of their names, every male by their polls; From twenty years old and upward, all that are able to go forth to war in Israel ... ' That exercise was repeated on the hostile plains of Moab, where it was realised that the different tribes of Israel – the sons of Simeon, Reuben, Gad and others – could mobilise for battle a total of 601,730 men over the age of twenty.

Taxation and war would be for millennia the main or only reasons for counting adult male populations. A census of property owners – and therefore of voters and potential soldiers, who were expected to own property – was taken in the Roman Republic for over 400 years. The most celebrated event in census history occurred at the very end of the years before Christ, when according to the apostle Luke 'there went out a decree from Caesar Augustus that all the world should be taxed'. The people of Israel customarily returned to the city of their birth to register for a poll tax, which demanded a headcount of the population. So the Nazarene carpenter Joseph and his pregnant wife Mary travelled the seventy miles from Nazareth to Joseph's family seat of Bethlehem, where 'she brought forth her firstborn son' who eight days later was circumcised and named Jesus.

There were possibly censuses for the purposes of taxation or assessing military strength in Pharaonic Egypt, ancient Greece and the first cities of Mesopotamia. Censuses were probably taken over 2000 years ago in India and in the fifteenth-century pre-Columbian Inca empire. There were certainly censuses in China during the Han Dynasty, in the seventh-century Middle Eastern caliphate and in the Caribbean and Latin American provinces of Spain in the sixteenth century. In 1471 the Bavarian city of Nuremberg held a one-off census because its rulers needed to know their human resources in the event of a siege. The rural population of Brandenburg-Prussia was counted in 1683, and the kingdom of Prussia took a general census between 1719 and 1725.

The pioneers of the modern, comprehensive, regular census were however the Scandinavian countries. The united kingdoms of Denmark and Norway enumerated their adult male populations between 1700 and 1703. Their dependency of Iceland, whose 50,000 people lived in poverty so abject that even observers in the late seventeenth century were shocked, simultaneously took a census which included all ages and both genders to assess the total scale of the island's misery. In 1769 Denmark/Norway conducted their first modern census of all citizens, men, women and children, and calculated that the federation had a total population of 1,528,000 people. They modelled that exercise on their neighbours Sweden and its province of Finland, whose government had conducted a first general census in 1749, revealing a combined population of 2,203,000, and repeated the process every succeeding decade.

There was therefore no shortage of precedents, even within the British Isles. After the Emperor Claudius's conquest in AD 43 most of England is unlikely to have escaped the imperial Roman censuses. No records of them remain, only the noun. The term census derives from the Latin word *censere*, which means to assess.

In 1085 another conqueror anxious to discover the taxable value of his new possessions, William I, king of England and duke of Normandy, 'sent men all over England to each shire to find out what or how much each landholder had in land and livestock and what it was worth'.

The results were published the following year, and amplified in what later became known as the Domesday Book. It was both geographically and demographically incomplete. It excluded much of Wales, all of Scotland and Ireland, several peripheral northern English shires and the tax-exempt cities of London and Winchester, as well as almost all women and all children, as taxable landholders tended to be adult males.

The Domesday Book was nonetheless able to tell its Norman commissioners that John Rickman's future home of Christchurch was in 1086 in the possession of King William himself, that it had thirteen ploughlands or arable fields, sixty-one acres of meadow and one mill, and that it was settled by thirty-four households containing the families of '21 villagers. 5 smallholders. 1 slave. 7 other.' The population of Christchurch just twenty years after the Conquest was naturally still dominated by such Anglo-Saxons as 'Almaer brother of Asgot; Alnoth the priest; Alsige the priest; Asgot ... Count Alan; Ealdraed; Earl Godwine'. The taxable value of Christchurch to the crown was 0.3 geld units a year.

In the following centuries headcounts were made piecemeal, by different authorities, for diverse reasons. Parochial surveys of families, servants, hogs and dogs were conducted in such places as Canterbury in 1565, Poole in Dorset, where in 1574 the constables of the town enumerated each householder, 'his wife', children and servants, and Marlborough in Wiltshire, where in 1601 the names of all men between seventeen and sixty years of age were gathered for the purpose of mustering a local militia to fight the Spaniards.

As taxation became more widespread, national military service more essential and churchwardens more literate and willing and able to record births, marriages and deaths, so the men and women of the British Isles were more regularly listed on one parchment or another. But nobody gathered them all together into a cogent single set of statistics. In 1590 Queen Elizabeth I's Lord High Treasurer, the extraordinary William Cecil, proposed to the Archbishop of Canterbury that a General Register Office be established to centralise and coordinate all this disparate information.

'There should be yearly delivered unto your honour,' wrote Cecil, 'and to every lord treasurer, for the time being, a summary of the whole. Whereby it should appear how many christenings, weddings and burials were every year in England and Wales, and every County particularly by itself, and how many men-children and women-children were born in all of them, severally set down by themselves.' The suggestion failed to secure the archbishop's favour and Cecil died two years later. In the words of the genealogist Colin R. Chapman, 'over 200 years had to pass before such a proposal fell on sympathetic ears'.

Those 200 years were not uneventful. In 1695 the Scottish Parliament imposed a poll tax, which required a list of all 'pollable persons' in the country. The lists for Aberdeenshire and Renfrewshire survived. In the same year the House of Commons announced a poll tax in Ireland. A Commissioner of the Revenue in Ireland consequently enumerated the population of the island and came up with the suspiciously precise sum of 1,034,102 Irish men, women and children. In 1696 the Window Tax demanded the name and address of each taxpayer in England and Wales, and later in Scotland and Ireland, along with the number of windows in his or her house (large windows counted as two), which offered an indication of the householder's social and economic status.

Throughout the late seventeenth century and the first half of the eighteenth, Britons in general and Londoners in particular discovered and then drank great quantities of Dutch gin, a product of the homeland of the new monarchy, the House of Orange. The result was the Gin Craze. Gin was cheap, its mass distillation assisted farmers of grain, and as the social reformer Francis Place later wrote, the poor had few enjoyments other than 'sexual intercourse and drinking ... [and] drunkenness is by far the most desired ...'

The social effects were visible to the naked eye and were immortalised by William Hogarth in his dystopian depiction in 1751 of a London slum, 'Gin Lane'. Hogarth's print was a caricature, but there is no doubt that despite a series of gin taxes and other panicked legislation a good deal of London was drunk for a good deal of the time, with an adverse effect on the city's commercial activities and moral and physical health. By the time of the passage in 1751 of the Sale of Spirits Act, or Gin Act, which severely limited the distribution of the beverage, Londoners were drinking an average of two pints of gin per head each week (which when abstainers, the sober bourgeoisie, the deserving poor and most babies were eliminated from the equation meant that somebody was drinking several other citizens' two pints of gin a week). In 1750 more than a quarter of all houses in the parish of St Giles, upon which Hogarth modelled 'Gin Lane', were gin shops.

Alarm at the Gin Craze reached crisis proportions when an examination of London parish records revealed that more people were dying in the city than were being born. Extrapolating from its largest centre of population to the rest of the country, where strong spirits were also drunk, it was presumed that Great Britain's population was in decline; that the nation was drinking itself to death. The logic of this theory was best expressed by the Scottish mathematician William Braikenridge, who wrongly but persuasively calculated that the population of London had fallen from 875,760 in the later 1730s to 748,350 in the early 1750s. As Braikenridge explained in a paper for the Royal Society, 'it is evident, that the number of inhabitants must always be in proportion to the number of births, and burials considered together'.

In hindsight, that was sloppy reasoning simply because it took no account of population movement. Fewer births than deaths certainly were recorded in most of London, but the size of the city was nonetheless increasing due to a steady stream of immigrants from other countries and other towns, and from the comparatively healthy English countryside. Without a comprehensive population survey it was impossible to confirm or deny those trends.

In 1753 Thomas Potter, the Recorder of Bath and Member of Parliament for the West Country constituency of St Germans, Aylesbury and Okehampton, proposed what would have been the first British national census. Potter's bill suggested 'An Act for Taking and Registering an Annual Account of the Total Number of People ... in Great Britain'. The survey would commence on 24 June 1754 and be repeated on the same day every following year. It would be taken by Overseers of the Poor, men whose profession presumed an intimate knowledge of their locality, who would go to every house in their parishes and record the number of men, women and children in each building on that date.

Thomas Potter's bill may have been handicapped by the fact that its sponsor, a son of an Archbishop of Canterbury, was an arrogant rake and a member of the orgiastic Hellfire Club. But it also met stiff opposition on the grounds of tradition, superstition and principle. Matthew Ridley, the coal magnate and MP for Newcastle upon Tyne, spoke in apocalyptic terms of 'a violent spirit of opposition to this Bill' which 'if it should be accidentally followed by any epidemical distemper, or by a public misfortune of any other kind, it may raise such a popular flame as will endanger the peace'.

Others considered, then and later, that while it might be useful for military reasons to know the size of the male population, such a calculation could misfire if it turned out that the population of Britain was smaller than was generally imagined. If, as seemed a strong possibility, the nation's manpower was also proved to be in decline such a revelation would give fresh heart to 'our enemies'. On a practical level, the leap from having no census at all to taking a full census every twelve months of a population of several millions was thought by some of Potter's more sympathetic opponents to be overly ambitious.

Then there was that stubborn old shibboleth, British liberty. While William Thornton, MP for York, was among those who believed that with the help of Potter's census 'our enemies abroad would become acquainted with our weakness', he reserved most of his outrage for the impertinent intrusions of census-taking. 'I was never more astonished and alarmed since I had the honour to sit in this House,' he said when the census bill was first presented, 'than I have been this day: for I did not believe that there had been any set of men so presumptuous and so abandoned as to make the proposal we have just heard.' A national census would 'molest and perplex every single family in the kingdom'. It was 'totally subversive of the last remains of English liberty ... calculated to divest us of the last remains of our birthright'.

Thornton assured the House that if anybody appeared on his doorstep demanding to know the 'number and circumstances of my family, I would refuse it; and, if he persisted in the affront, I would order my servants to give him the discipline of the horse pond'. If the bill became law, Thornton promised to leave the country and seek a place where men could live in freedom. 'A tame submission to this yoke,' he said, 'will prove indeed that the spirit of our ancestors is departed.'

Despite Ridley's fears and Thornton's resounding words, Thomas Potter's proposal for an annual census actually did pass through the House of Commons. It was then kicked into the long grass by the House of Lords in May 1754. William Thornton was spared his voluntary exile and Overseers of the Poor in the district of York were saved from involuntary immersion in his horse pond.

The matter was never likely to die, if only because each new generation discovered fresh reasons for discovering how many people lived in Britain. Until his death in 1762 William Braikenridge continued to compute the populations of the nations of Great Britain. He came to accept that immigration from Scotland and Ireland had a stabilising effect on the population of England, but obstinately calculated that thanks to fatalities in war as well as cirrhoses of the liver the number of people in the entire British Isles was, like that in London, falling.

Braikenridge's pessimism was picked up and carried through the rest of the eighteenth century by a much more influential character. Richard Price was a Welsh philosopher, a liberal theologian, a member of the Royal Society, a supporter of the French Revolution, a friend of both Benjamin Franklin and the cause of American independence, and a mentor of the feminist and author Mary Wollstonecraft, who said of Price that his 'talents and modest virtues place him high in the scale of moral excellence'.

Regardless of his moral excellence, Richard Price's tinkering in the subject of the British populace was as misguided as it was provocative. By the second half of the eighteenth century many theorists started from the root assumption that the population was in decline and then proceeded to convert the assumption into fact. Price was the most notable of them all.

In 1772 Price advertised one of his many treatises with the words, 'in this kingdom, it appears that, amidst all our splendour, we are decreasing so fast, as to have lost, in about 70 years, near a quarter of our people'. Later in the same year he reasserted his deduction that during the eighteenth century the number of people in the British Isles, excluding Ireland, had collapsed from about 6 million to a current low of 4½ million. Price was unsure whether London was growing rather than, as William Braikenridge had argued, slowly disappearing, but if the former was true 'this is an event more to be dreaded than desired. The more London increases, the more the rest of the Kingdom must be deserted ... Moderate towns, being seats of refinement, emulation and the arts, may be public advantages. But great towns, long before they grow to half the bulk of London, become checks on population of too hurtful a nature, nurseries of debauchery and voluptuousness; greater evils than can be compensated by any advantages.'

Price's presumptions and conclusions were questioned from several learned sources, but the man was unbowed. In 1780 he published an 'Essay on the Present State of Population in England and Wales'. Using Window Tax returns since 1697, he repeated his earlier observation that the number of occupied houses in England and Wales had fallen from 1,319,215 to fewer than 1 million. Even if his figures were reliable – and several arithmeticians pointed out that they were not – they need not automatically have indicated population decline. Aside from the fact that householders dodged the Window Tax in a variety of ways (bricking up their windows was one of the most popular, but as the raising of the tax continued – it was levied between 1697 and 1851 – new houses were built with fewer windows, to the detriment of both public health and the glass industry), if more people were crowded into them, as was the case in such growing cities as London, the number and size of houses was not perennially commensurate with the number of their residents.

Richard Price died in 1792 but the arguments and counter-arguments raged on, refuelled occasionally by the posthumous republication of his essays. In that intellectual climate in 1796, John Rickman sat down in his family's Christchurch home and struggled with the first draft of his own solution to the controversy, 'Thoughts on the Utility and Facility of Ascertaining the Population of England'.

Two years later a giant entered the fray. Thomas Malthus's *An Essay on the Principle of Population* was first published in London in 1798. In the following thirty years Malthus would revise his book before each of its several republications, but his principle remained the same. Malthus, who was yet another cleric, took for granted that the population was increasing, not only in Great Britain but throughout the world. Instead of welcoming that refutation of Richard Price's convictions, Malthus argued that unchecked or unconstrained (the qualifiers are important: Malthus nowhere suggested an inevitable future) population growth would lead first to a permanent, semi-starving underclass whose condition could not be helped, and ultimately to a 'Malthusian catastrophe' of famine or plague or both.

The impact of Thomas Malthus's intervention in the population debate would reverberate for a further two centuries and more, an advantage held by Malthusian theory being that as it was located in a possible future it could never be disproved. In the aftermath of its first publication, it led John Rickman to revisit his own 'Thoughts on the Utility and Facility of Ascertaining the Population of England' and include the essay in the June 1800 issue of *The Commercial and Agricultural Magazine*.

Rickman's 'Thoughts' were, compared to Malthus's epic prognostications, brief, modest and practical. In his laboured prose, Rickman listed twenty points in favour of 'Ascertaining the Population of England'. '[A]n intimate knowledge of any country,' he averred, 'can be the only foundation of the legislation of that country, and also of its political relations to other nations.' The 'grand basis of the power and resources of a nation' was 'an industrious population', which gave rise to the question, 'What is that population?'

In every war, he continued, 'it must be of the highest importance to enrol and discipline the highest number of men'. That could not properly be accomplished 'till the population is ascertained'. Similarly, in peacetime there was no way of knowing the number of experienced seamen who had been demobilised and had returned to their homes but could still be called upon.

His publication's specific themes of commerce and agriculture were also affected. The wildly fluctuating price of corn, which alternately enriched and then impoverished farmers and their labourers and was a source of grave concern in the eighteenth and early nineteenth centuries, could surely only be stabilised if the size of the market was known, wrote Rickman. 'No society can confidently pretend to provide the requisite quantity of food, till they know the number of consumers.' If that number was known, 'The influence of the price of provisions in different years ... would all be ascertained with tolerable precision.'

John Rickman was not and never would be a Malthusian, possibly because his acquaintance with agricultural improvements (one of his brothers was a farmer and he was after all, as Charles Lamb noted five months later, 'somewhat concerned in an agricultural magazine') gave him confidence that, properly managed, the food supply could keep pace with the population. But he also dismissed the fallacies of Richard Price, believing that 'the real number of inhabitants, in England, is far beyond the usual estimate ... I would guess, that Scotland and Ireland contain about five millions, England [including Wales] about ten millions.'

Rickman then made a conclusive plea to his fellow educated Britons of the Enlightenment. '[A]ll the authors,' he pointed out, 'who have written on the state and politics of any nation ... [have] assumed a certain population of the nation in question ... what superior value they might have given to their calculations, had they possessed a foundation of solid materials.'

Having rehearsed the why, Rickman turned to the how. He noted the Roman method of 'collecting [citizens] in their respective municipia'. That had doubtless provided a 'sufficiently accurate' headcount, although 'The inconvenience which affected Joseph and his wife, and caused their child to be laid in a manger, seems not to indicate much attention in this mode of procedure, to the comfort of individuals, who were dragged far from home, each "to his own city".'

Instead of summoning people back to their birthplaces, Rickman proposed counting his fellow citizens where they lived. He suggested that an Act of Parliament ('Some sort of compulsion is necessary') should oblige the ministers of every parish in the country to return 'a printed letter' which would detail 'the births, burials and marriages for the past ten years; distinguishing male and female, and anything else which may be thought necessary'. Having established an average ratio of births to deaths, wrote Rickman, a precise enumeration of the total current population of just 'three or four' parishes would then allow a numerate person 'to ascertain by a simple arithmetical operation, the population of the whole nation'. The whole process would take two years and would cost a trifling £740.

'Thoughts on the Utility and Facility of Ascertaining the Population of England' was neither a definitive nor an exceptionally persuasive treatise. Its suggested methodology was little more than a refined and expanded version of the kind of approximations which had informed Richard Price. Most significantly, Rickman did not in his essay propose a future census to be taken at regular intervals. He argued for a one-off or an occasional headcount, in line with most of its European predecessors. Wishing above all to refute the

22

Pricean thesis that the country had been in decline since the 1690s, Rickman looked instead to the more distant past, pointing out that his method could be backdated and used to assess 'the relative state of population at any period, from the days of Elizabeth'.

But it was published by the right person at the right time. John Rickman may have been an uninspiring essayist but he was an extremely persuasive man. As the eighteenth century gave way to the nineteenth, as the agricultural and industrial revolutions began noticeably to transform the country and as Britain locked in mortal combat with Napoleonic France, he discovered a more receptive audience than had Thomas Potter fifty years earlier.

Unsurprisingly, 'Thoughts on the Utility and Facility of Ascertaining the Population of England' fell into the hands of the Member of Parliament for Christchurch, to which town Rickman's 'foolish family ties' returned him frequently. George Rose was a 56-year-old Scottish economist with impressive and extremely relevant contacts. He had served as Keeper of the Records of Scotland in the 1770s before working at the Treasury under William Pitt the Younger. In 1788 Rose had been elevated to chief clerk of the House of Lords, and in 1790 he became MP for Christchurch.

George Rose did not need much convincing. The year 1800 saw an exceptionally poor harvest, which at a time of war greatly worried Rose and many of his colleagues. He would try, without much success, to persuade distillers of spirits to use as little grain as possible and allow the bulk of the harvest to be processed into food, but he was deeply frustrated by the facts that nobody knew how much grain there was in Great Britain, and that the trade itself was almost impossible to regulate due to its unrecorded complexity. The Christchurch MP wrote in his journal in October 1800:

> Of the corn sold in Mark Lane [the London corn exchange], of English growth, nine-tenths belongs to individual farmers, from the harvest-time till the summer months; thenceforward, probably about five-sixths; the remainder to middlemen. The whole is sold by factors on commission.
>
> The number of farmers for whom the sales are made are incalculable; many hundreds, even thousands, dispersed throughout the country, without knowledge of or intercourse with each other; sometimes the property of fifty farmers is in one vessel.
>
> We cannot state the number of middlemen who are dealers; in most sea-port towns there are several, and a few in inland ones, unconnected entirely with each other, and a constant jealousy amongst them.
>
> Of persons usually selling corn in Mark Lane, there are about twenty strictly corn-factors, and about fifteen who are also dealers or jobbers; besides the haymen, about fifteen in number, who sell the Kentish wheat.

Rickman's comments in 'Thoughts on the Utility and Facility of Ascertaining the Population of England' that 'No society can confidently pretend to provide the requisite quantity of food, till they know the number of consumers' and that in a census 'The influence of the price of provisions in different years ... would all be ascertained with tolerable precision' therefore chimed in perfect harmony with George Rose's disquiet. Rose passed the essay, along with a recommendation of Rickman himself, to his friend and fellow Tory reformer, the Member of Parliament for Helston in Cornwall, Charles Abbot.

Like George Rose, Abbot was already a convert. Metropolitan France, the mainland area of Great Britain's enemy, had long been acknowledged to be the most populous nation in Europe. Recent figures had credibly suggested that in 1800 First Consul Napoleon Bonaparte ruled over almost 30 million people between Calais and Nice, Brest and Grenoble; figures which helped to explain why his conscripted republican army had not only withstood counter-revolutionary assaults from the European monarchies but also could and would rapidly conquer much of the continent. Although France had forfeited control of the sea to Great Britain, the war would clearly have to be won on dry land. Military necessity in conjunction with scarcity of food had made it a matter of urgency to discover whether Great Britain contained 4½ million, 6 million or – as John Rickman controversially and uniquely guessed – 15 million people.

Charles Abbot did some perfunctory research. He maintained close contact with George Rose, and therefore indirectly with John Rickman. The United States of America had taken rough censuses in 1790 and 1800, which estimated its population, excluding slaves and Native Americans, at 3,929,326 and 5,308,483 respectively. Abbot called on the American minister, or ambassador to London, Rufus King early in November 1800 and asked for details of how that 'numeration' was acquired. He then wrote to the prime minister, William Pitt, and the Speaker of the House of Commons, Henry Addington, 'to apprise them of my intention to move for a Bill to ascertain the population of Great Britain'.

Two days later, on 7 November 1800, Abbot received a letter from Pitt requesting a meeting in Downing Street that same afternoon. The prime minister, Abbot told his diary,

> then proceeded to discuss the proposed Bill for ascertaining the population, &c, which he agreed to be a measure highly desirable; but only doubted how far it stood so immediately connected with the question of scarcity, as to make it fit to bring forward on the second day of the session, which would be intimating an opinion that this was considered as a sort of remedy for the prevailing evil: and that he should rather wish it to be postponed for a few days.
>
> I explained to him that my reason for bringing it forward so early was the disposition of people at present to accede to any measure having a tendency to furnish information, with the amount of the demand or the causes of the scarcity; and that, so far, this would show the extent of the demand for which a supply was to be made.

Abbot pressed his case for a census at times of food shortage and war, when an 'increase of tillage' might be discovered to be necessary. A regular repetition of the exercise, he argued, would also show whether the population of the United Kingdom was increasing or decreasing. The prime minister accepted his proposal. Charles Abbot then wasted no further time. He made plans to introduce a bill to Parliament within two weeks. It would be seconded by a friendly independent Member of Parliament who would be better remembered for campaigns against slavery: William Wilberforce.

This time the census bill sailed through both Houses of

Parliament. Abbot had been right when he told Pitt that the disturbing circumstances of 1800, the two dark riders of food shortage and war, had made people vastly more anxious than in the past for dependable information about the demographics of their country. With Pitt pulling levers from Downing Street, Abbot's bill for ascertaining the population attracted little substantive debate, let alone passionate condemnation from county squires anxious to preserve British liberties.

That is not to say that the national census was instantly embraced from coast to coast. It would in the following two centuries provoke dissent and boycott from several different politically recalcitrant bodies. In 1821 John Rickman would report: 'It has been reasonably supposed, that the first Enumeration of the People in Great Britain, especially as it took place in time of War, was rendered somewhat defective from backwardness or evasion in making the Answers required, inasmuch as direct taxation, and more obviously the levy of men in every place, might possibly be founded on the results of such an investigation.' Since, in fact, 'no such effect was perceived to take place, the Returns of the year 1811 were in all probability more full and accurate than those of 1801; and the War [for which taxes were levied] having now ceased, there remains no reason to suspect the least deficiency in the Return of 1821'.

Isolated and decreasing instances of peaceful or violent objections continued throughout the nineteenth century, but by the early twentieth the census was conducted unopposed. Only after the Second World War, which had been fought against a totalitarian state, were doubts seriously raised once again. As Sydney Bailey writes, 'In

1950, probably for the first time since 1753, there was some restrained parliamentary opposition to the fact that it was proposed to hold a census. One Opposition Member said that there were two objections to the census. "In the first place, it is going to cost a good deal of money, and, in the second place, it will cause annoyance to a considerable number of people."'

Another Member claimed that the government had failed to make a case for a new census. 'The British public today is regimented and documented far more than any other people in the world, except, possibly, those behind the Iron Curtain.' Some of the questions which it was proposed to ask were 'downright impertinent . . . People will object very strongly to being asked, for example, whether they were more fertile after their second marriage.' The government should postpone their 'grand snoop' until the country could afford it. Yet another Member urged the people of 'once free Britain' to 'strike a blow for freedom by putting the census forms on the fire'.

At that time there even appeared a reincarnation of William Thornton of York and his concern for 'the last remains of English liberty'. In 1951 Sir Ernest John Pickstone Benn of Oxted in Surrey, the first president of the Society for Individual Freedom and an uncle of the Labour politician Tony Benn, refused to fill out his census form or to give the required information to an enumerator. Instead he wrote across the form, 'In view of the critical state of the national economy, I must refuse to take any part in this unnecessary waste of manpower, money, paper and print.' Sir Ernest was summoned to court in Dorking, where his barrister informed magistrates that his client 'hates with a passionate hatred the encroachment of Government activity in the sphere of the individual'. Benn was fined £5 with £2 2s costs.

In 1800 there was some concern about the expense of the enumeration, and a delay occurred when the Scottish clergy petitioned to have their country omitted from the census because they did not consider it their duty to 'execute the civil office' of counting their parishioners. The second problem might have eliminated the first, as a census which excluded Scotland would be a cheaper exercise, and both Pitt and Abbot were prepared to leave out Scotland 'however unreasonable' they considered the Church of Scotland's objections.

But those objections were overridden by Pitt's and Abbot's fellow parliamentarians. Scotland would be included along with England and Wales. Scottish ministers were mollified by the amendment that north of the River Tweed responsibility for the census would not be devolved to the Church but would be taken by 'such Persons as shall be for that Purpose appointed by the Sheriff Deputes, Stewart Deputes, and Justices of the Peace'. In the event it was largely taken by Scottish schoolteachers. That was a satisfactory conclusion for John Rickman; as 'the official Schoolmaster of each Parish: an institution peculiar to Scotland, which has existed in full vigour since the year 1696; and as the Office of Precentor and Clerk of the Parochial Session for Poor Relief is often combined with that of Schoolmaster, the personal knowledge of the number of Children in every family appertains to the Schoolmaster in Scotland almost as effectually as to the Overseer in England'. Indeed, he added in 1831, 'the habit of regularity, together with the official knowledge of writing and arithmetic implied in the character of Schoolmaster, renders the Population Returns of Scotland quite as authentic, and obviously more methodical than those obtained from the Overseers of the Poor in England'.

Ireland, which did not formally become part of the United Kingdom until 1 January 1801, would be for the moment overlooked. On 22 December 1800 what had become familiarly known as the Population Bill passed through the House of Commons. On 27 December it passed through the House of Lords. On 31 December 'An Act for taking an Account of the Population of Great Britain, and of the Increase or Diminution thereof' received the assent of King George III and became law.

3

A Hazy Snapshot from the Air

'At my suggestion,' wrote John Rickman to Robert Southey, who was still in Portugal, on 27 December 1800, the day that the Population Bill won the approval of the House of Lords, 'they have passed an Act of Parliament for ascertaining the population of Great Britain, and as a compliment (of course) have proposed to me to superintend the execution of it.' He continued:

> Next March the returns will be made, and I shall be busy enough for a short time, I suppose. I suspect all this attention (it is more immediately from G. Rose) is intended as a decent bribe: which I shall reject, by doing the business well, and taking no more remuneration, than I judge exactly adequate to the trouble.
>
> It is a task of national benefit, and I should be fanciful to reject it, because offered by rogues. As they well know me for their foe, I cannot suspect them of magnanimity enough to notice me with any good intention.

Rickman's letter to Southey captured that moment when the bright young radical, in his thirtieth year, was seduced by an irresistible offer from Establishment 'rogues' and felt himself – having until recently anticipated no future of much remuneration – obliged to accept the 'bribe' in the interests of his fellow citizens, even if on his own uncompromising terms.

His Tory 'foes' in William Pitt's government gave John Rickman an office and a handful of clerks at the Cockpit by St James's Park in Westminster. A large 300-year-old leisure complex built by Henry VIII to house a bowling alley, a real tennis court, a jousting yard and an actual cockpit, where cocks fought, the Cockpit later became a theatre and, in the seventeenth and eighteenth centuries, government offices. When Rickman moved in the Foreign Office had just moved out and the Privy Council, under whose aegis he would be working, was still in residence.

In that building in the first three months of 1801 the first British national census was prepared. The 'Account of the Population' and its three successors in 1811, 1821 and 1831 have occasionally been dismissed as scanty and inaccurate, which to some extent they were. Their use to researchers of the twentieth and twenty-first centuries has been sadly limited by the fact that most of the first four census returns, those taken in 1801, 1811, 1821 and 1831, were destroyed by government order in 1904, leaving only the abstracts of returns and Rickman's general reports. (They were not the last to suffer. Irish census returns would prove particularly vulnerable. The full Irish census papers taken between 1821 and 1851 were almost all carbonised by a fire at the records office in Dublin in 1922 during the Irish Civil War, while the original Irish returns for 1861 and 1871 were unaccountably put out with the garbage shortly after their collation, and those for 1881 and 1891 were pulped during a paper shortage in the First World War. The 1931 census for England and Wales was also lost in a fire at its Middlesex storage depot in 1942.)

Partly as a result of that official vandalism, Rickman's qualities and accomplishments as a statistician have been denigrated by some later demographers. It is true that he was neither a professional demographer nor a professional statistician, but in 1801 those occupational nouns, let alone the careers themselves, did not exist. Later scholars who hail the work of the seventeenth century's John Graunt, the eighteenth century's Richard Price and the nineteenth century's Adolphe Quetelet may occasionally be guilty of neglecting the achievements of the hardworking polymath from Hampshire. Even as Rickman began his forensic work, others with little information to hand were still publicising their estimations. In December 1800 the mathematician J.J. Grellier, the secretary of London's Royal Exchange Insurance Office, announced that the total population of Great Britain was 7 million. Grellier was promptly contradicted by the economist and Regius Professor of Modern History at Oxford University, the Reverend Dr Henry Beeke, who guessed the population of England and Wales alone to be 'not much less than 11,000,000'.

'As I conceive it impossible to reconcile accounts which vary so very materially,' wrote one 'TB' from London to *The Monthly Magazine* in January 1801, 'I leave those who possess better means of information on these subjects to determine, which approach nearest the truth.'

If Rickman was not a mathematician or a statistician at the end of 1800, he became both within twelve months. As Charles Lamb had noted, he was exceptionally quick on the uptake. He was also, as would become apparent, a supremely efficient administrator. He had his own vision of the scope and purpose of an 'Account of the Population' and he was working to meet the instructions of a detailed Act of Parliament. It is also worth repeating that if it had not been for Rickman's knowledgeable and genial personality, the census of 1801 might not have been taken at all.

The forms were all to be completed on the same day, 1 March. As Rickman had told Southey, the returns were supposedly to be gathered in at the Cockpit the same month – by 10 March, to be precise. The 'Act for taking an Account of the Population of Great Britain' in 1801 was printed and mailed, along with empty forms for completion, to clerks of the peace and town clerks throughout most of England and Wales and to sheriffs' offices in Scotland (some offshore islands were, like the country of Ireland, initially neglected). In England and Wales those clerks then distributed them to county constables, who in their turn usually passed them on down to overseers of the poor '(or in Default thereof, some substantial Householder) of every Parish and Place', as Thomas Potter had suggested in 1753; in Scotland they were sent to whichever schoolmasters were appointed by the sheriffs. The expenses incurred by schoolmasters and overseers of the poor in completing each returned form would be compensated by the payment of either one shilling or one shilling and sixpence.

The process was therefore delegated down four or five levels of a small pyramid. A failure on any single level would, and did, result in a smaller or larger gap in the results returned to the Cockpit. Communications typical of this cumbersome process survive. W.E. Taunton, Clerk of the Peace of the County of Oxford, wrote on 30 April 1801:

Notice is hereby given that the Chief Constables of the County of Oxford, are required to transmit to me at my Office in Oxford, on or before the 8th. Day of May next, the printed Schedules or Returns which have been delivered to them within their respective Jurisdictions, together with a true and perfect List of the Names of the Overseers of every Parish, Township, and Place, or of the Householders therein, to whom such Schedules have been delivered, pursuant to the Directions of an Act passed in the last Sessions of Parliament, intituled an Act for taking an Account of the Population of Great Britain, and of the Increase or Diminution thereof.

On W.E. Taunton himself, of course, lay the responsibility of posting those returns back to John Rickman's office at the Cockpit in London.

The forms first established the exact location of their findings – their county, their hundred (a hundred was a Saxon parcel of land, of which more will be heard), their city or town and their parish. They then left space for six questions to be answered. Those questions were:

How many Inhabited Houses are there in your Parish, Township, or Place; by how many Families are they occupied; and, how many Houses therein are Uninhabited?

How many persons (including Children of whatever Age) are there actually found within the Limits of your Parish, Township, or Place, at the Time of taking this Account, distinguishing Males and Females, and exclusive of Men actually serving in His Majesty's Regular Forces or Militia, and exclusive of Seamen either in His Majesty's Service, or belonging to Registered Vessels?

What Number of Persons, in your Parish, Township, or Place, are chiefly employed in Agriculture; how many in Trade, Manufactures, or Handicraft; and, how many are not comprised in any of the preceding Classes?

What was the Number of Baptisms and Burials in your Parish, Township, or Place, in the several Years, 1700, 1710, 1720, 1730, 1740, 1750, 1760, 1770, 1780, and each subsequent Year to the 31st Day of December 1800, distinguishing Males from Females?

What has been the Number of Marriages in your Parish, Township, or Place, in each Year, from the Year 1754 inclusive to the End of the Year 1800?

Are there any Matters which you think it necessary to remark in Explanation of your Answers to any of the preceding Questions?

Other than the fourth question, which was designed to settle once and for all the vexing matter of whether the country's population had increased or declined during the eighteenth century, it was an inclusive although far from definitive modern census. Both genders were to be counted, although their names, ages and familial relationships would not yet be required. Uninhabited as well as inhabited houses were to be listed, to satisfy another general curiosity of the era. And the numbers of people engaged in the two broad spheres of early nineteenth-century occupation, agriculture or trade and manufacture, were to be assessed. Men in the armed services and merchant navy were excluded because they were already recorded in regimental or naval musters, and in 1801 the last thing that the government wanted was to distort the nation's military potential by counting them twice.

The 1801 census was designed to deliver a hazy snapshot – as from the air, through thin cloud – of the mainland of England, Scotland and Wales as it stood in March of that year.

John Rickman was the first to accept how hazy was his 1801 landscape. He told Southey during that summer of 'the incredible inaccuracy of the returns under the Population Act. I write hundreds of letters to little purpose, and have worked about 9 weeks without being able to say that anything is done.'

Essentially, far from every town clerk, overseer of the poor, sheriff's officer, minister, vicar, schoolteacher or other 'substantial houscholder' could be bothered to fill in and return the forms, even in exchange for one shilling and six-pence. The national census was, in early nineteenth-century Britain, an entirely new concept and an unprecedented exercise. Many of those who had been made legally responsible for its completion, and equally liable to punishment for its lack of completion, comprehended neither the purpose nor the urgency of those strange printed sheets delivered by the General Post Office from Rickman's headquarters in the Cockpit. Some who did understand were undoubtedly opposed to the intrusive notion of a census. A few were actually illiterate or otherwise incompetent. To more than enough of the recipients, it was junk mail.

As a result, when he came to compile his abstract of find-ings, despite several weeks spent chivvying recalcitrants in all corners of the kingdom, Rickman was obliged to note in his report to Parliament that in his surveys of fifty-one counties and shires in England, only thirteen were 'com-pleat'. Buckingham was missing seventy-three parish returns and 'the Clerk of the Peace has made urgent Application to the Defaulters'. More than half of Monmouth was 'wanting'. About a third of Somerset could not be included. In the twelve counties of Wales only Radnor and Merioneth had completed. About half of Anglesey, Flint and Glamorgan were missing. Only in Scotland were the forms filled in and returned with relative diligence but even there several large parishes and, perhaps unsurprisingly, the small islands of Rum, Canna and Muck failed to report. Rickman and his clerks were therefore obliged to spend several weeks studying comparable population returns and estimating the number of people in places like Somersetshire (which contained, they calculated, 190,223 men, women and children in March 1801) while omitting entirely such truants as Buckinghamshire and Monmouthshire.

He could not wait for ever. Charles Abbot had been appointed Chief Secretary for Ireland and had asked Rickman to become his private secretary. A ship to Dublin waited. Rickman rushed out a short preliminary report in June 1801 and left his clerks to attempt to fill in the gaps before conceding, from Dublin Castle – where he was in constant communication with the Cockpit – to an incomplete account of the population of Great Britain being published in December.

It was, for all that, a formidable manuscript. His summaries and abstracts amounted to almost 600 pages.

The headline statistics of the 1801 census were simple and, following rigorous retrospective analysis, as close to being accurate as would make little difference to students in future centuries. The total population of England, Scotland and Wales was, according to this first Rickman census, 10,901,236. There were 8,331,434 people counted in England, 1,559,068 in Scotland and 541,546 in Wales. There were also 469,188 men from all quarters serving abroad, at home or at sea in the army and the Royal and merchant navies. Most but not all of those men were British subjects. The large number of foreign nationals – at their peak in the first two decades of the nineteenth century 100,000 foreign men were estimated to be serving in the merchant navy – who were chiefly at sea on British ships, were nonetheless included in the total population headcount. Although comprising less than 1 per cent of the 10.9 million, and an even smaller proportion when Ireland was also counted, they could be said to compensate for the omissions or underestimates of actual natives in places like Somerset and Monmouth. Many of them would also, following demobilisation or dismissal, settle in Britain.

Even excluding Ireland, 10.9 million was a lot more people than the 4½ million and falling estimated three decades earlier by Richard Price. Early in 1802 Rickman's employer Charles Abbot was informed in Dublin by the anti-Catholic academic and parliamentarian Dr Patrick Duigenan that the population of Ireland was 3 million, and by John Foster, the last speaker of the dissolved Irish House of Commons, that it was 'above 4,000,000'.

Foster's was the more accurate estimate. Most notably, whichever sums were accepted, the totals not only ridiculed Price; they also came remarkably close to Rickman's assertion in his seminal published essay of June 1800 that the population of the United Kingdom was around 15 million, or half the number claimed to live in France. 'I would guess,' Rickman had written, 'that Scotland and Ireland contain about five millions, England [including Wales] about ten millions.'

The forms returned from parish records dating back 100

years put the last nails in the coffins of William Braikenridge and Richard Price. They showed that almost everywhere outside London, in every decade since 1690 considerably more baptisms than burials had taken place, and that in the second half of the eighteenth century the number of marriages had almost doubled. Taking two large sets of documented samples from parishes in Bedford and Berkshire, Rickman's clerks had counted in the ten years between 1690 and 1700 a total of 5075 baptisms and 3945 burials. By 1790 to 1800 the same figures had increased to 8212 baptisms and 6004 burials. In 1754 those parishes had witnessed 1167 marriages, which increased in 1800 to a total of 1829.

The numbers of marriages could be misleading. Not every mother was married and not every marriage was fertile. But the considerably greater number of newborns who lived to be christened over the total number of deaths presented indisputable evidence of a population which, in such regions, was very far from falling but instead had grown by almost 50 per cent in the previous 100 years.

London, the template from which Braikenridge and then Price had drawn their misleading conclusions, told an entirely different story. In that city throughout the eighteenth century more people did indeed die than were born. At the height of the Gin Craze between 1730 and 1740, Rickman's backdated parish register returns revealed that only 17,779 babies were baptised in the City of London, Westminster and Southwark, while 31,085 people were buried. It stood in stark contrast to the health of leafy Bedford and Bucks. But between 1700 and 1800 London contained no more than 7 per cent of the total population of the United Kingdom. The human resources of the 93 per cent in the rest of the nation were more than sufficient to replenish the capital and to keep the entire country's population on an upward trajectory.

With Braikenridge and Price discredited, John Rickman could study at leisure his sketch of the thriving United Kingdom as it appeared in the early spring of 1801.

Thanks chiefly to those half-million men serving in the British army and the navies, in every single county of each of the three countries there were marginally more women than men. Taken as a whole, the United Kingdom was still an agricultural nation. Slightly more than 2 million (2,078,807) of what would become known as its gainfully employed worked on the land. Another 2 million (2,136,726) laboured at 'trade, manufacture or handicraft', but most of the trade was in agricultural produce. Only in England did more men and women work indoors (1,789,531) than out in the fields (1,524,227). Scotland was still mainly rural; in Wales more than three times as many people worked in agriculture as in trade or industry. In all but one of the six hundreds of the county of Anglesey, between ten and twenty times as many men, women and children worked on the land as in trade or industry. Even the town of Holyhead contained four times more agriculturalists than trades or craftspeople. If Ireland had been enumerated the bias towards agriculture would have been even greater.

In some districts, however, the industrial turmoil of the near future was already evident. In such Yorkshire mill towns as Dewsbury the land was all but forgotten – in 1801 only eight of Dewsbury's citizens worked in agriculture, while 1058 were in trade or industry. Twenty miles to the west of Dewsbury was an ancient township on Saddleworth Moor named Quick. In one sense Quick was part of timeless England. It had appeared, as Thoac or Tohac, in the Domesday Book seven centuries earlier. In that manuscript Quick/Thoac/Tohac was part of the apentake (or wapentake, a Danelaw equivalent of the Anglo-Saxon hundred) of Agbrigg, and that, with variant spellings, was exactly how it was still described in the census of 1801. Almost forty years after the census, in 1838, Quick would be described as situated in 'a wild, bleak region'. But at the end of the eighteenth century and the beginning of the nineteenth, 'industry has accumulated in it a large number of inhabitants, who gain a comfortable subsistence by the manufacture of woollen cloth, for which the place is peculiarly famous'.

So it was that in March 1801, John Rickman's first census of the United Kingdom revealed that where for centuries only sheep and their shepherds had made a home, there were in the settlement of Quick a mere fifty-nine people still employed in agriculture. Those fifty-nine pastoralists were outnumbered on their wild, bleak moor by a further 3913 industrial workers and their families – most of whom had not been born there – who were taking wages from cotton mills. Unknown to almost everybody and remarked upon by few, Quick was both a survival and a microcosmic harbinger of the Britain yet to come.

Perhaps the outstanding feature of Great Britain as portrayed in the census of 1801 was that, even with the agricultural revolution approaching maturity and the industrial revolution in its frisky teens, the countryside was still littered with thousands of discrete old villages, many of which would in the next two centuries either be absorbed into the suburbs of larger conurbations, often leaving no trace but the residual name of a wood, a hill or a stream, a mansion house or a street, or be ploughed over by large farms and disappear altogether. Some fell into the sea or were deluged by man-made dams.

  Those small hamlets were no longer in 1801 home to the majority of the people, but between them they contained a million or more of the country's rooted rural population. Some 13,400 English towns and villages were recorded in the Domesday Book, at a period when almost everybody lived in small towns, smaller villages and isolated steadings. The 1801 census was taken after the Black Death had almost halved the fourteenth-century British population and after the bulk of the Enclosures which dispossessed much of the English peasantry. It was taken forty years after Oliver Goldsmith had seen a living village, Nuneham Courtenay in Oxfordshire, destroyed in the 1760s to make way for a manorial park, and thirty after he had written in his eulogy 'The Deserted Village': 'Ill fares the land, to hastening ills a prey, / Where wealth accumulates, and men decay . . . '

But the 1801 census (which admittedly surveyed much more of the country than its predecessor) still listed around 14,000 individual settlements and parishes in England's 50,000 square miles, most of which had also been among the 13,400 in the Domesday Book. The country consisted of an average of one singular if not self-contained city, town or village in every five square miles. Paddington to the west of London was a farming community of 1881 people, containing 158 agricultural workers. Fulham, with its 450 people working on the land and 391 in trade and manufacture, was an almost wholly rural parish. There were 163 agriculturalists living in Hanover Square. As late as 1867 the *Daily News* reported:

the Census enumerator . . . inquiring at each house who slept there on the previous night, puts all these important persons down to the credit of the districts where he finds them, and returns the City of London as a deserted place, tenanted chiefly by porters and housekeepers.

The official returns show that when the last Census was taken [in 1861] there were nine bankers and ten stock and share brokers in the City, but forty-four farmers, twenty-three gardeners, and one shepherd . . .

Ancient agricultural settlements would disappear in a number of different ways and for a variety of reasons. In Bedfordshire the village of Eaton Socon, with its 1625 people who in 1801 mostly worked the land, as they had done since the time of the Domesday Book, soon became part of St Neots and thereby of Cambridgeshire. The village of Moot in Cumbria, which in 1801 contained an almost perfect and extremely promising balance of 145 males and 146 females with no uninhabited houses, would disappear into the expanding boundaries of the town of Keswick, leaving only its old manor house as a memorial to those 291 men, women and children.

The township of Castle Martin in the hundred of the same name in the Welsh county of Pembroke contained in 1801 a total of 338 persons, 248 of whom were employed on the land. In 1939 Castle Martin would become part of an Army Training Estate. The whole surrounding area was evacuated. Most of the evacuees failed to return. Two hundred years later Castle Martin was home to half as many people as in 1801. Fifty farming people lived in the Wiltshire village of Imber in 1801. Similarly, Imber had the misfortune to be situated in the middle of Salisbury Plain. In 1943 its people were gathered in the schoolhouse and told to leave in order to make way for tens of thousands of American troops in training for the Allied invasion of Nazi-controlled Europe. Imber would never be repopulated.

The fates of those lost English and Welsh villages, as well as such as the Welsh settlement of Capel Celwyn which disappeared in the 1960s beneath a huge reservoir constructed to supply Merseyside with water, or the Yorkshire fishing community of Wilsthorpe, claimed by the North Sea, were dwarfed by the catastrophes which would shortly hit their equivalents in Ireland and the Highlands and Islands of Scotland.

Ireland being unrecorded in 1801, the student of John Rickman's first census was left to note that in the Scottish county of Inverness, which contained much of the north-western seaboard and many of the Hebridean islands, there were 74,294 people. It was the tenth most heavily populated of the thirty-three Scottish shires. Inverness-shire's glens and islands held 5 per cent of the total population of Scotland. It was roughly the same size as industrialising Renfrewshire and had half as many people as Lanarkshire, which included a place called Glasgow. Inverness-shire contained hundreds of healthy, growing villages which went by such names as Morsaig, Corodale, Boreraig and Hallaig. Those places and those correlations, which had changed little over the preceding centuries, would not last for very much longer.

Both politicians and the press accepted the results of Rickman's work first with curiosity and then with extraordinary fealty. Within months his 'Account of the Population' was being referred to in parliamentary debates as a census, and was being cited without question in discussions on such subjects as the size of the armed forces, electoral reform, the sustenance of the population and the clearance by landowners of people from their estates in the north of Scotland.

The regional newspapers jumped with delight on the returns from their local towns and parishes, most of which were calculated and published by John Rickman's clerks for the first time in 1801 and 1802. When the results for England and Wales were published in April 1802, the *Caledonian Mercury* in Edinburgh, while eagerly awaiting the final figures for Scotland, thought it safe to affirm in 'the United Kingdom of Great Britain and Ireland, that the population exceeds fifteen millions . . . and it appears . . . that our population has increased with very accelerated rapidity the nearer we approach to the present time'.

In February 1802 Charles Abbot was called back from Ireland to become Speaker of the House of Commons. He asked John Rickman to remain at his side as the Speaker's secretary. 'From attachment to England or to a young lady at Chidham', Rickman agreed. He sailed from Dublin to London and moved into New Palace Yard in the precincts of the old Palace of Westminster. His house there, which he would occupy for most of the rest of his life, was a three-storey dwelling by Westminster Hall among wooden buildings which dated from the time of Queen Elizabeth I, some of them so close to the River Thames that, as Rickman's daughter Ann would recall, 'at spring tide there was great pleasure to us children in dipping our fingers down into the waters from the sitting room windows . . .'

Rickman himself had good views of the Thames from his own ground floor, but his pride was his garden. It was, wrote Ann Rickman, 'a bright, pleasant piece of ground with a terrace and rails to the river, and the roses and other flowers grew luxuriantly', while against the end of Keeper of the Exchequer Mr Wilde's house on the terrace 'there was a Hamboro' grape; and we had gooseberries too and a Morella cherry besides a very pretty Bird cherry tree ... and there was a corner and a mound to bury the kittens and canaries in ...

'Papa very often in warm weather stretched himself down on the slope of turf that formed the terrace, in the centre of which were four stone steps: he generally went to sleep and we made daisy chains to dress him up, and looked at his pigtail, but we never quite made up our minds to pull it.' The lighthearted polymath Papa Rickman in his turn insisted that at the family dinner table his children should order their desserts in Latin.

The Speaker's secretary was a well-paid job, with material, social and political benefits which went beyond such comfortable accommodation. At home and at work, John Rickman was situated at the heart of government. New Palace Yard contained taverns and coffee shops. When Parliament was sitting members arrived there, gathered there and departed from there in their carriages. It was witness to such coronations in Rickman's time as that of King George IV. The Lord Mayor of London would embark annually from his golden barge at New Palace Yard. Music drifted and fireworks were seen from Vauxhall Gardens across the river. The unemployable, 'seditious' young radical had, within two years of arriving in London, entered what he continued for a short time to describe to his friends as 'vile employment' at the traditional heart of the British establishment.

Then, wrote Ann, there was the official church parade . . .

the Speaker and his wife, Mr and Mrs Abbot, [in] her
bright emerald silk pelisse trimmed with deep ermine,
a muff as large as a pillow with deep cuffs and a long
tippet en suite. The footman behind her with her prayer
book; Mr Abbott with pig-tail and broad-brimmed
hat, a black swallow-tail coat, tight grey pantaloons and
Hessian boots rather short with a tassel in front. Our
Father had much the same dress, but his boots varied,
and sometimes had a straight trim and no tassel, but there
was a pig-tail. Mamma had sable en suite, her pelisse was
'Waterloo-blue' silk . . .

'Mamma' was Rickman's 'young lady at Chidham'. After a
courtship of several years, in 1805 he married a tall, striking
and sociable woman from West Sussex named Susannah
Postlethwaite. Chidham was fifty miles along the south
coast of England from Christchurch. One of Rickman's
brothers farmed there and Rickman himself had known
Susannah since he came down from Oxford in the early
1790s. He wrote to Robert Southey of importing 'a wife
from the country by way of experiment', and Susannah
could hardly have been more of the countryside. Her new
husband's census of 1801 recorded Chidham as being an
agricultural parish of 209 persons within the Rape (an
ancient sub-division unique to Sussex) of Chichester.

Rickman was eager to reassure his male associates that
his marriage to Susannah had no sentimental foundations.
'[T]he main ingredient determining my choice,' he wrote
to Tom Poole, a West Country landowner and another
friend of such men as Coleridge and Lamb, 'was not love

or gain – but an esteem of very long standing – having been well acquainted with the lady who has consented to migrate hither rather more than a dozen years, and having always perhaps had so much influence over her as to cause her, sensibly or insensibly, to do and to think very much after my own taste.'

Besides, by 1805 he was thirty-four years old – 'half the age which David assigns to us'; he was bored with rattling alone around his house in New Palace Yard; he required a countrywoman to care for its garden as well as to bear him children (she would deliver four). He was also, finally, resigned to the fact that his future lay not in Southeyesque adventures overseas or in the ferment of domestic revolution, the very notion of which he soon came to abhor, but as a hired hand of the House of Commons. He was comfortable in and unashamed of his newfound conservatism, to the amusement but ungrudging respect of his radical friends. John Rickman came, wrote the unrepentant liberal Leigh Hunt, 'to represent among us the plumpness of office and the solidity of government'.

For almost four decades the supervision and preparation of the national census was not regarded as a full-time job. The census was not even considered to be a regular fixture on the calendar. Each decennial census was dependent on the passage through Parliament, every ten years, of a new Population Act. Nor, for that matter, was the secretary to the Speaker of the House of Commons expected to limit himself to those responsibilities. In the 1800s alone, Rickman found himself serving as secretary to the parliamentary commissions on building new roads and bridges in Scotland and on digging the Caledonian Canal from east coast to west through the Great Glen by way of Loch Ness. The engineer Thomas Telford sat on both commissions and was thereafter added to Rickman's long roster of close friends.

His colleague Charles Abbot being neutered in the position of Speaker of the House, in February 1811 the second bill 'for taking an Account of the Population of Great Britain' was introduced by the Christchurch MP George Rose. It was quickly passed, and responsibility for its execution was once again handed to Rose's former constituent and protégé, John Rickman.

That second time around, most parties to the enumeration being familiar with the process, the census was taken much more smoothly. Rickman himself was able finally to report to the House of Commons in June 1812, a year to the month after the first forms had been sent back to his office from all over England, Scotland and Wales, that unlike in 1801, 'The Enumeration of the whole Population may be considered as complete, no place being known finally to have omitted making Return.'

He followed exactly the same system, requesting county clerks of the peace and sheriffs' officers to delegate downwards to the overseers or educated large householders of their individual parishes or, in Scotland especially, schoolteachers. He made only one substantial change to the questions asked in the 1801 form. In that year householders had been asked for the number of persons employed in agriculture, in trade, manufacture or handicraft, or in neither of those two categories. The question had caused confusion. In particular, 'Miners, Fishermen, and those employed in Inland Navigation' had been sure that they were not agriculturalists, but unsure whether or not they were in commerce. Moreover, some householders had included their servants as members of their family when they should have appeared in the catch-all third class.

Rickman hoped to straighten all this out in 1811 by keeping a question which answered to the individual numbers and genders of the citizenry, while also asking for each family's chief source of income and confirming that coal miners, fishermen and servants, rather than being omitted altogether from the employment statistics, should be entered in classes two or three. He did not appear to care which one, although his third class had initially been intended to cover 'superannuated Labourers, and Widows resident in small tenements'. Unfortunately many families depended on various sources of income. A fisherman's wife might make and sell handicrafts, while his daughters could be household day-servants and his sons might work in a Cornish tin mine. It would not only be difficult to single out any one of them as the 'chief source' of family income; it would also omit the others from the national roster of working people. As the sociologist David Glass pointed out, 'the change in 1811 from occupations of persons to occupations of families is likely to have increased the errors'.

Rickman was right, however, to claim a greater accuracy in the overall statistics for 1811. They showed a booming population. The population of England had apparently grown by over 14 per cent to 9,583,827, that of Scotland by 13 per cent to 1,805,688, and that of Wales also by 13 per cent to 611,788. With 640,500 men – more than the entire population of Wales – serving in the army and navy as Great Britain fought both Russia and the Napoleonic European Empire and was about to go to war with the United States, that gave a total of 12,641,803, an increase of 1,740,567, 'or about Fifteen in a Hundred', in the previous ten years.

In fact the totals for 1801 had probably been understated by incompetent returns and the actual decennial growth was not quite so dramatic. But with an estimated Irish population of 5 million, that United Kingdom of 17.5 million people was clearly a nation on the march.

Where had they come from and what were they all doing? Those not at war were mostly still on the land. Almost 900,000 English, Welsh and Scottish families were in 1811 directly dependent on agriculture, with 1,130,000 in all of the different forms of commerce and 530,000 in other employment or no employment at all.

As the size of the average British family in 1811 was just under six people, it is probable that those 900,000 agricultural families represented a slight increase on the 2 million individuals who in 1801 were classified as working on the land. But the relative proportions with other occupations were changing. In 1801 only 3 per cent more of King George III's subjects had worked in 'trade, manufacture or handicraft' than in agriculture. By 1811 the household 'chief source of income' survey suggested that the gap in favour of commerce had increased to about 15 per cent. Probably it had not broadened so widely, or so quickly. The likelihood is that in most cases the source of income of the male head of the household was returned, and the employment of the rest of his family was unrecorded. So in 1811 the sons of carters or grocers who were still resident in the family home and who worked as farm labourers would be lost to posterity. An undeniable trend was, however, under way.

Places such as Wiltshire, Suffolk and Essex were overwhelmingly agricultural and their populations were relatively static. Middlesex, which included most of London, was even more overwhelmingly commercial and its population was growing. In such Midland and northern counties as Staffordshire, Lancashire, Northumberland, Durham and the West Riding of Yorkshire, and in the Scottish central belt, the industrial revolution was flexing its muscles. Their villages were swelling into towns and their market towns into small cities.

In 1801 the population of Bradford in Yorkshire had been 5073. Bradford was then no more than a small market town in the greater wapentake of Morley. Its population was chiefly commercial, with a high proportion of home weavers and spinners. By 1811 Bradford's population had risen to 7767. In 1831 it would be 22,223 and still growing. The population of Lanarkshire in Scotland had risen from 146,000 in 1801 to 191,000 in 1811. In 1831 Lanarkshire had 316,819 inhabitants. Its main city of Glasgow alone contained 202,426 people.

According to many theorists those statistics should have ushered in an early Malthusian catastrophe. They did not. As John Rickman understood, they were instead the result of a population growing apace to meet the hectic demands of a war economy and an industrial revolution which were both nourished by the rapidly increasing yields of an agricultural revolution. People had children for Darwinian reasons. Those children would mostly be fed and given employment. The average family size was in fact falling. Each family unit would in 1831 contain an average of just over five people, fewer than twenty years earlier. As that was the result of a conscious human decision to limit the reproduction of the species, it could be claimed to be a direct refutation of Malthusian principles.

The fluctuating size of average British families was always

difficult to estimate. Due partly to high rates of infant mortality, early nineteenth-century families were not always so large as later generations imagined. In 1821 John Rickman calculated that every 100 marriages resulted in 369 baptisms, which indicated an average 'live birth' rate and consequent family size of 3.69 children. Not every mother was married and not every baby was baptised, but Rickman's analysis suggested that the popular myth of a nation of rural cottages or urban slums overrun by a dozen or more offspring was groundless.

By 1871, when the Registrar General George Graham and his assistant William Farr were doing the sums, 'the pressure on subsistence is less than it was' and 'In England the children born in wedlock to a marriage are 4.3.' A hundred years later in 1971 there would be on average two children to each cohabiting couple in Britain. In the twenty-first century that family size would fall further to 1.8 children per household.

Averages were of course merely averages. Some mothers gave birth to sufficient children for eight or ten others. The most prolific couple in recorded British history was John and Mary Jonas of Cheshire. In 1839 Mary Thomas, a woman in her mid-twenties from Denbighshire in Wales, married a Chester chair maker named John Jonas. Mary was already pregnant and later in 1839 she gave birth to twins, one of whom survived. In the following two decades Mary Jonas would bear thirty-three children, including fifteen pairs of boy–girl twins. Only a dozen of them reached adulthood. As recorded in the national census, the Jonas family reached its peak size in 1861, when John and Mary, both by then in what was for the time advanced middle age, lived at 34 Foregate Street in Chester's old city centre with eight of their children, including two complete sets of surviving boy–girl twins.

Most remarkably, Mary herself survived that life of annual childbirth. By 1891 she and her husband were again living alone, both in their late seventies and sharing a modest end-of-terrace cottage in Chester's Churton Street. John Jonas died the following year at the age of seventy-eight; Mary passed away in December 1899 at eighty-five. Their shared gravestone in Chester's Overleigh Cemetery was inscribed:

In Memory

Of

JOHN JONAS,

Who Died February 24th 1892,

Aged 78 Years.

Also MARY JONAS,

The Beloved Wife Of The Above

And Mother Of 33 Children

Who Died December 4th 1899,

Aged 85 Years.

Nothing In My Hands I Bring

Simply To The Cross I Cling.

The most successful mother in British history was Mrs Ada Watson of Cambridge. Ada married a labourer from London named John Henry Watson. They settled in Cambridge and in 1904, at the age of nineteen, Ada Watson gave birth to her first surviving son. The couple suffered at least three infant mortalities before raising a further twenty-four healthy children, including three sets of twins, until 1931, when at the age of forty-five Ada ceased to reproduce. Like Mary

Jonas, she lived to a good old age, dying in 1974 at the age of eighty-eight.

The 1991 census would register in Liverpool six eight-year-old daughters of Graham and Janet Walton. Hannah, Luci, Ruth, Sarah, Kate and Jennie Walton were the first surviving British sextuplets, and the first set of all-female sextuplets in the world. At the time of the 2011 census the six 29-year-old women were all still unmarried. Their father Graham commented, 'They've all said they don't want joint weddings. But I try to talk them out of it anyway and say that people don't get married these days, it's old-fashioned. I tell them they can live in sin with my blessing – it'll save me a few bob!'

On several occasions early in the nineteenth century John Rickman encouraged his friends to criticise the irrepressible Thomas Malthus in print, or congratulated them on doing so. Aside from their opposing views on the feasibility and desirability of an increased population, he had good practical reasons for regarding Malthus as an irresponsible nuisance. In 1816 Rickman became secretary to the Poor Law Committee, which guided the distribution of relief to the impecunious of Great Britain. Malthus naturally held the opinion – and wrote – that any system of poor relief encouraged unsustainable overpopulation.

A colleague of Rickman's in the civil service, Simon Gray, writing in 1817 under the pen name of George Purves, used the statistics of Rickman's first two censuses to declare Malthus' work absurdly mistaken. Gray's antithesis received much publicity in the press of the time. As he stated, in terms which could have been drafted by Rickman himself, 'the population of every district of Britain had increased,

not even excepting the Highlands of Scotland, thinned by
constant emigration though they were.

'Allowing for the greater completeness of the enumeration of 1811, I am inclined to think, that the population of
Britain alone had increased between 1792 and 1815' – the
approximate duration of the wars with France and the
United States – 'full one fourth, or about 2,500,000 souls.
In this prodigious increase of her circulators, combined
with the unprecedented increase of really productive, that
is, profitable employment, we have the actual sources of
the astonishing increase in her income and capital, or her
wealth, during these 23 years ...

The Reverend Mr. Malthus has assumed, that there is
a constant tendency in all animated nature to increase
beyond the nourishment prepared for it.

This I consider as a mere and unwarranted imagination. But though it could be proved to be the fact in
nature, when applied to irrational animals, under all
their circumstances of character and kind, as it certainly
cannot, while the contrary is more probable, it would
not hold with respect to man, whom reason has made as
completely the regulator of the amount of subsistence, as
of clothing, lodging, and the rest ...

The other position, which has been maintained by
this reverend author, as well as by several other writers
of name, that there is a tendency in the increase of population rather to produce poverty, is equally contrary
to facts, whether applied generally or occasionally. The
reverse is uniformly true ...

The real and pleasing effects of a rapid increase of
population were seen in most brilliant display, during the

war, through the whole extent of our island, and gave as decisive a negation to the gloomy theory of the Reverend Mr. Malthus, as the employment created by the war did to that of the author of the Wealth of Nations [Adam Smith] . . .

In his home in New Palace Yard, John Rickman had become aware that he was capable of changing the course of British political philosophy, and therefore of British history. His presence at the centre of his country's turbulent early nineteenth-century life was on certain occasions illuminated in the most dramatic fashion. At 5.15 p.m. on 11 May 1812 a discontented petitioner shot the British prime minister, the first and only time in history that such a deed was committed.

As he entered the House of Commons lobby, prime minister Spencer Perceval was shot once in the heart by John Bellingham, an export representative who had spent several years in Russian prisons without afterwards being compensated by the British government. 'After he was shot,' wrote Rickman, Perceval 'walked on but 6 or 7 steps, as if unconscious, and so much in his usual gait as to be recognised by it through the crowd, when he approached the door of the Ho. Commons, he struck both his hands upon his breast, and fell prostrate.'

Bellingham himself sat calmly on a bench in the lobby before being taken away, tried at the Old Bailey and then hanged. Perceval was taken into Rickman's office, which was empty in the early evening, and propped up on a table and chairs until a surgeon arrived and pronounced him dead. The corpse was then carried onto a sofa in the Speaker's nearby drawing room before being returned to 10

Downing Street. 'Poor Perceval,' Rickman wrote to Robert Southey five days after the assassination, 'breathed his last on the green table in my Ho. Commons room, but I was at home, and saw none of the tragedy.'

For what it was worth, Rickman had held a low opinion of the unfortunate 'blockhead' premier. He told Southey mischievously that the persistently bad press coverage afforded to the prime minister had meant that even before the gun was fired, 'I expected Mr Perceval to be murdered.'

Perceval was replaced by Rickman's almost exact contemporary, Robert Jenkinson, the Earl of Liverpool, who would remain prime minister for a further fifteen years, eventually dying of a heart attack. Liverpool's term of office between 1812 and 1827 encompassed the maturity of Rickman's own career. In 1814 he was promoted from Speaker's secretary to the position of Second Clerk Assistant at the Table of the House of Commons, and in 1820 to Clerk Assistant. The Clerk of the House was a position which dated from the fourteenth century, and by the nineteenth century had developed into an impartial advisory point of reference on parliamentary procedure to all elected members. However impartially he exercised his duties, the seditious young man from Christchurch had by 1820 become a hard-headed middle-aged Tory.

In 1815 Rickman had been made a Fellow of the Royal Society in recognition of his 'contribution to the improvement of natural knowledge'. In 1816 he began his work on the Poor Law Committee. He entertained and corresponded diligently and at length on literary and other matters with such friends as Robert Southey, Charles Lamb and Samuel Taylor Coleridge. And every ten years he took a national census whose functions expanded by the decade.

Whatever his manifold other responsibilities, some of her father's work on the census may have been described by his daughter Ann when she wrote later of being as a teenager 'seated "square" . . . drawing papers from beneath Papa's hand, just so exactly that he could go on signing paper after paper without any pause, to the number of 500 perhaps'. Those papers may have been the forms sent out for the 1821 census, when Ann Rickman was fourteen years old. There were two notable additions to that enumeration. The first was to require a rough estimation of the ages of citizens. The second was that, for the first time, Ireland was included.

The ages of members of the population were and would remain a headache to census takers. Aside from the fact that people have always been sensitive about stating their age, many people had only the vaguest notion of the year of their birth and most birthdays were not an occasion of much note, let alone celebration, until later in the twentieth century. On an April day in 1861 a census enumerator would call at Osborne Palace in the parish of Whippingham on the Isle of Wight. He discovered there a large family of a husband, wife and several children. Unusually, the wife's name was placed at the top of their census form as the head of the family. She was described as Victoria R, forty-one years of age, and her occupation was The Sovereign. Beneath her was Albert, also forty-one and Prince Consort. There followed five princes and princesses between the ages of three and nineteen. The national census of 1861 estimated Victoria's birth year as 1820. The summary of the 1841 census, taken four years after she ascended to the throne, stated that Victoria had been born 'abt 1821'. She had in fact been born in Kensington Palace on 24 May 1819. If the national census could consistently get wrong the personal details of the Queen of Great Britain and Ireland and future Empress of India, what hope had anybody else?

With similar potential difficulties in mind, the age details requested by the 1821 census forms were realistic. Enumerators, the choice of whom by then had been boiled down to schoolmasters in Scotland, overseers of the poor in England and Wales and policemen in Ireland, were asked to obtain estimated ages within a five- or ten-year margin of error. To be precise, they were politely asked in the forms signed by John Rickman: 'If you are of Opinion that . . . the Ages of the several Individuals can be obtained in a Manner satisfactory to yourself, and not inconvenient to the Parties, be pleased to state (or cause to be stated) the Number of those who are under 5 Years of Age, of those between 5 and 10 Years of Age, between 10 and 15, between 15 and 20, between 20 and 30, between 30 and 40, between 40 and 50, between 50 and 60, between 60 and 70, between 70 and 80, between 80 and 90, between 90 and 100, and upwards of 100, distinguishing Males from Females . . . '

'It will be perceived, from the tenor of this Question,' Rickman later reported to Parliament, 'that the Answers to it were purposely left optional . . . In fact the Return of Ages embraces Eight-Ninths of the Persons enumerated; a proportion which shows so much general goodwill in execution of the Population Act . . . '

The exclusion of Ireland from the first two censuses, or 'accounts of the population', in 1801 and 1811 had been a cause of contention in Parliament, the press and other public discourse throughout those years. The exclusion of

1801 was explicable because the Population Act of late 1800 had passed a few days before Ireland was officially incorporated into the United Kingdom. The country's omission in 1811 had no such justification. In 1812 an Act had passed through the Houses of Commons and Lords at Westminster which supposedly enabled an Irish census. Its execution was devolved to a precocious young Irish statistician named William Shaw Mason, who faithfully adopted John Rickman's questionnaires. Between 1813 and 1815 Mason managed to wring some statistics from much of the country – enough to estimate the Irish population as exceeding 6 million – but made no headway whatsoever in returns from Donegal, Fermanagh, Galway 'and from several large towns and baronies of other counties'.

That attempt to take a census of Ireland was subsequently abandoned. It failed, in Mason's words, because in the absence of Irish poor laws and the shortage of schools there were no overseers of the poor and few schoolmasters, and therefore 'no constituted body was to be found possessing all or even most of the requisites for this duty'. It was eventually agreed to pass on the responsibilities to Ireland's boards of magistrates, who were delegated to appoint enumerators in May 1821 to every part of the country.

They did not have an easy task. As had been revealed between 1813 and 1815, large parts of Ireland remained unreconciled to the union of 1801. Mason wrote that 'a determined hostility to [the enumerators'] proceedings, which shewed itself openly in some districts, was the most formidable, as it affected the very basis of the Inquiry'.

As a result, letters were then mailed to every Catholic and Protestant clergyman in Ireland. 'In them they were made acquainted with the intentions of the Government, to carry the Population Act into effect; its object was clearly stated, and their aid requested, both for controlling the proceedings of the Enumerators in their respective Parishes, and for removing any prejudices, or other unfavourable circumstances, that might tend to produce an unkindly feeling towards them in the minds of the lower classes.'

Aside from their anti-union sentiments, the lower, Catholic Irish classes had good reason to mistrust many enumerators. The magistracies were correctly identified as representatives of the Protestant ascendancy, their appointees as Protestant factotums and police officers as enforcers of the Anglo-Scottish occupation. Ten years later, in 1831 in County Wicklow, one such official was observed diligently to count the members of Protestant households individually, but merely to estimate, or underestimate, in bulk the local Catholics as they left church on Sunday morning. He was reported, and was ordered to go back and make his enumeration again, but it is unlikely that he was an isolated malefactor.

The hostility would never disappear. In 1861 a police constable taking the census in County Offaly was shot and then bludgeoned to death on a lonely pathway in the course of his duties, although whether he was murdered for being an enumerator or for being a policeman never became clear. 'The shot was heard ... by several persons,' it was reported, 'but, owing to the unwillingness of the peasantry to afford information in all such cases, it is not at all improbable that the murderer will remain undiscovered.'

Involving the Roman Catholic Church was, however, relatively successful in defusing the reaction from grassroots Irish nationalists to the British census. As William Shaw Mason stated:

Whenever a tendency to opposition was reported by the Enumerator, letters on the subject, transmitted to the resident clergyman of the district, immediately led to a satisfactory explanation, by which not only the obstacle was removed, but a friendly sentiment substituted in its place, so as to turn the current of public opinion immediately and completely into the channel most desirable for the effectual attainment of the great objects of the Legislature under the Population Act.

The local knowledge of the Clergy, both with regard to the people, and to the several districts in which they resided, also gave ample means to guide and check the Enumerators; and a correspondence was accordingly maintained between them and the Population department, which afforded many valuable remarks and suggestions.

In a polity where Roman Catholics, by virtue solely of their religious denomination, were not allowed to vote or hold public office and where the Penal Laws which attempted to oblige them to convert to the Protestant Church of Ireland – laws which the Dublin-born Anglo-Irish politician and political philosopher Edmund Burke had described as a 'contrivance, as well fitted for the oppression, impoverishment and degradation of a people, and the debasement in them of human nature itself, as ever proceeded from the perverted ingenuity of man' – were still in place and in practice, it is unlikely that matters ever proceeded as smoothly as Mason suggested. But they proceeded smoothly enough for him, at the second time of trying, to produce an account of the population of Ireland to set beside John Rickman's accounts of England, Wales and Scotland. It was agreed that all completed forms would be stored in Mason's 'Record Tower' in Dublin

Castle rather than in London. They were, as we have seen, almost all destroyed by a fire at the Public Record Office in that city at the outbreak of the Irish Civil War in 1922.

It was finally determined that in 1821 the population of the island of Ireland was 6,801,827. Dublin, 'the metropolis', contained only 227,335 of them. The remaining 6.6 million were overwhelmingly agriculturalists and small trades-people, spread more or less evenly across the four provinces of Munster, Leinster, Connaught and Ulster. In not one of those provinces did more than 20 per cent of the population live in settlements of more than 2000, and in Ulster and Connaught the scattered rural population comprised over 90 per cent of the total.

Back in London, such intriguing details put to one side, John Rickman was able finally to announce an almost complete (some parishes still did not return their forms and some smaller offshore islands were still not counted) enumeration of the United Kingdom of England, Wales, Scotland and Ireland.

In 1821 there were 11,261,437 people living in England, which represented an increase of 18 per cent in ten years. The 2,093,456 inhabitants of Scotland marked a decennial increase of 15 per cent. There were 717,108 people in Wales, 17 per cent more than in 1811.

Part of that increase in the overall civilian population was owed to the Battle of Waterloo in 1815 and the end of the Napoleonic and American wars in the same year. The number of men in all branches of military service had sub-sequently halved from its 1811 level of 640,500 to 319,300 soldiers and sailors in 1821. The reintroduction of more than 300,000 fit and active as well as disabled men had not only increased the resident civilian population; it had also created levels of unemployment and unrest which the industrial revolution struggled to accommodate. The enlargement of the labour market caused increased competition for jobs, which employers were quick to exploit by slashing wages; this in its turn created yet more urban misery and dissatisfaction. A reverberating outrage of 1819, when cavalry killed fifteen protesters and wounded several hundred more while breaking up a large reformist gathering at St Peter's Field in Manchester, was quickly and pointedly dubbed the Peterloo Massacre to reflect its cause as well as the obvious black irony of British soldiers being deployed against the very citizenry on whose behalf four years earlier they had supposedly defeated Napoleonic autocracy at Waterloo.

So long as a Malthusian catastrophe had not yet occurred and for as long as he could keep the Poor Laws in effective operation, such radical expressions of social discontent were only of concern to John Rickman insofar as they confirmed his rapid progression to the political right. Rickman agreed with his Tory government that reform would lead to revolution and that the only proper response to reformism was repression. Everything was, after all, progressing at a healthy pace. The population of the British Isles, he could reliably inform its Parliament, from Kent to Galway and from Cornwall to the Shetland Islands stood in 1821 at 21,198,458 men, women and children. The Isle of Man and the Channel Islands having been canvassed for the first time, 'The Enumeration of the whole Population,' Rickman reported with satisfaction, 'may be considered as complete ...' Its evidence of extraordinary demographic growth would hopefully, he wrote privately to Robert Southey, 'put to flight for ever and aye' reformist complaints about 'the Distress of the Times'.

*

John Rickman passed his own fiftieth birthday shortly after the taking of the 1821 census. As well as his numerous other duties he was busily compiling reports on roads and bridges in the Scottish Highlands and on the progress of the Caledonian Canal, which was nearing completion. He would shortly accept the secretaryship of yet another Highlands and Islands commission, which examined the building of churches in that region and which reported in 1831, both a census year and the year of his sixtieth birthday. 'You have had more than your share of this world's business,' wrote Southey. 'I doubt whether any other man who has worked so hardly, has worked so continuously and so long.'

But Rickman was comfortable. He took his family on summer holidays to his brother's farmhouse at Chidham in Sussex, where they indulged in 'hay-making and the cherry season'. In 1824 he spent £3000 on building and furnishing a country house at Portsmouth, to which he would subsequently retire with his wife and children for up to two months in the year. He managed to escape London for Normandy to view the Bayeux Tapestry, and to the Netherlands in the company of Southey. By his sixtieth year he was nonetheless feeling the strain. 'What with the Popn. work,' he wrote to Southey in July 1831, 'the Highland Churches and the Reform bill' – the first Reform Act of 1832, which transferred the franchise from some rotten and pocket antique rural constituencies to certain affluent men in the new industrial towns and cities, and to which Rickman was privately opposed, was set in motion as a controversial parliamentary bill in March 1831 – 'I have more than enough to do and little time for thinking.'

His fatigue was reflected in the 1831 census. It contained

some additions but one substantial omission. The estimate of ages nervously introduced with some success ten years earlier, instead of being made more precise, was dropped altogether. 'The Question of the Age of persons,' wrote Rickman in December 1831, 'which succeeded beyond expectation in 1821, has not been repeated in 1831, not only as imposing too much labour ... but as unnecessary and inconclusive at an interval of no more than Ten years.' The first reason given was more convincing than the second. Co-opted schoolteachers, overseers of the poor and other enumerators had simply found the age question to be too much trouble, and Rickman was past arguing with them.

Instead the enumerators were asked to discover how many men were over twenty years of age – and then to find out almost exactly how they spent their working days. In place of the broad and often confusing three basic categories – agriculture, trade and industry, and anything else – the employment specifics were greatly enhanced.

Agriculture was expanded to include 'Graziers, Cow-keepers, Shepherds and other Farm Servants, Gardeners ... and Nurserymen'. Manufacture now included 'making Manufacturing Machinery'. Then there was 'Retail Trade and Handicrafts'. A list of 100 occupations which in 1831 fell into that category was helpfully distributed to the enumerators. As well as bakers, blacksmiths and butchers, it included such vocations as drysalter, scavenger, toyman and wharfinger. Drysalters sold such chemical products as glue and varnish and the materials, such as salt, for preserving food. Scavengers were street cleaners who made an income by collecting and reselling discarded or dropped items of either substantial or petty value, from lost jewellery to jettisoned rags. A toyman obviously sold children's toys. Wharfingers were small-scale harbourmasters who managed the shipping and trade which passed through wharves or docks. Rickman was slightly apologetic about the number of occupations listed. 'This List,' he wrote, '[is] known to contain far less than the entire number of Trades in large towns especially in the Metropolis, where in the result no less than 426 Subdivisions of trade were found to exist; but a greater number than one hundred would have been inapplicable and even perplexing in rural parishes ...'

Their job descriptions, if not the jobs themselves, may have disappeared from Great Britain by the first half of the twentieth century, but those were the embryonic lower middle classes. They were distinct both from the middle and upper middle classes of 'Wholesale Merchants, Bankers, Capitalists, Professional Persons, Artists, Architects, Teachers, Clerks, Surveyors, and other Educated Men', and from the manual working classes, including 'Miners, Fishermen, Boatmen, Excavators of Canals, Road Makers, Toll Collectors, or Labourers'. And finally there were the unemployed and unemployable: 'retired Tradesmen, Superannuated Labourers, and Males diseased or disabled in Body or Mind'.

The presumption being that adult male employment alone was significant (extremely rash in an age when women and small children of both genders worked long hours in mines and mills, in the fields and on the fishery docks), female household servants were the only employed women to be counted. There were 670,491 female servants in England, Scotland and Wales.

The creeping relative decline of the agricultural community, which nonetheless in 1831 still occupied 961,135 families in Britain outside Ireland, had already been noted by Rickman in 1821. In 1831 he drew attention to the burgeoning cities and towns: 'Manchester, Glasgow and Paisley, eminent in the Manufacture of Cotton; Birmingham, which relies on the Hardware trade, that is, the conversion of Metals to useful purposes; Leeds eminent for Woollens, Norwich for Crapes, and Nottingham for the Manufacture of Stockings. After these are placed the Commercial Sea-Ports; Liverpool, Bristol with its Suburbs ... Aberdeen, Newcastle-upon-Tyne with its Suburb of Gateshead (in the County of Durham); Hull, and the prosperous Town of Dundee: The two great Naval Arsenals, Plymouth and Portsmouth, close this explanatory Catalogue ... '

London, with 1,471,410 inhabitants, was of course the biggest conurbation in Britain. Although statistics, or even estimates, from China were not available to John Rickman at the time, London had probably just overtaken Beijing as the most populous city in the world, a position it would hold for a further 100 years until the British metropolis was itself overtaken by New York in the 1920s. It was followed in the United Kingdom of 1831 by Manchester with a population of 227,808, Glasgow with 202,425, Liverpool with 189,202, Birmingham with 142,206 and Bristol with 103,886.

Those totals represented breathtaking increases over the ten years between 1821 and 1831 of 20 per cent in London, 47 per cent in Manchester, 38 per cent in Glasgow, 44 per cent in Liverpool, 33 per cent in Birmingham and 18 per cent in Bristol, which was already established as a major entrepôt to and from the north Atlantic Ocean. The population of the 'prosperous town of Dundee', whose textile industry had suddenly expanded thanks to the fortunate discovery that whale oil, of which Dundee had a surfeit, could be used to lubricate the dry fibres of imported jute, had grown by no less than 48 per cent to 45,355 in the decade before 1831. The 1820s, John Rickman was indicating, were the years in which the British industrial revolution came of age.

In Ireland a civil servant named George Hatchell had been 'appointed by the Chief Secretary of the Lord Lieutenant for digesting and arranging the Population Returns' from what had been christened the 'Population Inquiry Office' at Dublin Castle. Like William Shaw Mason before him, Hatchell was not assisted by simmering Irish grievances. Most notably, in May 1831 an affray at the annual Fair Day at Castlepollard in the Irish midlands resulted in police shooting randomly with muskets into the unarmed crowd and killing thirteen men and women. Nineteen policemen were subsequently charged with causing the deaths. In July 1831 they were all acquitted.

Shortly afterwards the parish priest of eleven of the thirteen murdered civilians received from George Hatchell in Dublin Castle his standard request to assist with the population returns. The priest wrote furiously back to Hatchell:

I have been favoured with two copies of your census of the population ... I would wish to know what obligation the priests of Ireland owe either to you or to the Government, that we should assist your travelling servants, or look over your work. If you want clerical bailiffs, call on those whom you pay, and who have nothing else to do. With respect to you, we have neither time nor inclination to give you gratuitous services; no more than we should be inclined to disgrace ourselves by receiving your pay.

You want the census of my parish. All the information I can afford you is, that its population was reduced, in the last shooting day, eleven in number; and that we have laws which forbid me to characterize the deed as it deserves. The Government, which is supported at an enormous expense for the purpose, or under the pretence (which you know is the same thing) of preserving each man's right inviolable, calls upon me to help to number the rest of my flock, without attending, in the smallest degree, to those eleven whom I have lost. Does this government think I could so soon forget them, or that I can ever forget them, or that from my memory can be effaced the impression which their pallid countenances, distorted by expiring agonies, their stiffening limbs, their bodies smarting with the tepid current that gushed from their hearts, has stamped on my mind.

Sir, send your Orange messengers and enumerators to those to whom they are welcome; but let them not be annoying my little place with their unwelcome presence. I am too much affected by the loss of my parishioners, whom I regarded more than I do you, or any one belonging to, or connected with, the Irish government, to turn my attention to this display.

Despite such culls of the Catholic majority and the withdrawal of cooperation caused thereby, Hatchell was able to report a substantial increase in the population of Ireland to 7,734,365 men, women and children. They included five hackle-makers, all of whom were in Dublin manufacturing fibre combs from metal. After the hackles had been run through sheared wool or imported flax the material was handed over to tucker millers, who plucked out further imperfections by hand. In that year there were fifty-one tucker millers in Ireland.

In 1831, John Rickman was able finally to report, the population of Great Britain and Ireland was 24,132,294, and rising more quickly than almost anybody else had anticipated. Rather than drinking itself into oblivion, it had grown in a little over 100 years from a middle-ranking European country to the third largest after Germany and France, and it was closing rapidly on both of them.

Rickman had conducted his fourth and last census. Early in 1832 he considered retiring from his parliamentary duties in the Easter of that year. He was sixty years old when the average life expectancy of an Englishman of that age was sixty-five. By then contemptuous of politics and politicians of all parties, he wrote in February 1832, while working on the latest population abstract, that he had 'not slept above 3 hours in the 24 since Xtmas [Christmas 1831]'. He was tired.

Rickman did not and never would retire. 'My escape from the H. of C.,' he wrote in June 1832, 'is impeded by procrastinating manoeuvres of which I do not fully understand the motive and cannot overcome.' While his family and his ageing body may have been urging him to retire, both his colleagues and even his own weary intellect might have had another opinion. Above all, he was reluctant to desert his 'better occupation' of the population accounts. There were still, he wrote in the summer of 1833, 'mountebank theorists, praters and puffers' in the demographic arena, and he felt unable to leave the field clear for Thomas Malthus and his heirs.

Life in New Palace Yard also continued to offer a front row seat at the most momentous occasions of the nineteenth century. In October 1834 the Houses of Parliament in the medieval Palace of Westminster were almost completely destroyed by fire. The catastrophic blaze was not started by the kind of revolutionary mob from which Rickman had come to expect such atrocities, but by a chimney fire from the furnaces beneath the House of Lords.

Most of the Rickman family was in residence at the time. At 3.30 in the morning of 17 October a sleepless Frances Rickman wrote to her older sister Ann, who was away in the country, 'after near eight hours dreadful doubt, we seem all safe, though I am still partly lighted by the still blazing House of Commons!

I fear you will hear of the awful fire before this reaches you. ... I will give you as collected an account as I can, for my legs ache and I could not sleep, so I may as well write.

After dinner, at half past six this evening, Papa and Mamma taking a nap, in came Ellis, 'I think, Miss, there's a small fire broke out at the House of Lords.' I said 'Come with me to the leads to see it,' and there, even then, a volume of flame was blowing towards the Wildes'. Papa at first thought it could be got under, but soon it fearfully grew, and we had little doubt the Hall would catch. The House of Lords we could not see, but some heard that it and Mr. Ley's and the Library were destroyed: then the flames burst from the House of Commons windows, and sooner than I could believe the interior of that was destroyed ...

Poor Mamma was much overcome at first, but that made me stronger, as I felt I must look to everything, Papa being then rather provokingly easy. By this time we had many helps and constant knocking at the door ... the books were tied in sheets, drawers emptied, everything dismantled. Here (bow room) only a few chairs, sofas and the table remain . . . Fancy the whole house dismantled . . . Papa and Mr. Payne took me out to the corner of Palace Yard to see the Abbey, such a grand sight as I pray I may never see again; the bright moon in dark clouds, and the clear red and blue and yellow light. Oh! no one who did not see it can picture it . . .

Half past six. Daylight, and after a hard fight to save the Hall, the fire is all out . . .

Although most of the Palace of Westminster was reduced to scorched walls or rubble, the Rickmans' house in New Palace Yard was relatively undamaged and they were able quickly to return home with their possessions. 'The Ho. Commons . . . makes an excellent ruin' wrote Rickman to Southey. Rickman's own precious population forms and returns from 1801 onwards, being stored elsewhere, survived the fire, only to be destroyed by that careless official order seventy years later.

The rebuilding of the Houses of Parliament entailed the demolition of New Palace Yard, and in 1835 the Rickman family moved to 23 Duke Street, Westminster. The fire seemed somehow to represent the end of days. Rickman's friends Coleridge and Lamb both died in 1834. Susannah, the 'young lady at Chidham' who had become his wife, died in May 1836. 'Our long tragedy is now fast drawing to a close,' wrote Robert Southey to his lifelong friend and correspondent in October 1837 as Southey's own wife lay dying.

In 1840 Rickman began work on the following year's population accounts. That June he took to his bed with an ulcerated larynx. He continued to work on the census bill from his lonely home in Duke Street, but after what his daughter Ann described as a 'sad, painful struggle for breath', Rickman died on 11 August 1840 at the age of sixty-eight. He was buried beside his wife in St Margaret's Chapel, Westminster.

On 3 February 1841 tributes were paid to Rickman in the House of Commons which he had served for four decades. Joseph Hume, a Scot who had become the Radical MP for Kilkenny in Ireland and was therefore one of those politicians for whom the older John Rickman had developed a hearty distaste, said: 'I am unwilling to allow this vote to pass without expressing my humble approbation of the conduct of the late Mr. Rickman.

'I have never known a public officer so modest, so unassuming, possessed of such varied knowledge respecting the affairs of Parliament, and yet so ready to afford every information to others.

'The labours of Mr. Rickman generally in statistical matters, to which I have paid particular attention, have been highly valuable; and, specially as regards the preface to the Population Returns, will stand unrivalled in the amount of information and in the concise manner in which he brought it before this House. I therefore most cordially concur in expressing my sense of the value of his services.'

Two years later, in 1843, an engraving was published of a mature John Rickman at work. In the portrait he is standing by a desk with a quill pen in his right hand and a sheaf of papers beneath his clenched left fist. Below the engraving were inscribed the words, 'An Honest Man'.

4

The First Modern Census

In the spring of 1851, 38-year-old Norman MacRaild travelled eighty miles westward, over land and sea, from his home in the north of the island of Skye to the small island group of St Kilda.

MacRaild was accustomed to the journey. For the previous nine years he had been employed as factor by the landowner John MacPherson MacLeod, an upper-class Highlander who had amassed a small fortune from the East India Company and invested much of it in Hebridean estates. Those estates included the distant archipelago of St Kilda. While MacLeod was away in Bombay or London, his factor MacRaild had responsibility for the administration of his land and tenantry.

But in the spring of 1851 MacRaild was given an unusual task. Half a century after an 'Account of the Population' had first been taken in most of the British Isles he was instructed to include St Kilda, one of the few last unaccounted outposts, in the census enumeration.

It was an historical moment, the significance of which may have escaped Norman MacRaild. He was mailed a set of forms which he stowed in his baggage as he set off to sail from Skye to the Outer Hebridean island of Harris, and then from Harris into the north Atlantic Ocean. The skyscraping cliffs and sea stacks of the most isolated community in Britain became visible from the deck of his boat long before he entered the sheltered anchorage of Village Bay on the largest St Kildan island of Hirta.

MacRaild stepped onto the rocky shoreline. A hundred yards away, curving in a graceful arc through a few acres of greensward, its roofs leaking peat smoke, stood a detached terrace of low thatched cottages, their gable ends facing the sea.

The only permanent human settlement on the three islands of St Kilda stood sideways-on to a rough main pathway 'sufficient for at least two people to walk abreast'. The cottages, 'or at least the front ones, form a pretty regular line, though some are placed farther back or behind the others, so, as in these parts, to make the line double'. They had 'the appearance of being detached from each other, though sometimes two small dwellings join together ... The door-way is very low, and the great thickness of these double walls produces a space as you enter, which may be called a passage.

'There are generally two rooms together, each apartment being covered by a separate roof, although there are smaller single tenements for widow women and old maids.' The houses were peculiarly thatched, with the bottom edge of thatch tucked inside the outer walls to stop the Atlantic gales from gaining purchase and lifting off the roof.

Norman MacRaild walked along that rough main pathway holding a pencil and the sheets of printed paper mailed to him from the General Register Office in London. Calling at thirty-one adjacent cottages, he registered in his educated copper-plate a total of 110 people, all but one of whom had been born on St Kilda. The exception was 35-year-old Betsy MacDonald, from Lochinver in Sutherland on the mainland of Scotland. Betsy had arrived as Elizabeth Scott some twenty years earlier to keep house for a temporary minister of religion and had shortly afterwards married the St Kildan Calum MacDonald. Unlike her neighbours, Betsy had some conversational English, which made her for many years a point of contact between visitors and the Gaelic-speaking St Kildans.

The oldest inhabitant recorded by MacRaild in the 1851 census was the 79-year-old widow Marion MacCrimmon, a 'former birdcatcher's wife', who was in receipt of alms and lived alone in a small cottage appended to the larger MacCrimmon family home towards the southern end of the row. The youngest was the three-month-old daughter of another MacCrimmon family who lived in the middle of the street. The minister's manse was unoccupied; there was no resident minister and therefore no minister's family. Nor was there a schoolteacher; not a single child was registered as a 'scholar'.

The staple of the St Kildan diet was dried and boiled gannets and fulmars caught from the highest stacks and cliffs in Britain. Almost every man and teenage boy on the island offered as his 'Rank, Profession, or Occupation' the terms 'birdcatcher' and 'farmer', or in the case of the single male over seventy years old, Roderick Gillies, 'formerly farmer and birdcatcher'. Most of their spouses and mothers were listed as 'farmer and birdcatcher's wife'. Young St Kildan girls were usually 'employed at home'; young boys were sheep and cattle herders until the age of fifteen, when they became 'employed in the general service of the island – farming and birdcatching'.

When MacRaild had finished, returned to Skye and posted the papers back, and when they had been received and filed by the civil service in Edinburgh and then in London, the job was done. The great project initiated fifty years earlier was finally comprehensive. Its originator, the 'clearestheaded fellow' John Rickman, was not alive to see it, but his vision had become reality.

When Rickman announced in 1821 that 'The Enumeration of the whole Population may be considered as complete' he was not, as he must have been aware, being entirely accurate. He is likely to have meant that, at last, Great Britain had become accustomed to a decennial census and all of his forms from England, Wales and Scotland were being returned, and that Ireland was, however reluctantly, included in the project.

But the British and Irish archipelago consists of more than 6000 islands. Many if not most of those had at one time or another offered a home or a summer grazing or a fishery harbour or a sanctuary, however temporarily, to human beings. Early in the nineteenth century it is likely that more than 200 of Britain's islands were permanently occupied by a settled population. Only the very largest were canvassed by John Rickman's censuses.

Anglesey in Wales, which was a county in itself, the Isle of Wight in Rickman's family county of Southampton, such of the Hebrides as Lewis, which made up 700 square miles and contained a quarter of the population of the county of Ross-shire, and the substantial north Atlantic island groups of Orkney and Shetland were necessarily included from the beginning. In 1821 all of the Channel Islands, from the

28,600 people of Jersey to the one family of nine members living on Jethou, were counted, as were the 40,081 occupants of the 'Isle of Mann'. In the same year St Mary's parish in the Scilly Islands was enumerated with 2614 people.

Not until 1851 would the seven people living on the river islet of Looe in Cornwall be separately counted, however, or the four people on the offshore island of Barry, which was not yet connected by landfill to the Glamorgan mainland. In that same year, thirty-four inhabitants were listed as living on the island of Lundy in the Bristol Channel, whose proprietors had for centuries claimed to be without the jurisdiction of the United Kingdom. It was in the same early summer that Norman MacRaild arrived with the census forms on St Kilda, whose people had been attempting to win more jurisdiction, acceptance and services from the rest of the country.

An attempt had been made to enumerate every single citizen of the British Isles, complete with his or her full name, age, address, birthplace, family and occupation. Every populated corner of the country – even its most remote hundred Gaels clinging to its most fantastic cluster of rocks – was known. If there was any irony in St Kilda's embodiment of that completion, it lay in the fact that the most traditional, undeveloped and in many respects medieval community in Britain was eventually enumerated by a nation which was otherwise rapidly shucking off its past.

In 1837, three years before John Rickman's death, the office of Registrar General of Births, Deaths and Marriages for England and Wales had been created. The General Register Office was based in Somerset House, a forty-year-old neoclassical mansion on the south side of The Strand. Its first holder was a well-connected 37-year-old novelist named Thomas Henry Lister.

John Rickman was still alive and working, and Lister's job description did not initially include taking the national census. The General Register Office was to be a holding centre for records of births, marriages, deaths and other civil registrations, exactly as had been recommended by William Cecil in 1590. It was established after an 1833 parliamentary Select Committee on Parochial Registration had reported that the current system, which was both ramshackle and overly dependent on Church of England records and which therefore dealt inadequately with the births, marriages and deaths of nonconformists and Roman Catholics, was in urgent need of reform.

England and Wales were consequently divided into 619 civil registration units. Each unit had a superintendent registrar, and most were subdivided under local registrars. All of those men reported back up the pyramid to the Registrar General in London.

While Rickman was ailing at his Duke Street home in the summer of 1840 it became apparent to the government that even if he lingered on, the founder of the census would be incapable of administering its fifth edition the following year. They therefore contracted a respected Anglo-Indian lawyer and civil servant named John Elliot Drinkwater Bethune to help to prepare the 1840 Population Bill and to suggest an alternative administrator for the 1841 census.

Bethune inevitably turned in June 1840 to the Registrar General. Thomas Lister proved to be both willing and full of ideas. Sensitive to the fact that, despite being on the point of death, from his sickbed John Rickman was still firing off memoranda about the forthcoming enumeration, Lister wrote to Bethune that he did not wish to criticise 'any other plans that may have been proposed for taking the Census', but he had 'my own notion of the manner in which in England and Wales I think that object may be most easily and effectually accomplished'.

Lister proposed, logically enough, that the new regional registrars were best placed to supervise the census. They could not be expected actually to take the survey, as many of them were doctors and other men with full-time professional responsibilities, and anyway most of their districts were too large for one person to enumerate. But 'they are peculiarly qualified by the local knowledge which they must necessarily possess' to oversee the division of their localities 'into smaller districts convenient for Enumeration' by 'a certain number of Persons competent and willing to be Enumerators and resident within the district'.

As for the contents of the enumeration, Lister, like Rickman before him, was anxious not to overburden the enumerators. The Registrar General nonetheless recommended that for the first time the census form should include 'every house, and the name, age and occupation of every Inmate. The names should be written at length.'

Two months later Rickman was dead and buried and Lister officially took over the 1841 census of England, Wales and Scotland. He was assisted by two commissioners: a thirty-year-old London barrister, Edmund Phipps, and the 42-year-old House of Commons librarian, Thomas Vardon. Thomas Henry Lister would live to be recorded by name in his own census, with his aristocratic wife, two children, even more aristocratic mother-in-law and ten servants at their home in the City of Westminster, but he died of tuberculosis in June 1842, leaving Phipps and Vardon to finish the job.

There was not and would not be until 1854 a Registrar General for Scotland, and so in 1841 and 1851 the place of Welsh and English local registrars in collecting material and returning it to Lister, Phipps and Vardon was taken chiefly by schoolmasters who reported back to the county sheriff-substitutes – 'substantially the same as . . . [in] former years', wrote Phipps and Vardon.

The 1841 census of Ireland was conducted on behalf of the Lord Lieutenant by three commissioners: William Tighe Hamilton, Henry John Brownrigg and Thomas Askew Larcom. The first two were respectively a senior civil servant and the inspector general of the Irish Constabulary. The third, Larcom, had as a lieutenant in the Royal Engineers and an official of the Ordnance Survey recently helped to supervise a survey of the antiquities of Ireland. They deputed police officers to carry out the groundwork; 'where the constabulary were not sufficiently numerous', coastguards or other literate civilians were drafted. Hamilton, Brownrigg and Larcom agreed that 'a Census ought to be a Social Survey, not a bare Enumeration' but found themselves 'restrained by the apprehension that jealousy and prejudice might be excited'.

Because it recorded for the first time each individual's name, as well as his or her age in single years rather than decades or quinquennia, and occupation, and whether or not they had been born in their county of residence or in another part of the United Kingdom; because it was almost entirely executed by lay personnel; and because it and its successors in England, Scotland and Wales were not pulped or burned in 1904 or 1922, the 1841 account of the British population became celebrated as the first modern census.

According to the final report of Edmund Phipps and

Thomas Vardon in August 1843, 35,000 enumerators were employed to conduct that 1841 census in England, Scotland and Wales. The clerks at the General Register Office received 'upwards of one hundred millions of separate facts' which required 'more than three hundred and thirty thousand separate calculations ... For many months the clerks worked twelve hours a-day.'

Their bare returns showed a continuing rise in the population to just over 15 million in England, 8,175,238 in Ireland, 2,620,207 in Scotland and 911,603 in Wales. The population of the British Isles in June 1841 was therefore 26,707,091 men, women and children.

Those statistics once again indicated a substantial increase of over 10 per cent in the preceding ten years. Phipps and Vardon were however obliged to note that the rate of increase was smaller than in the previous two decades, and that Irish population growth in particular had slowed dramatically to a little more than 5 per cent.

There were manifold causes. The number of men in the armed forces had fallen from 640,500 at the height of the Napoleonic Wars thirty years earlier to 188,453 as the fire blanket of the Pax Britannica was draped across much of the world by the Royal Navy in 1841. But also, for a wide variety of reasons, more people were leaving Great Britain and Ireland than ever before. 'The apparent falling off in the rate of increase of population ... in the ten years ending 1841 ... ' concluded Phipps and Vardon, 'has been influenced more by the progress of emigration, than by any causes affecting the natural increase by the excess of births over deaths.'

The Emigration Board informed the Registrar General that between 1832 and 1841 an unprecedented 429,775 people had left the ports of England and Wales alone for foreign shores. 'Of this number,' wrote Phipps and Vardon, 'a large proportion were natives of Ireland, who sailed from the Ports of England, particularly from Liverpool ... it is notorious that the greater part consist of persons in the prime of life.'

In addition to those Britons making for a new life in Canada, Australia and the United States of America, hundreds of thousands of Irish people had moved to England, Wales and Scotland. Of them, reported Phipps and Vardon, 'there are nearly 300,000 in England and Wales alone, or a proportion of nearly 2 per cent of the whole population; while, in Scotland, they amount to 126,000, and are in a proportion of nearly 5 per cent of the population: in the latter country they rise in four counties to upwards of a tenth of the whole number enumerated'.

From Dublin Castle the commissioners Hamilton, Brownrigg and Larcom confirmed that 'Emigration has ... operated to a very great extent. It is to be remembered that Ireland is an agricultural country, and devoid of the means of providing employment for its rapidly growing population ... A valuable outlet for its excessive numbers is therefore found in the manufactories of England and Scotland.' They calculated that between 1831 and 1841 a total of 428,471 Irish people had also emigrated to the British colonies.

Those were, it should be stressed, the years before An Gorta Mor, the Great Irish Famine. Worse, much worse, was to follow. By way of contrast, in 1841 Scots themselves 'barely form a thousandth part' of the total population of England and Wales. Even the border counties of Northumberland and Cumberland had no more than 4 per cent of Scottish-born residents.

It is significant that Oliver Goldsmith's eulogy 'The Deserted Village' was written in 1770. The 42-year-old Goldsmith had by then spent many years visiting and writing about English country villages which were being destroyed by the Enclosures, which removed access to good traditional common land from rural inhabitants and put it in the private hands of farmers or landowners. The process had been going on piecemeal for centuries, but it accelerated with the help of parliamentary legislation in the late eighteenth century. As we have seen, Goldsmith actually saw one living village, Nuneham Courtenay in Oxfordshire, destroyed in the 1760s to make way for a manorial park.

But Oliver Goldsmith had been born in 1728 in the Irish midlands. The apparently placid agricultural environment of his upbringing in the counties of Longford and Roscommon concealed deep and ominous grievances. Landowners and large farmers were intruding their livestock upon traditional peasant smallholdings, causing substantial unrest. In the words of the Archbishop of Dublin, writing to Jonathan Swift, 'Lands of late have been raised mightily in their rates, and the poor people not being able to pay when demanded are turn'd out of their farms, and one man stocks as many as ten, twenty or perhaps an 100 inhabited, these poor people are turned to stock-slaying or starve, for the Land will yield a great deal more when there is found only a shepherd or cowherd to pay out of it, than it can yield when some inhabitants are first to be fed out of it . . . '

That was an analysis in Goldsmith's native Ireland of the Enclosures which he later discovered in England, and a fore-warning of the clearances which were shortly to depopulate much of the north-west of Scotland. Following Goldsmith's death in 1774 greater damage was to be done to rural society in both Ireland and northern Scotland. By the second half of the nineteenth century, the process was complete in an England which was largely, if not yet completely, transformed into a society of industrial towns and cities.

Most of the kingdom was more or less contentedly settled. In 1841 80 per cent of the people of England, Scotland and Wales still lived in the county of their birth; in Cornwall, Devon and Anglesey the proportion of natives rose to 94 or 95 per cent. But among more than a million people in Middlesex nearly 500,000 had been born somewhere else in the British Isles. The same county, which contained so much of the conurbation of London, had almost 60,000 Irish immigrants. The county of Lancaster, which included Merseyside, in 1841 was home to over 100,000 Irish people, 50,000 of whom formed 17 per cent of the population of Liverpool. Between 1885 and 1929, following the enfranchisement of most male Irish immigrants and descendants of immigrants, uniquely in the mainland of the British Isles the misleadingly named Merseyside parliamentary constituency of Liverpool Scotland returned as its Member of Parliament Thomas Power 'Tay Pay' O'Connor, a man from County Westmeath who represented not the Tories, Liberals or Labour who dominated the rest of mainland Britain, but the Irish Nationalist Party.

So in 1841 the elderly Mick and Maria McCartney, two of a dozen Irish Liverpudlians to carry their surname, were to be found lodging in Liverpool's Pine Court near the city centre. There were also a dozen Lennons nearby, including John Lennon, who had been born in Ireland thirty-five years earlier and in 1841 lived in the Irish enclave of St Thomas with his wife Anne and their two sons. Bridget

Harrison, an unmarried 27-year-old who had travelled from her Irish home to find work as a domestic servant on Merseyside, lodged in an Irish household on Vincent Street. To complete the quartet the 51-year-old Irishman John Starkey, one of half-a-dozen Starkeys in the Liverpool of 1841, ran a lodging house in Queen Street.

No bloodlines or connections other than their family names and their country of origin should be inferred. But more than a century later another Liverpudlian Starkey would change his stage name to Starr and would become the drummer in a pop group called The Beatles. Ringo Starr recalled of his inner-city Liverpudlian boyhood, in words with which Mick and Maria McCartney, John and Anne Lennon, Bridget Harrison and John Starkey might have identified, 'You kept your head down, your eyes open, and you didn't get in anybody's way.'

The deceased Thomas Lister was replaced in 1842 as Registrar General in England and Wales by 41-year-old George Graham. It was not an auspicious appointment. Graham was the younger brother and private secretary of the Home Secretary, Sir James Graham. His only previous administrative experience was two years spent as a military secretary in Bombay. George Graham would nonetheless become the longest-serving Registrar General in British history, holding the office for almost four decades and conducting three censuses.

The large and apparently bumbling Graham, a man of huge physical bulk, proved to be a capable overseer and an energetic administrator. A sympathetic character with an active mind, he had the good sense to patronise and promote the career within the General Register Office of the remarkable William Farr. Following Graham's retirement Farr would write of his former superior: 'For more than 37 years I have had the pleasure to serve under Major Graham, and had constant cause to admire and respect the energy, ability, personal attention to details, and capacity for organisation which marked his successful control of civil registration. No one acquainted with his duties, or with the way in which they were performed by Major Graham, can either describe his post as a sinecure or refuse to recognise the value of the services of the late Registrar General ... '

The origins of the two men could hardly have been more different. Graham was the fourth son of a Cumbrian baronet, while Farr was born to impoverished parents in the isolated village of Kenley in Salop, or Shropshire. When Farr was three years old in 1811, John Rickman's second census had identified Kenley as a hamlet of 261 people, almost all of whom were agricultural workers.

Owing to his parents' destitution and his own obvious promise as a child, Farr was adopted by a local squire and given an education at which he excelled. He studied medicine in Paris and London and then practised as a doctor. In 1837 he assisted the Scottish economist John Ramsey McCulloch in compiling the latter's 'A Statistical Account of the British Empire'. Having lost his young wife to tuberculosis after just four years of marriage, Farr also became acquainted with an authority on that disease, another Scot who would shortly become both Queen Victoria's physician and a baronet, James Clark of Banffshire. The influential Clark noticed Farr's fascination with medical statistics and may as a result have recommended him to the new General Register Office, where Farr began work under Thomas Lister in 1838.

Farr, 'a somewhat stocky figure, bald head, large nose and deep eyes', gave help to Lister, Phipps and Vardon with the 1841 census. George Graham subsequently promoted him to assistant commissioner for the censuses of 1851 and 1861 and commissioner for the 1871 census. During his substantial career Farr was also a member of the Statistical Society and of the British Medical Association, a Fellow of the Royal Society, a colleague of and adviser to Florence Nightingale and a contributor to *The Lancet*. He was the author of a history of medicine in antiquity and late antiquity before the fall of Constantinople, and of exhaustively researched and elegantly written papers on subjects as diverse as the 'Mortality of Lunatics' and the 'Pay of Ministers of the Crown'.

There is more than a hint of the character of John Rickman in a contemporary's description of the indefatigable Farr as 'of a simple disposition ... endowed with a vastness of ideas and a philosophic mind'. Farr would eventually be memorialised as the 'most significant medical epidemiologist and statistician of the Victorian era'. If Rickman is correctly credited with establishing the census of the British Isles, the unlikely partnership of George Graham and William Farr was responsible for developing and refining the survey in the high Victorian period. No census conductor who followed those three men would be able – indeed permitted – to shape the survey so completely to match their own vision.

It was no coincidence that distant St Kilda was finally included in the first census to be taken by the diligent Graham and the acutely painstaking Farr. The two men and their colleagues between the 1840s and the 1870s were nothing if not thorough. They were ideally chosen and perfectly placed to put on record the most painful and pitiless progressions of the nineteenth century, when the United Kingdom of Great Britain and Ireland wrenched its remaining toes out of the Middle Ages and stood squarely in modern times.

5

Seamstresses, Prostitutes, Billiard-Markers and Footballers

As would be noted by the census in due course, 1851 was a year of escalating horror in one large part of the British Isles. It was also a period of blithe celebration among the governing classes of the mainland nations of Great Britain. A country which just forty years earlier had been in danger of becoming no more than the wettest and windiest province of a French European empire, found itself standing alone as the most powerful and prosperous nation on earth.

The most visible, and most popular, demonstration of that status was a Great Exhibition of the Works of Industry of all Nations, staged between May and October 1851 in an enormous but temporary Crystal Palace in Hyde Park. Its explicit purpose was to enable 'Great Britain [to make] clear to the world its role as industrial leader'. Enthusiastically organised by Queen Victoria's consort, Prince Albert, it attracted more than 6 million visitors. Among them was a 34-year-old woman from Yorkshire, who recorded what she saw in the following terms:

It is a wonderful place – vast, strange, new and impossible to describe. Its grandeur does not consist in one thing, but in the unique assemblage of all things.

Whatever human industry has created you find there, from the great compartments filled with railway engines and boilers, with mill machinery in full work, with splendid carriages of all kinds, with harness of every description, to the glass-covered and velvet-spread stands loaded with the most gorgeous work of the goldsmith and silversmith, and the carefully guarded caskets full of real diamonds and pearls worth hundreds of thousands of pounds.

It may be called a bazaar or a fair, but it is such a bazaar or fair as Eastern genii might have created. It seems as if only magic could have gathered this mass of wealth from all the ends of the earth – as if none but supernatural hands could have arranged it thus, with such a blaze and contrast of colours and marvellous power of effect. The multitude filling the great aisles seems ruled and subdued by some invisible influence. Amongst the thirty thousand souls that peopled it the day I was there not one loud noise was to be heard, not one irregular movement seen; the living tide rolls on quietly, with a deep hum like the sea heard from the distance.

The writer of those resonant lines, Charlotte Brontë, had travelled from Parsonage House in Haworth, where she lived with her 74-year-old father Patrick. Charlotte had in 1851 already been revealed as the author of *Jane Eyre* and *Shirley*. Under 'Rank, Profession, or Occupation' on that year's census form either she, or her father on her behalf, entered 'None'.

While the Crystal Palace was being erected, George

Graham and William Farr were planning the sixth statistical account of the nation and the first of which they had fully taken the reins. Well aware of their responsibilities in that year of all years, Graham and Farr pulled out the stops. They were happily able to report to the Home Secretary, Viscount Palmerston, that the English, Scottish and Welsh nations of Great Britain, excluding some bothersome statistics from Ireland, had doubled in size since John Rickman's first headcount in 1801 and stood five decades later at 21,186,010 people. That population boom carried at least two heartening national benefits: 'The males at the soldier's age of 20 to 40 amounted to 1,966,664 in 1821, and to 3,193,496 in 1851; the increase in the thirty years is equivalent in number to a vast army of more than twelve hundred thousand men (1,226,832). The women at this fruitful age of marriage (20 to 40) were then 2,119,385 in number; they have increased by 1,243,073, and now amount to 3,362,458.'

The average English male life expectancy at birth was forty years and four months. Women could expect to live for an additional ten months. There were however gross disparities which the Registrar General urged Parliament to address. Graham and Farr were alarmed to note that 'of 100,000 children born in Liverpool, only 44,797 live to the age of 20, while in Surrey that age is attained by 70,885 out of the same number of children born: the probable lifetime is about 6 years in our unhealthiest towns, 52 years in Surrey, and other comparatively healthy parts. In Manchester, where the mortality is high, 100,000 annual births only sustain, at the ages 20–40, a male population of 38,919; while in all England and Wales, where the mortality is now much lower, the same number of births produces a constant force of 61,215 men at that age . . .

'The prolongation of the life of the people must become an essential part of family, municipal, and national policy,' insisted Graham and Farr.

> Although it is right and glorious to incur risk, and to sacrifice life, for public objects, it has always been felt that length of days is the measure, and that the completion by the people of the full term of natural existence is the groundwork, of their felicity.
>
> For untimely death is a great evil. What is so bitter as the premature death of a wife, – a child, – a father? What dashes to the earth so many hopes, breaks so many sweet alliances, blasts so many auspicious enterprises, as the unnatural Death? The poets, as faithful interpreters of our aspirations, have always sung that in the happier ages of the world this source of tears shall be dried up.

While he was patronised and encouraged first by Thomas Lister and second, and more significantly, by George Graham, that concern of the General Register Office with monitoring the physical health of the nation was the work of the son of poor Shropshire farmworkers, William Farr. It had profound results. He was able, as in the paragraphs above, to identify unregulated urbanisation and crowded city slums as ideal breeding grounds for contagious and epidemic diseases. His work as a medical statistician contributed substantially to the creation of sewage systems and supplies of fresh, clean water to London and then to other British cities. His introduction to the census of questions about serious infirmities resulted in the realisation that, in 1851, one British person in every 979 was blind – an extraordinarily common affliction which Farr attributed in large part to the proliferation of smallpox. In 1853 an Act of Parliament made smallpox vaccination compulsory.

Farr, and the successors who used his templates, were also able to identify the most and least healthy of occupations. Farr approached this subject from a variety of directions. The dangers faced by fishermen and other seafarers, for instance, were highlighted in 1851 by the numbers of widows they left behind. The average percentage of adult women who were widows was 7.2 in England and Wales, 8.4 in Scotland, and 9.1 in the offshore islands of the British seas. However:

> The widows exceed 15 per cent, in the following districts: in Canterbury they are 15.3, in Bury St. Edmunds 15.3, Yarmouth 16.4, Salisbury 16.2, Plymouth 15.4, Stoke Damerel 16.3, Truro 15.9, Falmouth 16.2, Helston 15.5, Redruth 17.1, Scilly Islands 16.5, Bath 15.5, Bristol 16.6, Weobly (Hereford) 15.5, Tenbury 16.2, Hull 15.8, Whitby 16.3, South Shields 15.9, Tynemouth 15.7, Alston 21.4, Whitehaven 15.7, Cockermouth 15.5, Carmarthen 15.3, Narberth 15.2, Cardigan 15.2, Aberayron 15.2, Dolgelly 15.1.
>
> [In Scotland] they numbered 16.8 in Bute; in Renfrew it was 16.3; Lanark 15.6; Edinburgh 16.2; Forfar 15.0; Aberdeen 15.1, Argyll 15.9 . . .
>
> The great number of widows in the ports indicates the loss of great numbers of men at sea, of whom little other record is left than these relics.

The striking exception to that rule in the townships listed was the landbound town of Alston in Cumbria, which stands 1000 feet above sea level and has no seagoing tradition. More than one in every five of Alston's adult women were nonetheless widows: easily the highest proportion of any town in Britain. That was possibly, suggested Farr in a footnote, linked to the fact that in Alston 'Of 1,765 males of the age 20 and upwards, 1,038 are lead miners.' In the whole of Britain in 1851, 16,680 men, 4937 youths, 400 women and 513 girls worked in lead mines. A century later the medical statistician at the General Register Office, W.P.D. Logan, would consciously echo Farr's findings about the dangers encountered by miners of base metals by reporting that 'In 1930–2 the occupation with the highest mortality was that of tin- and copper-mine workers below ground, with a mortality experience 242% above the average for all males.' By way of comparison, Logan noted, 'Medical practitioners had mortality rates 6% and coal-miners (all men, engaged in coal-mining) 7% above the general average.'

William Farr's diligent exploration of the ubiquity and causes of epidemic and occupational diseases in the census and elsewhere led him to develop a close friendship with Florence Nightingale, another early supporter of the use of statistical data in medical science. It would be written in 2007, on the 200th anniversary of his birth, that Farr's 'contributions to epidemiology were both broad and deep.

His creation of a vital statistics system, role in the formation of the International Classification of Diseases, and prominence in resolving the mode of communication of cholera in Victorian England were each seminal to modern epidemiology. The same can be said for his development of the concept of surveillance. Sir Isaac Newton famously observed, 'If I have seen further it is by standing on ye shoulders of Giants.' In epidemiology, it is upon William Farr's shoulders, among others, that we stand today.

It was suggested that the great semicentennial census of 1851 should for the first time ascertain the religious beliefs of the British people. It did so in a half-hearted manner, requesting only voluntary replies. Outside Roman Catholic Ireland, most people confessed to being Anglicans, but no fewer than 5 million citizens chose not to answer the question. To further complicate matters, the figures for Mormons and Catholics were accidentally transposed, which did nothing to appease the justified paranoia of the nineteenth-century British Catholic community.

The question was pursued once more in 1861, again attracting hostility from those outside the Church of England. 'The Nonconformists, for their part,' writes Sydney Bailey:

claimed that no reliance could be placed on the total for the Anglicans. A person either was a Baptist or was not a Baptist: but nobody could say this about an Anglican. A person might never enter a church after the day of his baptism and yet might still assert that he was a good Anglican.

One Member [of the House of Commons] reported that on one occasion a prisoner, being asked his religion, replied indignantly: 'Religion, Sir; I am of no religion; I belong to the Church of England'. The prisons, lunatic asylums, and workhouses were full of people who professed to be Anglicans. Another Member had visited a pauper lunatic asylum and found that 62 per cent of the inmates were Anglicans, 28 per cent Nonconformists and 8 per cent Roman Catholics; yet he knew for a fact that the inmates came from a district which was overwhelmingly Nonconformist. Again, of the delinquent soldiers committed to Millbank in 1878, 1,316 were described as

Church of England, 104 as 'other Protestants' and 568 as Roman Catholics. 'Of course, I am not to be understood as maintaining that Church teaching makes an undue proportion of imbeciles or of criminal soldiers.'

Another Member asserted that, generally speaking, the more dissolute a man was, the more loyal he was to the Established Church. 'Men who have betrayed every friend who ever trusted in them, men who are drunk every day of their lives – the worse they are, the more loyal to the Church ...'

It was not until 1910 that the preponderance of Anglicans amongst convicts was satisfactorily explained. John Burns, MP for Battersea, explained that when he had been in prison and had been asked his religion, a more experienced fellow prisoner had interrupted with the words 'Church of England, governor'. When he asked why, he received the answer, 'Three services on Sunday, and excellent hymns'.

The question 'What is your religion?' would be reintroduced to the censuses of 2001 and 2011. In 2011, 60 per cent of the entire United Kingdom population replied 'Christian', with their strongest concentrations in Northern Ireland and the Western Isles of Scotland. Christianity in the whole of the UK was followed by Islam, Hinduism, Sikhism, Judaism and Buddhism in that order. But over 20 per cent of the population professed no religion or refused to answer the question, and 176,632 Britons claimed to be affiliated to the faith of the Jedi Knights which had been popularised by the *Star Wars* science fiction films. That represented a substantial decline in the Jedi community. In 2001 it had 390,127 affiliates, making it briefly the fourth largest faith or creed in the United Kingdom. The Jedi were especially numerous in Brighton, where they accounted for 2.6 per cent of the population. They were fewer in both absolute and relative terms in Scotland, where only 14,000 Jedi identified themselves. These included eight serving officers in the Strathclyde police force.

Whatever their manifold hazards, the extraordinary variety of occupations created by what Graham and Farr regarded as the unique genius of the British people in the year of the Great Exhibition was sufficient, they considered, to explode the reductionary pessimisms of Thomas Malthus. They echoed John Rickman in asserting that if Malthus had been in any sense correct, his catastrophe would already have occurred. Instead, 'The United Kingdom is now covered by twenty-eight millions of people; and has thrown out towards the west a long line of colonies, and independent states, that speak her language, that preserve the purity of the English family, that have lost none of the courage or industry of their race – but furnish this country with supplies of food, as well as with the materials of manufactures, in exchange for wrought produce.'

That apparently boundless capacity for job creation was most evident in the middle of the nineteenth century, when so many of the old trades still existed alongside the astonishing novelties of an industrialising nation. It seemed to manifest a racial destiny, wrote Graham and Farr, that

the whole of the new population could not be employed in mines, in canals, or in agriculture – in the production of fuel or of food for mankind. Other wants existed; other occupations had to be created.

And it happened, as it always will happen in this nation, that as the millions of additional people grew up to manhood, inventors were found, in the lowest as well as the highest ranks, to discover new machines for their use in new employments; and also men, in all classes of life, of perhaps still rarer qualities, who could organize the people, lead them out to new enterprizes, and employ them profitably in the Old as well as in the New World.

Graham and Farr pointed proudly to Josiah Wedgwood's revolutionary industrialisation of the manufacture of pottery and his introduction to one of the world's oldest crafts of new glazes and finishes. They hailed James Hargreaves' spinning jenny, Richard Arkwright's water frame and Samuel Crompton's spinning mule, all of which had mechanised and vastly increased the production of yarn. They noted that 'The force of steam was placed at man's disposal by James Watt.' Such manifestations of British imagination were apparently limitless and guarantors of the nation's future:

> All these machines – of which the exquisitely regulated, incessant, and accurate movements cannot be contemplated without admiration – and others of little less ingenuity, in the hands of the inventors, and of the Peels, Marshalls, Strutts, Greigs, Ashtons, and masters scarcely less famous, produced a thousand different wares, yielding in value millions sterling yearly, and so offering occupation and subsistence to the population.

In the Great Britain of 1851 there were '1,038,791 domestic servants – 133,626 males and 905,165 females'. Agriculture employed 2,390,568 persons. There were also woodsmen and a small but 'peculiar race of men; silent, circumspective, prompt, agile, dexterous, enduring, danger-defying' who called themselves hunters. The 'trades, mechanical arts, handicrafts, and manufactures, including mining' employed '2,250,369 men, 615,961 youths, 550,759 women, and 299,328 girls under 20 – or collectively more than 37 hundred thousands . . . '

Among male occupations, 'The dress of both sexes comprises 11,895 hairdressers and wigmakers, 13,426 hatters, 1,510 furriers, 135,028 tailors, 2,534 shawl-manufacturers, 3,617 hosiers and haberdashers, 35,423 hose (stocking) manufacturers, 4,539 glovers (exclusive of silk-glove makers), 243,052 shoemakers, 3,819 patten and clog makers; 2,340 umbrella, parasol and stick makers; and 2,164 rag gatherers and dealers'. Among females there were '20,538 straw hat and bonnet makers, 7,628 bonnet-makers, 4,793 cap-makers, 1,959 furriers, 17,644 tailors, 3,299 shawl manufacturers, 267,425 milliners or dressmakers, 72,940 seamstresses or shirtmakers, 12,769 staymakers, 30,076 hose (stocking) manufacturers, 25,343 glovers, 31,418 shoemakers, 1,081 rag gatherers and dealers, 1,797 umbrella, parasol, stick makers; and, finally, 145,373 washerwomen, manglers, laundry-keepers, of whom no less than 136,582 are women of 20 years of age and upwards. This great class comprises 2,420,173 persons; of whom 632,713 are men, 1,787,460 are women . . . '

There were 285,686 men and 100,345 boys employed as carriers on the roads, canals and railways or on the sea or river. A total of 265,198 persons were employed in coal, 'either extracting it from the earth, distributing it amongst the consumers, or manufacturing it into coke and gas'. Almost three times as many people – 782,213 – were involved in the hemp, flax and cotton industries, most of them in cotton mills.

No fewer than '763,336 persons – 624,503 men, 121,928 boys, and only 11,617 women, 5,288 girls ... are engaged in the higher class of mechanical and chemical arts; are intimately connected with artists and men of science; from whom they frequently, either directly or indirectly, derive materials, direction, or inspiration. They multiply copies of original works. The matter in which they deal comes from the animal and vegetable as well as the mineral kingdom; but it is no longer living. They do not breed animals nor grow plants. They make things, and use tools or machines.' There were in Britain 4388 male copper-plate printers and engravers ... and 1366 lithographers or lithographic printers.

Four hundred and twenty-seven men and ninety youths, 1541 women and 1452 girls made artificial flowers. 'On watches and philosophical instruments, 17,899 men, 4,008 youths, and 471 women and girls, are employed ... The manufactures of arms employ 5,945 men and 1,820 youths, as gunsmiths, armourers, and sword-cutlers, and bayonet-makers. 54,819 males, or 44,563 men and 10,256 youths, are employed in making machines and iron tools of various kinds. The makers of carriages comprise 16,431 coach-makers, of whom 13,872 are men of 20 years of age and upwards. The saddlers and harness-makers are 16,890 males, the whipmakers, 1,005.'

The civil service employed 37,698 people, '29,785 ... in offices of local government; while 3,708 are officers of the East India government'. There were 18,348 policemen and 1838 gaolers and prison officers. There were 183,255 men in the army and navy. There were 30,047 ministers, priests, religious teachers and students of divinity, 18,422 lawyers and 22,383 men in the medical professions.

'The authors, writers, and literary men ... number 2,866; including, however, men who called themselves Graduates and Fellows of Colleges. 436 are authors; 1,302 editors or writers. The artists, in the wide sense comprehending all who devote themselves to the fine arts, are returned at 8,600; including, however, 4,915 painters, some of whom generally call themselves artists, but are often called by others drawingmasters. Many of the 2,971 architects are undoubtedly builders ...'

There were exhibition keepers, conjurors, ventriloquists, equestrians, pedestrians, billiard-table keepers and markers, shooting-gallery keepers, racecourse officers, cricketers and cricket-ball makers, archery-goods makers and fishing-tackle makers, while '1,260 men and 373 youths, 710 women and 166 girls, are engaged in making and dealing in toys'.

And so the roll-call continued, with 200,000 men, women and children in 'drinks and stimulants' industries, and over 3000 French polishers. 'The blade forgers and makers are 1,579 men, cutlers 6,433, knife makers 1,152, fork makers 433, and a large proportion of youths and boys. In the manufacture of needles 4,727 persons are employed; namely, 1,896 men, 880 youths, 1,215 women, 736 girls. Besides 116 youths and 115 women and girls, 183 men are makers of fish-hooks. There are makers of scissors 894 men, awls and bodkins 255 men, of tuning forks, shears, phlemes, steel tags, a few; of makers of snuffers 130 men, scythes and sickles 677 men, shovels and spades 594, steel mills and coffee-mills 31, springs 385, razors 777, grinders 1,635 (of unspecified branches), sawsmiths 937 men. The steel-pen makers are 134 men, 74 youths, 652 women, 476 girls. Skates and harpoons have also special makers.'

'In the early stages of society,' wrote George Graham ten years later in his 1861 census report:

the occupations are so simple that whole tribes have been designated hunters, shepherds or agriculturalists, according as the members live on the produce of the chase, on the produce of their flocks, or on the produce of the cultivated land. There is in such cases but one chief occupation, and the subsidiary occupations are few, employing comparatively few numbers. How different, and how much more complicated the social organization of Great Britain is in the present day . . .

The general tint of the map is green – to indicate the diffusion over the country of agricultural population, comprising the landowners, the farmers, the graziers, and the various classes of workmen either in or out of doors; watching the flocks on the hill pastures, managing the herds in the hill meadows, working with the horses the arable fields, or labouring in the various buildings for carrying on the multifarious processes of production, which are now branches of agriculture.

. . . another large class of the population surrounds the inhabited islands of Great Britain, and is constantly employed in drawing sustenance from the river and the deep waters of the sea; or in constructing, animating, and directing ships that connect the islands and the continents of the earth, and are at once the carriages and the highways of the ocean. The Celt on the hills, the Anglo-Saxon in his farm-house, and the Scandinavian in his ship – all find suitable occupations. They are diffused over land and sea ...

Besides agriculturalists, fishermen and seamen, the trades common to towns are as widely diffused as the towns themselves ... Thus ships are made at Woolwich. In London silk is manufactured; watches are constructed; ale and porter are brewed; pottery, and engines and machines are made in a large way: gardens surround it for the supply of vegetables; on both sides of the Thames paper is manufactured. Straw-plait, lace and shoes employ the people in the South-midland counties; the silk manufacture extends to Bucks, to Suffolk, to Norfolk – particularly around Norwich – to Coventry, Nottingham, and Macclesfield, with the districts surrounding the towns. Silk now employs hands in Manchester and Bradford. Glovers abound about Yeovil, Barnstaple, Worcester and Woodstock. Thus the seats of the principal manufacturers can be traced: the miners and the manufacturers of the principal metals; quarriers; the people spinning and weaving wool, silk, cotton and flax; the manufacturers or makers of hats, stockings, gloves, shoes, watches and clocks, guns, engines, machines, tools, ships, chemicals, soap, combs, skins, leather, ale, toys, straw-plait, ropes, nets, thread, paper, glass, jewellery, locks, buttons, wire, nails, anchors, boilers, files, cutlery, needles and pins.

In 1861 the Registrar General also noted the passing of most of the old trade and guild costumes. 'In the present day,' wrote Graham, 'costume is not in extensive use to distinguish one class of people from another. The soldier, the seaman, the policeman, the beadle, the footman, the butcher, the turncock, have peculiar dresses; the peer, the judge, the barrister, the clergyman and the alderman assume costumes in discharging the particular duties of their offices: but few people in trades are now easily distinguishable by the colours or qualities of their clothing.' A turncock was the man on the ground for the water companies; he turned the supply on or off and wore his company's uniform. Butchers wore large aprons, frequently with red and white stripes, and straw boaters. The other occupational costumes listed by Graham, such as those of policemen, judges and the clergy, were still identifiable in the twenty-first century.

Graham reported that 'The ancient office of executioner has one representative left in England.' That was sixty-year-old William Calcraft, who in 1861 was living in Tower Hamlets with his wife Louisa and their granddaughter Louisa Gibbs. Calcraft trained as a cobbler before being appointed in 1829 official Executioner for the City of London and Middlesex, and later of the whole United Kingdom. Executions were carried out in public until 1868 and it was never clear whether Calcraft's ghoulishly extended terminations (he frequently had to haul down on his victims' legs to finish them off) were the result of incompetence, drunkenness or a desire to entertain. He executed an estimated 450 people before retiring in 1874. That amounted to an average of ten a year, insufficient to identify hanging people as his primary trade – he offered his occupation on the census forms as 'shoemaker'.

Several new technologies displaced their older predecessors. The number of professional photographers boomed from 45 in 1851 to 2634 in 1861. As a direct result the old craft of engraving had begun its slow decline, from the 4948 practitioners recorded in 1851 to 3715 ten years later. In the village of Stoke Damerel in Devon in 1851 there lived a 68-year-old Cornishman named John Friend. John registered himself as a 'superannuated hoyman', which meant that his antique vocation had been overtaken by progress. Until the railway arrived he had carried goods up and down the rivers of the West Country and around its coast in his hoy, or small sailing boat.

In 1851, 67-year-old William Garner of the parish of St Martins in Birmingham could count himself the last snuffer maker in the Midlands. He manufactured the small hand-held devices which had been used since time immemorial to extinguish the flames of candles. In 1861 Susan Mason of Govan in Renfrewshire and Henry Stephens of Edinburgh both registered their occupations as 'amanuensis'. They were among the last people in the British Isles who made a primary living by writing letters or other documents for their illiterate fellow citizens. In 1851 a 26-year-old named Magnus Jamieson from Lerwick in the Shetland Islands was the last recorded 'abecedarian' – a freelance teacher of the alphabet – in the United Kingdom. Amanuenses and abecedarians were made redundant by the introduction of universal compulsory education in the early 1870s.

There were several Acremans or Akermans in the 1851 and 1861 and later censuses. Their surnames indicated ancestors who had been acremen, or bonded ploughmen on another person's land. There were still hundreds of bond-agers in England in 1851. Insecure cottars of both genders who were bound in return for their housing to labour for the landowner or farmer and who had no tenure, they had disappeared from England by the close of the nine-teenth century but were still plentiful in Scotland into the twentieth.

*

By 1881 the variety of British occupations was so extensive that the new Registrar General, Brydges Henniker, confessed his confusion, writing:

> In the first place, the number of distinct manufactures and industries in such a country as this is enormous.
>
> Moreover, most of these manufactures and industries are sub-divided with great minuteness ... not infrequently by several different designations in different localities.
>
> These designations in a large proportion of cases give no indication whatsoever as to the character of the business to those who are not possessed of some special acquaintance with technical terms. Here, for instance, are a hundred, – all names of occupations in current use, and yet such that in all probability an ordinary educated man would know at most but one or two of them, and often would not know a single one.

The list which followed included 'Bat-printer', 'Blabber', 'Camberel maker', 'Crutter', 'Fluker', 'Learman', 'Oliver man', 'Spragger' and 'Whitster'. 'The abstracting clerks could not,' Henniker argued, 'of course, be expected to know the meaning of such names as these, and consequently it was necessary to make a dictionary for their use, instructing them how to deal with each name that might occur.

'It was found that the dictionary in use for past censuses, and which had been constructed, we believe, chiefly on the basis of the directories of London and other large towns, had become obsolete. A great many terms that occurred in it had ceased any longer to be used, and, what was of more importance, several thousands that are now used had no place in it at all. Under these circumstances we determined to make a new dictionary of the names of occupations – a work, it need hardly be said, of very great labour, especially as we could lay no claim to special knowledge in the matter of trades.'

As a result, 'leading manufacturers' were circulated with requests for information about what certain specific trades and occupations were called in their areas. The resulting completed dictionary of late-Victorian occupations contained 'between eleven and twelve thousand different occupations . . .'

Earlier such dictionaries had contained only 7000 occupations. 'The great change in the nomenclature of occupations that appears to have occurred since the former dictionary was compiled,' explained the clerks of the General Register Office, 'is partly due to new branches of industry having sprung up, and greater sub-division having been made; but probably also in great part to the fact that many of the names in current use are scarcely more than nick-names, which have but short lives, but which nevertheless it was necessary for our purposes to take into account as being actually used in the schedules.'

The third or fourth largest paid occupation of Victorian women was never included in a General Register Office dictionary and never fully credited in any census or by any registrar general. Census enumerators who visited Allens Yard, a short, narrow, ramshackle two-storey terrace on the west side of Falmouth Bay in Cornwall, in the second half of the nineteenth century found there, and duly recorded, a busy community of women whose professed vocation was 'prostitute'.

Prostitution was not respectable in Victorian Britain. Within regulations concerning sexually transmitted diseases, until 1886 it was however mostly legal ('mostly' because prostitutes were always vulnerable to police persecution on such spurious grounds as loitering or moral corruption). Between 1858 and 1888 the police estimated that there were, at any given time, about 25,000 prostitutes in England and Wales, of whom 6000 to 7000 were in London.

It was certainly an underestimate. Part-time or full-time prostitution may have occupied up to 400,000 women in the nineteenth century. It was one of the largest female trades, but was as impossible to tally in the 1880s as it is in the twenty-first century. Only a few hundred women, and no men or boys, were registered as prostitutes in the censuses of 1871 and 1881, and most of them were in prison or in lunatic asylums, where their guards and keepers had offered their occupations to the enumerators. They were in prison not for prostitution itself, but for other offences such as theft or because prostitutes who were diagnosed with (or accused of spreading) venereal diseases were imprisoned until it was considered safe to allow them on the streets again. They were in asylums as a result of family or legal intervention. People of more favoured classes frequently considered prostitutes to suffer not from poverty, but from excessive sexual appetites as a result of mental imbalance. Understandably, most prostitutes did not advertise their jobs to agents of the government. Instead such occupations as 'seamstress' were given to the census enumerators. Not every seamstress recorded in late-Victorian Britain was a prostitute. But many were, and many others were both, as almost every woman was obliged to be a seamstress in an age of handmade clothes, whatever else they did with their lives.

A few free, practising prostitutes nonetheless declared themselves honestly to the census takers, and they included those who worked out of Allens Yard in Falmouth. The town had been a fishing and trading port for centuries. In 1858 a dockyard was opened there, and five years later the Cornwall Railway connected Falmouth Docks to London by way of Truro and Devonport. By 1881 Falmouth was a busy little working port, dockyard and West Country resort of 25,000 people, whose male industries were sufficient to sustain the women of Allens Yard.

In that year seven women and one boy lived in the adjacent small houses of Allens Yard, and six of the women were prostitutes. They were all Cornishwomen. Twenty-seven-year-old Agnes Curley from Penzance lived with her thirteen-year-old schoolboy son. Twenty-eight-year-old Elizabeth Rayworth from Falmouth lived with her elderly mother, whose occupation was charwoman. There was forty-year-old Catherine Clarke, also from Falmouth, thirty-year-old Annie Baker from Camborne, 24-year-old Annie Borrows from Perranwell and 42-year-old Martha Bishop from St Gluvias. Curley, Clarke and Bishop were all married women; Annie Baker was a widow and Borrows and Rayworth were unmarried.

As prostitutes were less likely than most other citizens to volunteer accurate names and other details to census enumerators, tracing the backgrounds and later lives of those women is unusually difficult. It is nonetheless reasonable to say that they were all the products of hardscrabble Cornish town or village nineteenth-century life in an age when women had no property rights and few opportunities.

Elizabeth Rayworth of Allens Yard had been born and raised in her mother's home town of Falmouth. Her father John Rayworth, a Nottinghamshire man, was a Chelsea Pensioner, which in the middle of the nineteenth century meant no more than that he and his family survived on a small army pension administered and issued from the Royal Hospital in Chelsea. John and Mary Rayworth were forty and thirty-nine years old respectively when Elizabeth was born and in 1870, when Elizabeth was in her late teens, John died at the age of about fifty-seven.

A year later, in April 1871, the census enumerator found nineteen-year-old Elizabeth Rayworth living and working as a prostitute in Allens Yard. She was still there in 1881, by which time Elizabeth had been joined by her mother Mary, who was in her late sixties and carrying on her occupation of charwoman.

The frankness, or what would have been called shamelessness, of the inhabitants of Allens Yard was unrepresentative, but it was far from unique. In the same year twenty-year-old Mary Ann Day of St Thomas Street in Doncaster declared herself to be a 'brothel keeper'. Mary Ann shared her house with a 35-year-old male chimneysweep, a 23-year-old female general servant and two prostitutes. That transparency would not see out the decade. In 1885 the Criminal Law Amendment Act made 'further provision for the Protection of Women and Girls, the suppression of brothels, and other purposes', and unincarcerated prostitutes disappeared from the census of the United Kingdom.

Other less respectable professions were also occasionally recorded with unnerving frankness. In 1881 an elderly married couple named John and Elizabeth Annis, who were boarding with an agricultural labourer in the hamlet of Great Staughton in Huntingdonshire, each offered their 'Rank, Profession, or Occupation' to the enumerator as 'tramp & beggar'. John Annis, who was eighty-two years old, qualified his entry by adding 'labourer sometimes'.

Slavery, which had been so commonly recorded seven centuries earlier in the Domesday Book, was effectively outlawed in Great Britain by the end of the eighteenth century. While bondagers, villeins and cottars, whose fettered positions were only a few rungs further up the social ladder than slaves, abounded throughout the British Isles, there were therefore no slaves recorded under 'Rank, Profession, or Occupation' in the nineteenth century.

Early in the twentieth century, however, the rank of slave made a comeback. In 1911 Mrs Alice Maude Mary Ayers of London registered herself as a 'White Slave'. Born in Battersea forty-six years earlier, in 1911 she was the wife of a photographer's assistant and auxiliary postman named Ben Ayers. Alice and Ben had three adult children and lived in a five-bedroomed house in Chelsea.

Alice Ayers was not alone. In the same spring census of 1911, 48-year-old Mrs Elizabeth Bond of Cambridge listed her 'Profession or Occupation' as 'Domestic Slave', while 52-year-old widow Lucy Gilbert of Bermondsey, who had her adult son, three grown-up daughters and three boarders under her roof, described herself simply as a 'Slave'; and Rosina Elizabeth Pentelow, a 48-year-old married woman with three children in Watford, was a 'slave for the family'.

A couple of hundred variations on the same theme could be found throughout Great Britain, with 'domestic slave' the most popular. Those women, and in some cases their sympathetic husbands who completed and returned the census forms, were suffragists, or suffragettes as they were more commonly known. They were engaging in the first concerted attempt to use the census as a means of protest.

Outside the Isle of Man, where property-owning women had been enfranchised in 1881, in 1911 no British woman was allowed to vote. Having begun in earnest in the second half of the nineteenth century, by 1911 the women's suffrage movement was approaching the height of its formidable activities. It engaged in a wide variety of both violent and non-violent campaigns, of which subverting the national census was among the most imaginative.

British suffragists frequently compared the position of unenfranchised women in western society to that of slavery. 'Because women are voteless,' said the suffragette leader Emmeline Pankhurst in 1913, 'there are in our midst to-day sweated workers, white slaves, outraged children, and innocent mothers and their babes stricken by horrible disease.'

The comparison attracted criticism, not least in the United States of America. British suffragettes were unapologetic. Pankhurst told a meeting in Hartford, Connecticut, 'You won the civil war by the sacrifice of human life when you decided to emancipate the Negro. You have left it to women in your land, the men of all civilized countries have left it to women, to work out their own salvation ... I think I have the right that all oppressed people have to ask for practical sympathy of others freer than themselves.' Pankhurst would write:

Men make the moral code, and they expect women to accept it. They have decided that it is entirely right and proper for men to fight for their liberties and their rights, but that it is not right and proper for women to fight for theirs. They have decided that for men to remain silently quiescent while tyrannical rulers impose bonds of slavery upon them is cowardly and dishonourable, but that for women to do that same thing is not cowardly and dishonourable, but merely respectable. Well, the Suffragettes absolutely repudiate that double standard of morals. If it is right for men to fight for their freedom, and God knows what the human race would be like to-day if men had not, since time began, fought for their freedom, then it is right for women to fight for their freedom and the freedom of the children they bear.

The decision to target the census was taken in the early spring of 1911, when Parliament was once more on the verge of selling the suffragettes short. 'The Census,' wrote Pankhurst to *The Times*, 'is a numbering of the people. Until women count as people for the purpose of representation in the councils of the nation as well as for purposes of taxation, we shall refuse to be numbered.'

Their campaign was three-pronged. Pankhurst recalled in 1914:

Our plan was to reduce the value of the census for statistical purposes by refusing to make the required returns . . . The first and most important was direct resistance by occupiers who should refuse to fill in the census papers. This laid the resister open to a fine of £5 or a month's imprisonment, and thus required the exercise of considerable courage. The second means of resistance was evasion – staying away from home during the entire time that the enumerators were taking the census. We made the announcement of this plan and instantly there ensued a splendid response from women and a chorus of horrified disapproval from the conservative public.

The third means was to return the census form while making their political point. Emmeline Pankhurst, who was living in Manchester but had travelled to be in London on census enumeration day, does not appear in the 1911 census records. She had earlier returned her form with only the words 'No vote no census' written across it, as a result of which it was nullified and scrapped. Other women followed that example with similar messages. The scientist Hertha Ayrton wrote: 'I will not supply these particulars until I have my rights as a citizen. Votes for Women.' Dorothy Bowker of London wrote: 'Dumb Politically, Blind to the Census. Deaf to the Enumerator.' A Birkenhead woman filled in the blank with full information about her single manservant, and added that there were 'many women but no more persons in her household'. In contrast, the otherwise uncontroversial returns of those who had declared themselves to be 'slaves' were accepted.

'Many thousands of women all over the country refused or evaded the returns,' reported Mrs Pankhurst. 'In Birmingham sixteen women of wealth packed their houses with women resisters. They slept on the floors, on chairs and tables, and even in the baths. The head of a large college threw open the building to 300 women. Many women in other cities held all night parties for friends who wished to remain away from home. In some places unoccupied houses were rented for the night by resisters, who lay on the bare boards. Some groups of women hired gipsy vans and spent the night on the moors.'

Emily Wilding Davison, who would sacrifice herself by

walking into the hooves of King George V's horse at the Epsom Derby two years later, hid in a House of Commons broom cupboard for forty-eight hours on either side of enumeration day. She was discovered there and her address was duly noted on one census form as 'Crypt of Westminster Hall, Houses of Parliament, Westminster'. At Davison's home address in St Pancras her landlady Charlotte Bateman simultaneously admitted, probably in some confusion, to her tenant's residence, with the result that in 1911 Davison was counted twice.

Emmeline Pankhurst described other of the suffragettes' activities:

In London we gave a great concert at Queen's Hall on Census night. Many of us walked about Trafalgar Square until midnight and then repaired to Aldwich skating rink, where we amused ourselves until morning. Some skated while others looked on, and enjoyed the admirable musical and theatrical entertainment that helped to pass the hours. We had with us a number of the brightest stars in the theatrical world, and they were generous in their contributions. It being Sunday night, the chairman had to call on each of the artists for a 'speech' instead of a song or other turn. An all-night restaurant near at hand did a big business, and on the whole the resisters had a very good time. The Scala Theatre was the scene of another all-night entertainment.

There was a good deal of curiosity to see what the Government would devise in the way of a punishment for the rebellious women, but the Government realised the impossibility of taking punitive action, and Mr John Burns, who, as head of the Local Government Board, was responsible for the census, announced that they had decided to treat the affair with magnanimity. The number of evasions, he declared, was insignificant. But every one knew that this was the exact reverse of the facts.

Women over the age of thirty with property were enfranchised in 1918. Ten years later, in 1928, the genders achieved representational equality when all women over the age of twenty-one were given the vote. Whether the suffragette boycott of the census had been significant or not, it was the first deliberate mass sabotage of the project, and would be the last until 1991. In his report of that year's census, Eric Thompson, the director of statistics at the Office of Population Censuses and Surveys (OPCS), into which by 1991 the General Register Office had been absorbed, wrote, 'There has rightly been discussion about the level of undercoverage in the 1991 Census ... It has been estimated that 97.8 per cent of the people resident in the country on Census night are represented in the census output tables ... '

In 1991 a missing 2 per cent of the population amounted to a million people. Thompson's 'discussion about the level of undercoverage' in that year revolved around the poll tax effect. The local government poll tax, or community charge, had been introduced by the Conservative government of Margaret Thatcher in 1989 in Scotland and in 1990 in England and Wales. It was resoundingly unpopular. After leading directly to the prime minister's downfall in November 1990, its abolition was announced by her replacement in March 1991. That was too late to halt a boycott of the 1991 census by hundreds of thousands of people who mistakenly believed that if they did not figure in the national records, they would be able to continue evading the community charge or its replacement, as the recalcitrants of 1801 and 1811 had thought that by avoiding the new national census they could escape taxation to pay for the Napoleonic Wars.

In the event, an under-enumeration in 1991 of 965,500 people was confessed by the OPCS. The under-enumeration ten years earlier, in the pre-poll tax year of 1981, had been estimated to be 214,000 people, which was the usual proportion of less than 0.5 per cent of the population. The OPCS said that in 1991 there had been 'an apparent shortfall of people aged 1 to 44 ... particularly males aged 20 to 29, in the census who also eluded the census validation survey interviewers'. Some 220,000 men in their twenties were guessed to have dodged the 1991 census enumerators. Although their absence from the national census returns had no effect on their local authority taxation claims, which were made regionally, it did, and would continue to, omit many of them from the national electoral register. They therefore had one thing in common with the women of 1911. The poll tax protesters of 1991 were disenfranchised.

By the time they achieved equal voting rights in 1928, some women had been census enumerators for over half a century. The first female enumerator was appointed in London in 1871. She was reported by the Registrar General to have 'discharged the duties very efficiently'; ten years later in 1881 a number of other women were consequently entrusted with the task. That hilarious state of affairs elicited a saloon-bar lampoon from the men at the *Hull Packet and East Riding Times*:

Neatly-dressed woman of an uncertain age, with big book under her arm and pen in hand, rings the door-bell. Young lady appears at the door.

Census enumerator: 'Good morning. Lovely morning. I'm taking the census. You were born –'

Young Lady: 'Yes 'm.'

Census enumerator: 'Your name, please. What a pretty dust-cap you have on. Can I get the pattern? It's just like the one the lady in the next house has. Let's see, your name?'

'I haven't the pattern. Don't you get awfully tired walking round taking the census?'

'Oh yes, it's wearisome, but I can pick up a great deal of information. How nice your dinner smells cooking. Plum pudding?'

'No. I haven't plum pudding today. I'm looking for a new recipe –'

'I've got one that I took down from a lady's cookery book across the way. Are you married?'

'No. Want an invitation to the wedding, don't you? It will be a long time before you get it. You can keep your plum pudding recipe, thank you.'

'I sh'd think 'twould be some time. Have you chil— oh, of course; I forgot. This hall carpet is just the pattern of Aunt Prudy's. She's had it more than twenty years. How many are they in your family?'

'If this hall carpet don't suit you, you can get off from it and go about your censusing.'

'Well, you're an impudent jade, anyhow. You haven't told me when you were born, or what's your name, or when you expect to get married, and there's a £5 fine for not answering the census-taker's questions, and if I were you I wouldn't be seen at the door in such a slutchy morning dress – so there.'

'Oh – you hateful thing. You can just go away. I'll pay £5 just to get rid of you, and smile doing it. It's none of your business, nor the census either. No, it isn't. You can keep your pattern, and your plum pudding, and your saucy, impudent questions to yourself – I – I –'

'Good morning. I must be getting on. I haven't done but three families all the forenoon.'

Emmeline Pankhurst, Emily Davison and their sisters had reasons not to underestimate the witless obduracy of too many of their husbands, brothers and fathers.

The careers open to men became more varied and, largely, immune to satire as the Victorian era matured. As George Graham and William Farr had noted, there were even livelihoods to be carved out of recreational sport. In the 1861 census the 34-year-old bachelor John Wisden, who was living with his sister and his cousin in New Coventry Street in the City of Westminster, recorded his 'Rank, Profession, or Occupation' as 'cricketer'. Wisden, born into a working-class family in Brighton, had played chiefly for Sussex, where he made his name as a fast underarm bowler and a very good batsman.

Wisden would retire from playing cricket in 1863, after which he opened a number of cricket equipment shops. He nonetheless told the enumerator in 1871, perhaps as much in pride as the strictest of accuracy, that he was a professional cricketer. Only in 1881, two years before his death at the age of fifty-eight, did he concede to a chief employment as 'cricketing outfitter'. Nowhere did he mention the *Cricketer's*

Almanack which he had been publishing annually since 1864 and which, as the oldest and most famous sports reference book in the world, would carry Wisden's name into the twenty-first century.

Pedestrianism was an athletic pursuit which had evolved since the eighteenth century from long-distance walking into something close to twentieth- and twenty-first-century track contests. The great pedestrians of yore, such as the two Scots Robert Barclay Allardice and Donald MacLeod, had become celebrated, and had made money from wagers, by walking absurd distances such as, respectively, a thousand miles in a thousand hours, and from London to York – a feat enhanced in MacLeod's case by his claiming to be over 100 years old at the time of his hike.

By 1881, when the 26-year-old Newcastle man John Angers told the census enumerator that his occupation was 'pedestrian', and 24-year-old Henry Coleman of Shoreditch in London listed his vocation as 'proff pedestrian', they were as likely to be runners as walkers. Pedestrianism was a popular spectator sport in the second half of the nineteenth century. But it was no longer confined to the open road. Events were staged 'for several large money prizes' of £5 to £25 at venues such as Salford Borough Gardens and the Grapes Running Ground in Newcastle upon Tyne. Some of these were still walking races, but increasingly the public turned up to see, and bet upon, the likes of John Angers and Henry Coleman run in makeshift head-to-head, all-comers and even handicapped sprints of 120, 200 or 440 yards.

Prizefighters, or bare-knuckled boxers, had also been scrapping out a livelihood since before the eighteenth century. Most of them travelled with circus troupes and spent their days taking on, and knocking over, a queue of local bloods who paid for the privilege. Contests between full-time prizefighters were relatively infrequent and usually illegal, but extremely popular. In the days before the introduction of the Marquess of Queensberry rules, which were broadly although far from universally applied by the 1870s, they were brutal, no-holds-barred matches which ended only with the concession, serious injury or death of one of the fighters.

It was neither a secure nor a respectable profession, which explains why so few Victorian prizefighters admitted the fact to census enumerators. James 'Jem' Mace, the most successful British prizefighter of the nineteenth century and an accomplished violinist, was already fighting for cash at fairs and racing meetings when he was nineteen years old in 1851, but listed his occupation as 'musician'. In the spring of 1861, when he was only a couple of months away from beating twenty-stone Sam Hurst in eight rounds for the championship of England and a purse of £200, Mace had moved from his native Norfolk to London and become, at least nominally, a hat presser. He was wise. Later in the 1860s Mace would twice be arrested and once imprisoned for engaging in prize fights.

Thereafter Mace spent most of his time in the United States, Australia and New Zealand and consequently evaded both the British police and the British census enumerators. Only in 1891, by which time he was back in England and had embraced the Queensberry Rules, did the 59-year-old dare to admit that his 'profession or occupation' was '(champion) pugilist'. Mace also lopped three years off his age.

No such modesty was required of billiard-markers, men who allocated tables and kept scores in public billiard halls.

The 1911 census reported that there were 11,139 billiard-markers in England and Wales.

Billiards was a popular sport. But it had also been popular forty years earlier in 1871, when the two countries contained just 250 billiard-markers. There had been no comparable surge in the use of billiard halls between 1871 and 1911. There had however been a marked increase in the number of soccer and rugby players who were forbidden by their ruling bodies to be paid for their performances on the pitch. The Northern Rugby Union, for instance, conceded in 1895 that players could be compensated for lost earnings – in what were known in all such codes of sport as 'broken-time' payments – if only they could demonstrate that rugby had torn them away from their actual profession.

The job of billiard-marker was a perfect foil. It was extremely difficult for the authorities to confirm or deny that an individual followed that occupation. Rugby players in Lancashire and Yorkshire usually had no objections to spending time in billiard halls. Those same halls were at their busiest at weekends, when rugby matches were played, which made sizeable compensation claims appear to be valid. Many of those 11,000 billiard-markers in 1911 were actually players of one of the football codes which since the late nineteenth century had blossomed as spectator sports.

The role of billiard-marking in early British shamateurism spread to the unlikeliest quarters. Even after professional association football, or soccer, had been legalised by the Football Association, there remained an extremely large rump of unreconstructed amateur bodies. The British Army, which had its own association, was obviously amateur and in 1890 even threatened to disqualify any regimental player rested for a big game by being 'kept off duty for more than seven days prior to the match'. According to an army referee of the time, Captain William Simpson, the Brigade of Guards football team evaded this regulation in the days before matches by putting their best players to undemanding work as billiard-markers in the officers' mess. But on 5 April 1891 a 29-year-old Scot who was boarding at 72 Knowsley Street in Preston told a census enumerator that his occupation was 'professional footballer'.

It was a doubly significant entry. Nicholas J. Ross, originally of Edinburgh, was the captain of Preston North End. He had signed for Preston from Heart of Midlothian in 1884, when professional football was outlawed in both Scotland and England. Initially the formidable Preston club chairman Major William Sudell, the owner of a local cotton mill, found Nick Ross a job as a slater. It is unlikely that Ross mounted many slates; as the soccer historian David Goldblatt writes, 'Under-the-counter payments, jobs in local firms, mock testimonials and a variety of other devices hidden on the club's balance sheets were used to pay players.' Occasionally no subterfuge whatsoever was employed. It was said of Sheffield's Billy Mosforth, who throughout his playing years in the 1880s and 1890s told the census-taker that he was a 'publican' or a 'licensed victualler', that 'He was once stripped to play for Hallam against Wednesday [but] when a supporter called "ten bob and free drinks all week, Billy, if you'll change your shirt", he returned to the dressing room to re-emerge in Wednesday colours.'

In 1885, a year after the arrival of Nick Ross at Preston, the Football Association found itself faced with such blatant subversion in and threatened secession by many northern clubs that it relented and permitted men to be paid for playing soccer in England. In 1888 Ross, who was one of the best defenders in the game, transferred to Everton where he was able to earn the dizzy sum of £2 10s a week. He returned to Preston after just one season, in time to captain the club to its second consecutive league title. In 1889 Ross moved into the forward line, where he joined his younger brother Jimmy, a formidable inside forward who scored eighty-five goals in 130 competitive senior fixtures with North End.

By the April of 1891 Preston had relinquished their league title. Nick Ross was nonetheless still the captain of the dominant team in the early years of English professional football. The most accomplished and successful all-round footballer of his day, he was probably earning around £2 a week from Preston North End. It was just enough to keep him in shared lodgings in a Preston terraced house, the home of a middle-aged fellow Scottish exile, printer-compositor Thomas McNeil.

He was also, that April, among the first few dozen players who were able openly to declare their profession without fear of banishment from the sport. Nicholas J. Ross, the captain of the best club football team in the world, did not have to pretend to be a billiard-marker. Players of rugby union were not allowed the same freedom from fake occupations until 1995.

6

Lathes and Rapes

Having both studied and taught mathematics – without pay – as a young woman at Queen's College, London, in 1861 a 21-year-old Englishwoman named Sophia Jex-Blake travelled to the United States, where she worked at the New England Hospital for Women and Children in Boston.

Upon her return to Britain she determined to acquire a medical training. Believing, correctly, that a Scottish university would be more likely than Oxford or Cambridge to admit a woman, she applied at the age of twenty-nine to the medical faculty of the University of Edinburgh. After an initial rejection she raised a public furore and her application was accepted. She qualified, practised, and in 1874 helped to establish the London School of Medicine for Women. Jex-Blake became the first practising woman doctor in Scotland and only the third in the British Isles, the previous two having qualified overseas. In 1877 women were allowed onto degree programmes at other British universities. 'Dr Sophia Jex-Blake has made the greatest of all contributions to the end attained,' wrote her friend and supporter James Stansfield, the eminent Liberal MP for Halifax.

Two curious details usually, and understandably, overlooked in accounts of Sophia Jex-Blake's courageous and accomplished life were her birthplace, in 1840, in the Rape of Hastings in the County of Sussex, and her childhood home, Sydenham in the Hundred of Blackheath in the Lathe of Sutton-at-Hone in the County of Kent. She herself would have paid little or no attention to those regional nouns: rape, lathe and hundred. They had always been there. But two of them would become extinct before her own death early in the twentieth century, and the third would fall into disuse.

When John Rickman was raised at the end of the eighteenth century, most of the southern English counties were subdivided into districts known as hundreds, while in large parts of the Midlands and the North, wapentakes or apentakes were the equivalent divisions. That had been the case for more than a thousand years.

They were venerable units. John Rickman himself was fascinated by such survivals. 'The further Division of the Southern parts of England,' he wrote in 1811, 'into Hundreds is ... unquestionably of Saxon origin.' As evidence of that assertion he was able to cite the Roman historian Tacitus, who in the first century AD had written of contemporary Germany: 'Eliguntur et principes qui jura per pagos vicosque reddunt: Centeni singulus ex plebe comites, concilium simul et auctoritus, adsunt.' ('In these same councils they also elect the chief magistrates, who administer law in the cantons and the towns. Each of these has a hundred associates chosen from the people, who support him with their advice and influence.')

'At least one hundred (which in Saxon numeration means one hundred and twenty),' continued Rickman, 'Free Men, Householders, answerable for each other, may be supposed originally to have been found in each Hundred.' The Saxon origin of the hundreds was further attested by the fact that when the Domesday Book was compiled the earliest Saxon counties of Kent and Sussex 'contained more than Sixty Hundreds, as they do at present'. In Lancashire, however, 'a County of greater area than either' but with far less of a Saxon tradition, 'there are no more than Six Hundreds ... '

In certain northern counties, wrote Rickman, 'formerly exposed to hostile Invasion, Wards and Wapentakes stand in place of Hundreds'. The 'hostile invasion' had come from Scandinavia. Within the Danelagh, or Danelaw, which at the ninth- and tenth-century summit of its power reached from modern Yorkshire and Lancashire through the eastern Midlands to Hertfordshire and East Anglia, hundreds were either replaced by or coexisted alongside wapentakes. The term wapentake derives from the Old Norse *vapnatak*, *vapna* being a 'weapon' and *tak* meaning 'take', which suggests the raising of a number of armed men at an assembly or in pursuit of conflict. As Cambridge University's Department of Geography reported in the twenty-first century:

Hundreds and their northern equivalents (wapentakes and wards) were one of the principal and most enduring units of administration in England ... and to a lesser extent Wales (16th to mid-nineteenth centuries). The importance of the hundred as a unit of administrative geography is manifest in the volume and quality of the historical data associated with it. For example, taxation returns ordered under hundreds survive for six centuries ... and the hundred was the administrative unit used for parliamentary enquiries into poor relief expenditure in the eighteenth and early nineteenth centuries.

Such antiquities were still a part of everyday life in the time of John Rickman as well as that of Sophia Jex-Blake. If Jex-Blake paid them as little attention as any other mundane part of her family's landscape, Rickman had cause to examine them closely. He personally – the last Clerk of the House of Commons to wear the medieval costume of a stiff neck stock and knee breeches when on duty at the table of the House – saw no good reason to do away with them. 'Innovations are really unnecessary,' he would tell Parliament; 'to alter the Names or Limits of the ancient Hundreds would really be equivalent to inventing and learning a new and changeable language, instead of retaining in use that which has been established for ages.'

Indeed, Rickman even regretted the earlier abolition of the *cantrefi* and *cymydau*, or commotes, of Wales, which had divided and subdivided that nation into distinct cultural and legal entities until the sixteenth century, when they were officially replaced by hundreds. That particular interference with tradition, he thought, 'was attended with much unexpected difficulty', and 300 years later 'the abolished Cantrefs and Commots are not yet quite forgotten and occasionally cause confusion.'

The established fabric of the islands did not extend only to hundreds, wapentakes and *cymydau*. North of the Danelaw, in Northumbria and Cumbria, as Rickman had written, administrative divisions were known as wards, a term which clearly derived from a form of guardianship, and which would survive in Britain and other parts of the English-speaking world to describe electoral districts.

South of the Danelaw, uniquely in those earlier Saxon shires of Kent and Sussex, hundreds were still contained within those larger formations known as lathes and rapes.

A Kentish lathe in Old English was a *laeth*, or an estate. A Sussex rape probably came from the Old English *rap*, or rope, which commemorated a typical method of dividing land. Across the kingdom, other areas known as liberties were traditionally districts outside the walls of a city or a town which were nonetheless under the jurisdiction – or guaranteed their liberty – by the urban centre.

As John Rickman had pointed out, such millennial units could not be made to disappear overnight. Lincolnshire was divided into the three Parts of Holland, Kesteven and Lindsey, as the French origin of the word 'part' suggests had been the case since the Norman Conquest, until local government reorganisation in 1974. The Scandinavian *thrithings*, or three Ridings, of Yorkshire would survive in common usage into the twenty-first century despite their abolition as administrative units in 1974. The hundreds were never formally abolished and would maintain a single degraded usage: 'taking the Chiltern Hundreds' (the three hundreds of Stoke, Desborough and Burnham in Buckinghamshire) became and remained a means by which Members of Parliament could resign from their seat in the House of Commons – stewardship of the Chiltern Hundreds having been a profitable Crown office, the occupation of which has been forbidden to sitting MPs since 1701. The Isle of Man was and would remain uniquely divided into six sheadings, a term whose origin remains unclear. It could be Norse, from *skeid*, a ship's crew, from the Middle English *scheding*, an administrative unit, or from the Irish word for six, *seu*, whose soft 's' is pronounced 'sh'.

But almost all such terms fell out of use during the nineteenth century, and most of the remnants disappeared at least from official terminology in the following hundred years. 'Hundred courts' were still sitting in the middle of the reign of Queen Victoria, but the judicial purpose of the hundreds and wapentakes was made anachronistic by the establishment of county courts in 1867. Inhabitants of a hundred were anomalously obliged to provide compensation for damage caused by riots within their region for a further nineteen years, until that legal liability was removed in 1886. William White of Sheffield produced a series of county directories and gazetteers from the 1820s onwards. In White's directory of Lincolnshire in 1882 wapentakes were described as 'now of little practical value'. That little remaining value was removed by the Local Government Act of 1894, which established urban and rural elected councils.

However irrelevant they had become, hundreds, wapentakes, rapes and lathes were still recorded in the census of 1881. Ten years later, in 1891, they had all but disappeared. The Rape of Hastings had become a borough within the administrative county of East Sussex. The Hundred of Blackheath in the Lathe of Sutton-at-Hone had become part of the civil parish of Lewisham within the registration county of London. By the time of the death of Sophia Jex-Blake in 1912 the thousand-year-old lathes, rapes and hundreds in which she had been born and raised would appear to have belonged not so much to another century as to another country.

7

Two Parrots, One Canary and Innumerable Mice

The refinement and expansion of the decennial census in the Victorian era was not universally understood or welcomed. In 1851 Matthew Reed of Sinnington in Yorkshire, given the opportunity as head of his household to fill out the forms himself, listed under 'livestock', 'tu poll parets [poll parrots], tu cats, on Canare [canary], and how mane meas [mice] I don't know.'

With better spelling but less wit, in the same year the satirical magazine *Punch* published a cartoon ridiculing the likes of Matthew Reed. Titled 'Filling up the Census Paper', it portrayed a small, meek man seated at a writing desk sucking nervously on the end of a quill. Before him stood a huge matriarch sternly brandishing a completed form. 'Upon my word, Mr Peewitt!' says his wife. 'Is this the Way you Fill up your Census? So you call Yourself the "Head of the Family" – do you – and me a "Female?"'

A census enumerator in the era of George Graham and William Farr was required to be 'intelligent and active, able to read and write well, not younger than 18 years of age or older than 60; they were to be respectable persons likely to conduct themselves with strict propriety and courtesy in the discharge of their duties, and well acquainted with the district in which they were to act.' Those qualifications omitted to mention that a census enumerator should also be male; that was taken for granted. Even after the appointment of the first female enumerator in 1871, the work was usually done by John Rickman's tried-and-tested local clergymen or by professionals such as schoolteachers and clerks.

Their job was clearly defined. The census enumerator's business, 'as a preliminary and very essential duty, must be to obtain a thorough and minute knowledge of the District which he has undertaken to enumerate'. In the week before the day of the census the enumerator should 'deliver to each Householder and Occupier in his District, a Householder's Schedule ... He must leave a separate Schedule with each Occupier – understanding by "Occupier" either the resident owner or any person who pays rent ... He should intimate that he will call for it on the following Monday, and that IT MUST ON NO ACCOUNT BE LOST OR DESTROYED.'

Schools, hotels, inns, lodging houses, prisons and asylums should be asked to list the people resident on their premises on census day, along with those individuals' details. On the dawn of the day itself, armed with 'a pencil or pen and ink – blotting paper – a portfolio or piece of strong paper', the enumerator should begin his rounds. When handed a completed schedule he would copy it into his portfolio. Wherever an incomplete schedule was returned he would endeavour to fill it in himself by personal inquiry. Only after each and every form had been fully completed could an enumerator retire to his bed. If the occupants of a building proved to be particularly reclusive he was allowed to return the following morning. Only then might the letters 'N.K.' – Not Known – be admitted. In 1861 the Registrar General George Graham employed in England and Wales alone 31,144 enumerators, paying them a total of £45,755 12s 4d. They had each been responsible for recording an average of 670 people.

They had become a common, if occasionally mystifying and sometimes controversial, feature of the British landscape. The caricaturist George Cruikshank's *Comic Almanac* calendar for 1851 included an illustration labelled 'Taking the Census'. It showed a top-hatted enumerator in the doorway of a room crowded with men, women and children of all ages. 'What! Not made out the list yet?!' says the enumerator to a middle-aged man at the front of the throng.

'Why, no,' replies the man, counting on his fingers, 'it is not such an easy matter as you may think for; However, let me see; there's John & Tom & Bill & Susan & Harry & Sarah & Dick & Eliza & George & Septimus & Peter & Jane & Augustus & Decimus & Charles & Betsey & Harriet & Rebecca & Emma & Bob & James & Emma & David & the two Gran'mothers & Father & Mother & my wife's Father & Mother & Cousin Alfred & the three nurses, two housemaids, the Cook & the boy & & & hang me if I can recollect em all so it's no use to try!'

From the back a woman with a swaddled infant in each arm calls out, 'John, dear, don't forget the two babbies!'

Resistance among certain individuals to the enumerators' enquiries still persisted. During the taking of the 1861 census, reported the *Morpeth Herald*, an elderly lady in the Northumbrian village of Alnmouth 'could not conceive' why her enumerator needed to know her age. 'She knew her own age and nobody had anything else to do with it.' Informed by a local worthy that the information was necessary as the enumerator had been appointed by the government to take an accurate account of the population of the country, she replied, 'Population indeed! Fine times truly. We were far better off lang since, when there was nae population at a'.'

The *People's Journal* of 6 May 1871 reported too briefly that William Collett of Hammersmith 'has been fined £2 for caning a census enumerator'. Meanwhile, George Graham reported to Parliament of residual resistance to the 1871 census:

A spinster in the country of rather advanced age, very wealthy, fastened up her doors and windows, forbidding access to the Enumerator, and saying a fine of 20s would not induce her to give him the required particulars. In answer to a soothing letter, she sent the Registrar General her schedule privately.

A gentleman of landed property declared he would pay a fine of any amount, indeed would rather cease to exist, than commit the offence for which David suffered, as recorded in the Old Testament. His religious scruples were respected, and the particulars of his family were nevertheless recorded with tolerable accuracy.

One Enumerator states that he was insulted and assaulted, so much so that he summoned the householder before the Magistrates, who inflicted a fine.

No prosecution was instituted by the Registrar General; but a few recusant householders appear to have been proceeded against in the country, and fined at the instance of Enumerators.

Ten years later in Glasgow another enumerator, named John Murphy, called at a house in the city's Princes Street. As

Murphy was conferring over details with the householder a young lodger called John Macdonald appeared, 'cursing and swearing'. Macdonald told Murphy that he had 'no right to take the census' and threatened to knock him down. Murphy called in the law and Glasgow central police court quickly fined Macdonald one guinea.

Citizens were not always uncooperative. In south Ayrshire in 1871 an enumerator received a form upon which was written this autobiography:

Thomas Moran boran In ireland county of armaugh Silver Brigs eage 303 years. To the best of my nolege i Am that eage, and i am married the secunt time the furst wife Mary Conolly be longed to ireland in county armaugh the Secent Wife be longed to County Dereay hur name is elen Moran but she run a way From me five years and ten months since and i dont now wheare she is for if she is dead or not i havent hard . . .

before now my father was a Farmer and had a great power of land in Ireland and when i came to scotland it was a navvy i was working In the Coll Pitt but sure i am not working no place now for i got my legs broken 5 weeks and 3 days since gon tomorrow . . .

For the most part, in England, Scotland and Wales the census evoked less hostility than curiosity and even wonder. In 1861 a journalist in Nottinghamshire found himself calculating that as an inch of space was allocated to each name in the survey of that year, 'Supposing the population of Great Britain and Ireland to be 30,000,000, the list of names would thus be 177 1/2 miles long; and if the sheets were bound so as to contain 30 names on a page, they would make 2,090 volumes of 500 pages each.'

When, as usually was the case, the enumerators were able to go about their duties unmocked, unhindered and unmolested, they found themselves recording in those 177 miles of completed names individual personal details which collectively described national developments of international significance. Edgar Chapman and Mary Burgess, born in the parish of Glastonbury in the Hundred of Glaston Twelve Hides in 1798 and 1811 respectively, became unlikely representatives of the greatest European demographic upheaval in the nineteenth century.

They were each of the rural middle class. Edgar's father was a property owner, Mary the daughter of one of Glastonbury's two surgeons. Their childhoods on the rolling meadows of the Somerset Levels were spent in an English pastoral idyll which was, early in the nineteenth century, apparently immutable.

Inoculated by their families' relative affluence against the hardships and diseases of agricultural life all around them, Edgar and Mary were raised and schooled in the heart of Anglo-Saxon England. Beneath Glastonbury Tor and the ruined medieval church at its summit, in the immediate vicinity of the vestiges of Glastonbury Abbey, they grew to adulthood amid rumours of Arthur and Guinevere and Lancelot and Avalon, Joseph of Arimathea and even of Jesus Christ: rumours which were circulated more widely after 1808 when William Blake first published his astounding verse 'And Did Those Feet in Ancient Times'.

Edgar's and Mary's young feet may not have followed those of the Holy Lamb of God, but they certainly walked in the steps of such local Anglo-Saxon eminences as Centwine, king of Wessex, the abbot Aethelwold, St

Dunstan and Eadwig, king of England. It was an inheritance they acknowledged in 1844 when they christened their third son Athelstan, after the most celebrated pre-Norman king of England.

The Glastonbury of their day was composed of terraces and rows of houses, new and old, large and small, running off an elegant main square. The town contained some 2000 people, a few of whom were tenants of Edgar's father and several of whom were patients of Mary's. They were smiths and saddlers, carpenters, innkeepers, tailors, grocers and laundrywomen, bakers, butchers and drapers. There were freeholding agriculturalists who still registered themselves as 'yeomen' in the census's 'Profession, trade, employment' column. There were four attorneys, an auctioneer and an accountant.

Some attempted to make money from pilgrims and other visitors to the abbey and the Tor by selling them holy curative water which had flowed through the abbey precinct. There were also fourteen alehouses. A long-established brickworks exploited the district's substantial reserves of clay.

Glastonbury's level of education was unusually high for early nineteenth-century England. 'In 1818,' write Siraut, Thacker and Williamson, 'it was reported [from Glastonbury] that in addition to the four charity schools there were two Church Sunday and weekday schools teaching 150 boys and 150 girls, a National school for 80 children, probably that known as the Madras school founded in 1815, a Quaker Sunday school for 30 girls, and a Dissenting Sunday school for 10 boys and girls. About 1825 the Church Sunday and day school had a total of 187 children, with a further 30 in a preparatory Sunday school ... by 1833 there were

13 schools in the town.'

There were almshouses and a Benevolent Society. Sewers were laid early in the nineteenth century. The six-year-old Edgar Chapman and his friends may have experienced a frisson of fascination and fear in 1804, when some French prisoners of the Napoleonic Wars were briefly detained in St John's Church. There was a monthly market which 'attracted horned cattle, horses, sheep and pigs, nursery shrubs and trees, cheese and other agricultural products', and there were three fairs a year.

Local government, which had earlier been routinely corrupt, was substantially reformed at the end of the eighteenth century and the beginning of the nineteenth. Shambles wardens, who policed the quality of butcher's meat on sale, and tithingmen, a thousand-year-old term for an area representative, were still appointed. By 1811 the civic authorities had agreed to ban thatched roofs from the town (in built-up districts they posed a fire hazard which the small horse-drawn parish fire engine might not cope with), levied rates to pave the streets and introduced parking restrictions for carriages on the narrow roads.

To the middle classes of Jane Austen's day, Glastonbury was a civilised, safe and respectable place to live and to raise a family, just as the Burgesses and the Chapmans had raised Mary and Edgar and their siblings there. It was the epitome of Austen's 'large and populous village, in a situation not unpleasant ... in her heart she preferred it to any place she had ever been at, and looked with great admiration at every neat house above the rank of a cottage, and at all the little chandler's shops which they passed'.

Mary Burgess married Edgar Chapman at St John's Church in 1832. They moved into Mary's parents' large house on the High Street and Mary quickly gave birth to six children, including young Athelstan. The boys and girls were all put into school between the ages of seven and thirteen, at a time when only half of the country's young were educated, and when that lucky half spent an average of just two years at elementary school. Edgar had built up a small business as a journeyman carrier – the 'journeyman' prefix meaning that he had completed an apprenticeship and was fully qualified in his vocation. Before long he was accepted into the Carriers Guild and became a master carrier. He was then in a position to employ and train his own apprentices, and after completing their schooling his four sons duly followed him into the carrier trade.

In the first third of the nineteenth century Glastonbury was a good place for a carrier. It had modest imports and exports to be hauled by Edgar Chapman's growing fleet of horses and carts and Edgar was the only carrier in his parish. The Chapman family should have had a comfortable future there. At any time in the previous few hundred years they would have had a future as well as a heritable past in Glastonbury.

In 1834, however, a canal was opened from Glastonbury to the nearby River Parrett, down which barges could make their way northwards to the south bank of the Bristol Channel and from there to Bristol itself, the region's main city, trading centre and port, twenty-three miles away. Canals were specifically designed to transport goods cheaply and this presented a clear threat to Edgar Chapman's carriage business. The canal was ultimately unsuccessful, but as its towpath was replaced by a railway line twenty years later, Edgar could take little consolation.

Edgar and Mary Chapman appear to have spent the

later 1830s and early 1840s assessing the damage done by the canal to their professional prospects. When they decided that they had no economic future in their home town, despite the fact that Edgar in his late forties was on the verge of early-Victorian old age, they packed all their belongings and children on their wagons and removed themselves 120 miles east to the market town of Saffron Walden in Essex.

Saffron Walden was surrounded by the farmland of north Essex, Cambridgeshire and East Anglia. It was just forty-three miles from London, the destination of most of its local produce, and it had no canal or, as yet, railway line. What was more, Saffron Walden was booming – the town recorded its highest-ever population of 21,000 in 1851 due largely to its growing role as a goods exchange and distribution centre for the metropolis. In the 1851 and 1861 censuses, Saffron Walden contained more agricultural workers than all other male occupations or professions combined.

The Chapmans must have done well in Saffron Walden. But the centripetal force of London, which Edgar came to experience for the first time in his life, was inescapable. If a master carrier could make good money transporting food and other materials from a small corner of Essex to London, how much better would he do if his business was located in the capital itself, with its myriad manufactured exports as well as its consumption of produce from all four corners of the south of England. They moved again, this time to London.

On Sunday 7 April 1861 a census enumerator knocked on the front door of a large terraced house in Abbey Street, Bermondsey. He recorded as living at 2 Abbey Terrace the 62-year-old master carrier Edgar Chapman, his fifty-year-old wife Mary and their four sons, all but one of whom were employed by their father as carriers. Every one of the Chapman family had been born in Glastonbury, Somerset, apart from the eleven-year-old schoolboy Edward, who had first opened his eyes in Saffron Walden.

They were a tiny part of an epochal upheaval. When the official report of the 1861 census was presented by Registrar General George Graham to Parliament two years later, in 1863, it noted that for the first time in history – for the first time in the history of any substantial nation on earth – more citizens of England and Wales lived in towns and cities than in the countryside.

The figures were indisputable: 10,960,998 English and Welsh men and women lived in urban areas. Almost 2 million fewer – 9,105,226 – lived in rural villages, isolated cottages and farmsteadings in country parishes. Temporarily losing sight of Wales, Graham wrote, 'The English nation then, without losing its hold on the country, and still largely diffused over 37 million acres of territory, has assumed the character of a preponderating city population.' The classically educated Graham and his co-authors and assistants from the General Register Office, William Farr and James Hammack, could not resist references to Nineveh and Tyre. 'It enjoys the advantages of the cities of the ancient world,' they said, 'in the proximity of its citizens for intercourse, for defence, for counsel, for production, and for the interchange of commodities ...'

It was not that the countryside had been abandoned. The number of people living in rural parts in 1861 was actually much greater than sixty years earlier – in fact, it was slightly greater than the total population of England and Wales in 1801. A line of demarcation was not easily drawn: coal miners, for instance, despite being involved in heavy industry, frequently lived in isolated villages around a pithead erected in open countryside. But there were still over 2 million men and women employed in agriculture: 1,631,652 males and 378,802 females. Most of them – 958,265 people – were agricultural labourers, but there were also a quarter of a million small farmers and an equal number of indoor farmers' servants. There were also in 1861 eight professional trufflers and fifty-five full-time cultivators of watercress.

The national population had more than doubled since 1801. Thanks to the industrial and agricultural revolutions most of the increase had occurred in the new towns and cities. Birkenhead on Merseyside had grown from a village with 667 inhabitants in 1801 to a substantial town of 51,649 in 1861. Bradford in the West Riding of Yorkshire, a small market town of 5000 people in 1801, was a manufacturing city of 106,218 sixty years later. In the same six decades the population of Liverpool had grown from 80,000 to 443,938, and that of Manchester and Birmingham from 75,000 to 357,979 and from 74,000 to 296,076 respectively. The population of the industrialised county of Lanarkshire, which included Clydeside and the city of Glasgow, had increased from 147,692 in 1801 to 631,566 in 1861. In 1861 a total of 4,828,399 British men and women were recorded as working in some branch of industry. Until the twentieth century the rural population had merely expanded less dramatically and at a much slower pace.

That is one reason why some of the most celebrated eulogies of the abandoned paradise of English rural life were not written and published until the end of the nineteenth century and the first half of the twentieth.

*

Flora Timms was born in December 1876 in the hamlet of Juniper Hill, 'on a gentle rise in the flat, wheat-growing north-east corner of Oxfordshire'. She was to be found there in 1881, a four-year-old girl living with her 26-year-old stonemason father Albert, her 27-year-old mother Emma and her one-year-old brother Edwin. They were surrounded entirely by farm labourers and one shepherd. The few families in Juniper Hill in 1881 were insufficient to merit a separate entry in the population returns; they were instead listed as being among the 240 people of the village of Cottisford, a mile away across the fields, where Flora walked to and from school. The Education Acts of the last third of the nineteenth century were another reason why country people of that era set down on paper accounts of their childhoods: they could write.

In the early summer census of 1891 the fourteen-year-old Flora Timms was still living in Juniper Hill. Eleven-year-old Edwin had become a labourer, her seven-year-old sister May had followed her to school in Cottisford and her parents were also raising three children between the ages of six months and four years. It was time for Flora to leave her little rural home and find work.

Flora's mother's cousin Kezia had married a blacksmith named John Whitton in the town of Fringford, three miles from Juniper Hill. John and Kezia had between them taken over the Fringford post office, where John became the nominal postmaster and Kezia the assistant postmaster who ran the place. In 1891 John and Kezia were respectively sixty and fifty-six years old and had no children of their own. They already accommodated three boarders, two of whom were men helping John Whitton at the smithy. When Emma

Timms asked Kezia Whitton if she could find room and work for the bright young Flora at Fringford post office, the Whittons happily agreed.

So Flora Timms moved from bucolic Juniper Hill to the village of Fringford, with its mansion house occupied by the Withington family and their servants, its grocer, miller, dressmakers, laundress, shoemaker, butcher, baker, schoolteacher, wheelwright, clergyman and another 400 people, and its proximity to the even busier town of Bicester. It was not a long walk from Juniper Hill through Cottisford and the woods and meadows to Fringford and Flora was able regularly to revisit her home. She had nonetheless, when barely a teenager, moved into another world.

Many years later, as an adult, Mrs Flora Thompson would write partly fictionalised accounts of her Oxfordshire childhood. In those bestselling memoirs Juniper Hill became the tiny, age-old agricultural settlement of Lark Rise, and Fringford the developing conurbation of Candleford Green.

The *Lark Rise to Candleford* books were published in three volumes between 1939 and 1943 – the last one appearing just four years before its author's death in 1947 at the age of seventy – at a time when the embellishment and even the invention of British tradition and identity were considered to be essential in a struggle for national survival. Forty years later the academic Barbara English accused *Lark Rise* of being 'a very skilful piece of special pleading. Thompson told her story with a purpose: the changes of facts or changes of emphasis . . . were made in order to reinforce her theme. For she too was caught up in the "Old England" legend . . . Whatever her aims and intentions may have been, she constructed a past which never really existed.'

In fact the village of Juniper Hill had been stripped of

its common heath by enclosures at the unusually late date of 1869. As a result most of Flora Timms' actual childhood neighbours were semi-itinerant labourers from elsewhere who moved in and then departed to other hires. The minority of settled villagers over the age of thirty could however remember vividly when the common land had given people a decent, self-sufficient and proudly independent living rather than an insecure labourer's pittance. Flora Thompson did not ignore that fact in her books, any more than she ignored poverty and disease and brutality. She was extremely well placed to describe the hardships as well as the pleasures of the last years of an isolated English rural community before it was entirely transformed, even if she did so from a distance and through the soft prism of old age. By contrast, Stella Gibbons, who subverted the rural romance so magnificently in *Cold Comfort Farm* seven years before *Lark Rise* was published, was born at the beginning of the twentieth century and raised in an affluent professional family in north London. When she wrote her most famous novel Gibbons was working as an editorial assistant at the women's society magazine *The Lady*.

It was not Flora Thompson's fault that her millions of readers did not buy *Lark Rise* for stringent social history. They bought it to share the unfeigned joy of a girl who 'longed to go alone far into the fields and hear the birds singing, the brooks tinkling, and the wind rustling through the corn, as she had when a child. To smell things and touch things, warm earth and flowers and grasses, and to stand and gaze where no one could see her, drinking it all in.' If it was erroneous to suggest that during the long history of rural Britain there was never something nasty in the woodshed, it was equally mistaken to imagine that such natural ecstasies had not been available and appreciated for centuries, and had subsequently been lost to little girls in the stews of nineteenth-century Glasgow and Birmingham.

Thompson wrote of Lark Rise/Juniper Hill in the 1880s:

Some of the cottages had two bedrooms, others only one, in which case it had to be divided by a screen or curtain to accommodate parents and children. Often the big boys of a family slept downstairs, or were put out to sleep in the second bedroom of an elderly couple whose own children were out in the world. Except at holiday times, there were no big girls to provide for, as they were all out in service. Still, it was often a tight fit, for children swarmed, eight, ten, or even more in some families, and although they were seldom all at home together, the eldest often being married before the youngest was born, beds and shakedowns were often so closely packed that the inmates had to climb over one bed to get into another.

But Lark Rise must not be thought of as a slum set down in the country. The inhabitants lived an open-air life; the cottages were kept clean by much scrubbing with soap and water, and doors and windows stood wide open when the weather permitted. When the wind cut across the flat land to the east, or came roaring down from the north, doors and windows had to be closed; but then, as the hamlet people said, they got more than enough fresh air through the keyhole.

There were two epidemics of measles during the decade, and two men had accidents in the harvest field and were taken to hospital; but, for years together, the doctor was only seen there when one of the ancients was dying of old age, or some difficult first confinement baffled the skill of the old woman who, as she said, saw the beginning and end of everybody. There was no cripple or mental defective in the hamlet, and, except for a few months when a poor woman was dying of cancer, no invalid. Though food was rough and teeth were neglected, indigestion was unknown . . .

A letter from a correspondent to the London *Standard* in September 1861 illustrated the contrast between routine ill-health in the countryside and the terrifying new causes of varieties of sickness and death which were thriving in the urban slums:

> Seeing in your paper of last evening an account of the death of four persons in one house in Eagle-street, Holborn, I am induced to draw attention to the densely-populated state of that locality, and to ask why some measures are not taken by the officers of health with a view to its relief.
>
> In one house in Eagle-street there were, on the night of 7th April last, 53 people sleeping, and in many others more than 30; while on the premises of Mr Smith, mentioned in your account, there were 13 cows! Surely the presence of 13 cows in premises adjoining a house containing 13 persons, cannot be conducive either to the health of the animals or of the individuals, and one can scarcely wonder at the small-pox making its appearance there.
>
> I am enabled to state this from having been a census enumerator.

London was the colossus overshadowing them all, the

provincial industrial towns and cities and the lonely thatched hamlets alike. In 1801 John Rickman's first census had reasonably estimated the capital's population to be 958,863 people. In 1861 the organised enumerators and their experienced superiors put it at 2,803,989. In the previous thirty years alone the size of London had almost doubled.

The new Londoners were not all ambitious bourgeois families from the Somerset Levels. They were farm labourers uprooted by the agricultural revolution, coal miners from the north seeking a safer and more comfortable life, girls and women sent from West Country or Scottish parishes to be maids and housekeepers. It was a nation on the move. Only 62 per cent of Londoners had been born in the city. 'The stream to London from the South grows larger,' noted George Graham, 'and the counties of Cornwall, Devon, Somerset, Dorset and Wilts send 128,442 of their natives to be enumerated in London – 70 natives to every 1000 of the inhabitants of these South-western counties.'

But London was not boosted mainly by immigrants from the West Country such as the Glastonbury Chapmans. Still more arrived from the south Midlands and from the south-eastern counties, but mostly they came from the eastern counties of Essex, Suffolk, Norfolk, Cambridgeshire and Lincolnshire, which lost to the capital an average of 133 natives out of every thousand – or 13.3 per cent of their population – in the years between 1851 and 1861. 'Proximity to the metropolis, and the absence of manufactures at home,' judged George Graham, 'first drew the natives of these counties to London, and the migration continues to flow thither in unabated force.'

Wholesale, as opposed to partial, abandonment of the English countryside was not in fact noted until early in

the twentieth century. It was due largely to the mecha-
nisation of agriculture. The word 'tractor' was first used
in 1901. In his report of the census of that year Registrar
General William Dunbar noted that 'there were five English
Counties – Oxfordshire, Huntingdonshire, Herefordshire,
Rutlandshire and Westmorland, and five Welsh Counties –
Cardiganshire, Brecknockshire, Montgomeryshire, Flintshire,
and Merionethshire, in each of which the enumerated population had diminished since the previous Census. These 10
Counties, all of which are of limited dimensions and may be
generally described as agricultural Counties, lost by migra-
tion not only all their natural increment, i.e., the excess of
Births over Deaths, in the ten years, but also a further portion
of their population.'

In the twenty years between 1881 and 1901 the number
of agricultural labourers in England and Wales fell from
1,200,000 to 870,000. In the same period the numbers of
railway workers rose from 165,500 to 320,500, of roadworkers from 341,000 to 595,000, of metalworkers from 775,000
to 1,200,000 and of mineworkers from 610,000 to 937,000.
The first category nonetheless continued to feed the second.

The symbiotic relationship between the agricultural
and industrial revolutions continued. The initial period of
agricultural improvements in the eighteenth century had
nourished the first groups of factory workers. Machines
developed in those factories during the nineteenth century
were then turned loose upon the land, replacing human
and equestrian labour and substituting ranches for farms,
but increasing still further the production of food, which
in turn enabled even more of the population to work for a
wage without ever milking a cow or turning a sod of soil.

That phenomenon had been noted as early as 1881, when

the census report commented: 'Some small indication, however, of a reason for the decline in the number of agricultural labourers is perhaps to be found in the fact that the Proprietors of, and Attendants on, Agricultural Machines, who only numbered 2,160 in 1871, had increased to 4,260 in 1881, that is to say, they had doubled in number in the course of the ten years. Machinery had taken the place of hand labour.'

Thirty years later, Registrar General Bernard Mallett wrote that 'while in 1851 the numbers of persons living under urban and rural conditions were, broadly speaking, evenly divided, in 1911 no less than 78 per cent of the population were living under urban, and only 22 per cent under rural conditions'. Between 1891 and 1911 the agricultural counties of Rutlandshire and Montgomeryshire each lost 8 per cent of their populations, while Westmorland lost 4 per cent. Where there was a growth in the absolute, rather than relative, rural population it was usually due to certain industries being opened in the countryside. The number of coal miners active in rural England and Wales, most of whom lived in new colliery villages beside pits sunk on the hillsides and among the fields and hedgerows, grew from 292,455 in 1901 to 493,816 in 1911.

The pendulum would swing back. By the time of the census of 2011, just 200,000 people in the whole of Great Britain were recorded as working in the combined category of 'agriculture, forestry and fishing'. And the number of coal miners working anywhere, in rural or urban districts, in Scotland, south Wales or the north-east of England, had fallen to below 4000.

Meanwhile, throughout the nineteenth and twentieth centuries and into the twenty-first, there was always Ireland.

8

The British Babel

When in 1841 the three Irish census commissioners William Tighe Hamilton, Henry John Brownrigg and Thomas Larcom reported their concern that the population of Ireland was rising much more slowly than that of England, Scotland and Wales, it was at least still rising.

In that year 8,175,238 people lived in Ireland. It would prove to be the largest number in the island's history.

Ten years later, in 1851, Ireland also had a Register Office in Dublin and the island's census was supervised by Registrar General William Donnelly. The son of a gentleman merchant from Armagh, Donnelly was educated at Trinity College, Dublin and trained in the law in London. He was assisted as census taker by a secretary called Edward Singleton and by the surgeon and scholar William Wilde, whose marriage to the nationalist suffragette poet Jane Francesca Agnes Elgee in that census year would result three years later in the birth of a son christened Oscar.

William Donnelly was thirty-nine years old when he became Irish Registrar General in 1844. He was guided by the philosophy of his predecessors Hamilton, Brownrigg and Larcom that 'a Census ought to be a Social Survey, not a bare Enumeration', an ambition which would quickly inspire George Graham and William Farr on the other side of the Irish Sea. The next three Irish censuses taken on Donnelly's watch were the most comprehensive social surveys yet attempted anywhere in the United Kingdom. They would therefore record in cold detail what could be described as the only Malthusian catastrophe to occur in the British Isles in the modern era.

The 1851 Irish census, the first to be taken since the beginning of the Great Famine in 1845, observed that in ten years the island's population had fallen from 8,175,238 to 6,552,385. That extraordinary loss of 1,622,743 people was, wrote Donnelly in his census report, published in 1856 – having been delayed in order to give Donnelly and his colleagues sufficient time to make some statistical sense of the shattering events in Ireland – inadequate to express the catastrophe. Donnelly noted that the recent English and Welsh censuses recorded on average one birth for every thirty-one people and one death for every forty-one. Had the same ratio applied to Ireland as it did to the rest of the United Kingdom, he reported, the population of Ireland on 30 March 1851 would probably have numbered 9 million instead of 6,552,385, and consequently, the loss of population between 1841 and 1851 could be computed at the enormous number of almost 2.5 million.

'The population removed from us, by death and emigration,' he wrote, 'belonged principally to the lower classes – among whom famine and disease, in all such calamitous visitations, ever make the greatest ravages.' Donnelly supposed that around a million people had died from hunger or from famine-related diseases in Ireland during the ten years following the potato blight in 1845. It is a figure that became broadly accepted, although Donnelly himself confessed in his 1856 report that it was impossible accurately to count the fallen and he may have underestimated.

Another million Irish men, women and children emigrated. Donnelly produced detailed statistics to prove that no fewer than 152,000 people had left Ireland in one eight-month period, between 1 May and 31 December 1851, that 190,325 had emigrated in 1852, 173,148 in 1853 and 190,556 in 1854. The vast majority of the emigrants were farm labourers and their families, although they took with them 112 blacksmiths. The viscera had been torn out of rural Ireland.

It can therefore have come as no surprise to Donnelly when he examined the 1861 census returns to discover that the population of Ireland had collapsed yet again, by almost another million people to 5,764,543. Most of the missing who were still alive were on the north-eastern seaboard of the United States of America. But tens of thousands were also in Glasgow, Liverpool, Manchester, Birmingham and London. 'It is probable that the immigration of Irish has contributed to the increase of the population in England,' said his 1861 census report. It was in fact certain.

At the other side of Bermondsey Square from the Chapmans' family residence on Abbey Street ran the Long Walk. Forty years later in his journal, the philanthropist and author of *Life and Labour of the People in London*, Charles Booth, would categorise this area as being 'Very poor', its inhabitants exhibiting 'Chronic want'. (Abbey Street by contrast was 'Mixed. Some comfortable others poor.')

A stroll up the Long Walk in 1861 revealed laundresses born in rural Dorsetshire, leather workers from the island of Guernsey, a 69-year-old 'scavenger' (or garbage collector) who was a native of Bermondsey, and then Thomas and Elizabeth Meagan and their daughters Ann, Mary and Ellen. Thomas and Elizabeth were both labourers; their oldest daughter, eighteen-year-old Ann, worked at a glue yard. They were refugees from Fermoy in County Cork. Ten years earlier the Meagans had been nowhere near Bermondsey. They had been in the south-west of rural Ireland. In 1863 William Donnelly would report that the combined populations of the villages of Ballyhooley, Carrig, Watergrasshill and the other seventeen townships which made up the small Union of Fermoy in Cork had fallen between the Irish censuses of 1841 and 1861 from 63,340 to 37,960.

One of the many poignant entries in two centuries of the United Kingdom's national census was taken at 4 and 5 Smith's Place, Bermondsey in 1861. There, living in the Catholic School established in two conjoined houses by a family of Hogans from Tipperary and County Clare to meet sudden local demand, was a person whom the enumerator could only describe as 'An Elderly Woman, about 60' who had been born in Ireland. Over the decades many people were unidentifiable to the census enumerators for many different reasons. But it is worth recalling that, as confirmed by William Donnelly's Irish census, in that elderly woman's lifetime a third of a million Irish people spoke no language other than Irish Gaeilge.

They also were among the dispossessed and, in places like Bermondsey, the incomprehensible. Which helps to explain why many of them, such as a sixteen-year-old Irish girl named Margaret Hurley, found themselves in one of the worst places in Europe to live. Jacob's Island in Bermondsey was among the most celebrated and lawless 'rookeries', or slums, of Victorian London. A cluster of sordid shanties on the south shore of the River Thames into which only armed policemen dared occasionally to enter, built over and beside underground rivers and filthy ditches, Jacob's Island was, wrote Henry Mayhew in 1852, 'a patch of ground insulated by the common sewer . . . Across some parts of the stream, rooms have been built, so that house adjoins house; and here, with the very stench of death rising through the boards, human beings sleep night after night, until the last sleep of all comes upon them, years before its time.'

As Mayhew noted, life expectancy was short in Jacob's Island. By the time of the 1871 census, when she should have been twenty-six years old, Margaret Hurley had disappeared from the public record.

We do not know which languages were spoken by young Margaret Hurley. We can be almost certain that Thomas and Elizabeth Meagan and even their deracinated daughters were native speakers of Irish, or Gaeilge. That guess can be hazarded because the Meagans came from rural County Cork and in the middle of the nineteenth century almost everybody in rural County Cork spoke Gaeilge.

The historian John Ranelagh estimates that of the 8 million people counted in Ireland in 1841, fully one half, or 4 million, still spoke only Gaeilge or were bilingual in Gaeilge and English. Those 4 million speakers of one of Europe's oldest surviving languages were spread across the country but were heavily concentrated in the southern and western provinces of Munster and Connaught, the traditionally rural regions most seriously injured by the potato blight, the famine, the lack of famine relief and the result-ant enormous numbers of deaths and emigrations. The rural population of Donegal, reported William Donnelly, 'was less by 241 to the square mile in 1851 than in 1841 . . . In Mayo, the rural population diminished from 475 to the square mile of arable land, in 1841, to 255 in 1851 . . . In Kerry, the population decreased from 416 to 216 . . . to the square mile of arable land.'

'The famine . . . ended,' writes Ranelagh, 'the widespread use of the Irish language.' He quotes Douglas Hyde's subtly different judgement of 1891 that 'The Famine knocked the heart out of the Irish language.' But we know from Donnelly's 'Social Survey' censuses that the famine did not kill Gaeilge.

Donnelly became the first census taker in the British Isles to count the number of speakers of one of the archipelago's native languages other than English (Scottish Gaelic was obliged to wait until 1881 and Welsh until 1891). So the 1851 Irish enumerators, who were still chiefly drawn from the ranks of the constabulary, were asked to append 'the word Irish to the name of each person who speaks Irish, but who cannot speak English, and the words "Irish and English" to the names of those who can speak both the Irish and English languages'. In 1851 Donnelly, Wilde and Singleton calculated that 1,524,205 of the remaining 6,552,385 residents of Ireland had Gaeilge. Most Irish speakers were bilingual but 319,602 of them, mainly in Connaught and Munster, could speak no other language. By 1861 that total had fallen to 1,077,087 among 5,764,543. At face value, in the space of just twenty years the proportion of Gaeilge speakers in Ireland had plummeted from 50 to 18 per cent.

But a million surviving speakers did not signify the imminent death of the language. Irish would still be spoken by both natives and learners in the twenty-first century. The scholar and future president of an independent Ireland, Douglas Hyde, had meant to suggest in 1891, as Ranelagh writes, that the confidence and legitimacy of Gaeilge, the combined qualities which would much later be described as the image of the language, had been destroyed by the national trauma of the famine. It would henceforth be regarded by too many Irish people as regressive rather than aspirational. 'Speaking Irish had become firmly identified with poverty and peasanthood, with famine and death ... English was identified with success and well-being. It was the language of commerce, and the language of likely more prosperous emigrant relatives too.'

The Union of 1801 had finally established English rather than Gaeilge as the language of government in Ireland. The 1831 Irish Education Act made English the medium of primary school instruction. It is possible if not probable that by the time of the censuses of the second half of the nineteenth century many speakers of Gaeilge chose not to admit their cradle tongue to the census enumerators, preferring instead to present themselves to the state's representatives as fluent users of modern English, uncontaminated by the miserable past. The biblical devastation of the famine, as recorded so faithfully in William Donnelly's censuses, delivered the coup de grâce to the reputation of Irish Gaeilge among Irish people themselves. It also killed disproportionate numbers of Irish speakers and left the survivors fully aware that if emigration was their children's only future, they had better be taught English in order to survive in Australia, the United States of America or the mainland of the United Kingdom.

*

Irish Gaeilge was far from being the only 'minority' indigenous language to be spoken in the British Isles. A thousand years earlier the islands, like most of the rest of Europe, had been a Babel of mutually incomprehensible vernaculars and dialects. Pictish people speaking their Brythonic variety of Celtic, akin to Welsh, were present throughout Scotland and in parts of the north of Ireland. Norse immigrants from modern Denmark and Norway were busily reconfiguring the place names of eastern England and the north and west of Scotland respectively. The inhabitants of the islands of Shetland and Orkney and part of the northern Scottish mainland spoke a localised Norse dialect known as Norn. Saxons, Jutes and Angles had imported their central European tongues to eastern England and south-eastern Scotland. Frisian islanders in the modern Netherlands and Germany on the east coast of the North Sea could easily communicate with speakers of Old English in the west (an eighth-century missionary from the East Riding of Yorkshire became the first Christian Archbishop of Frisia), but neither would understand a sentence of Cornish. Latin was still the language of the Church and of much civil administration. Soon Norman French would become the medium of the crown, the court and the landowning aristocracy, as well as of the ordinary citizens of those remnants of France within the United Kingdom, les Îles de la Manche, the Channel Islands.

By the nineteenth century most of them had, or were assumed to have, died as everyday spoken languages, been assimilated into English, or were simply regarded as too small and irrelevant to be taken account of by a national census. But others still had, like Irish Gaeilge, too large a constituency to ignore.

In the 1870s educated Scottish Highlanders exiled to Glasgow, Edinburgh and London established associations, published magazines and began to lobby on behalf of their blue remembered hills. The long-serving Scottish Registrar General, William Pitt Dundas, who had occupied the post since it was established in 1854, was asked to include an enumeration of Scottish Gaelic speakers in his 1881 census. Dundas was an unsympathetic member of Edinburgh's landed professional classes. He was also eighty years old, had conducted two previous Scottish censuses without feeling the need to assess the condition of Gaelic and was only reluctantly overseeing his third because a predecessor as registrar general had lasted for just six months in 1880 before dying on the job. Dundas rejected the approach.

Undeterred, Charles Fraser Mackintosh, the Member of Parliament for Inverness Burghs and a founder of the Gaelic Society of Inverness, asked the Home Secretary, William Harcourt, in the House of Commons to overrule the Scottish Registrar General. Such a gesture was the least that might be offered, Mackintosh said, to a linguistic group who were, unlike the Irish, 'a peaceable and orderly people who seldom obtruded their wishes on the House'. He was speaking, said Mackintosh, 'for educational and other purposes, on behalf of the Federation of Celtic Associations of Scotland, the Committee of the Free Church of Scotland in the Highlands, both largely representative bodies, as well as by others'.

English Liberal Home Secretary William Harcourt spent many of his summers yachting around the Hebrides and was openly more appreciative of their people than was William Pitt Dundas. He was also reluctant to interfere in a matter which was devolved to Scottish authorities in Edinburgh, and at first he refused Mackintosh's request. In January 1881, by which time the census schedules had already been printed without reference to Gaelic, the ten-year-old Gaelic Society of Inverness entered the fray.

The society wrote to the Home Office: 'A census of the Gaelic speaking population of Scotland, such as has more than once been taken of the Irish speaking population of Ireland, would be of great practical value in connection with several important questions affecting the Highlands, and would hereafter be considered a valuable historical record.'

William Harcourt, who was by early 1881 becoming concerned about widespread land hunger leading to social and political discontent in the Highlands and Islands, relented. It was too late to alter the printed census questionnaires but the survey on 4 April was mostly taken orally, and the 1881 national census enumerators were instructed to ask people resident in Scotland if they spoke Gaelic 'habitually'. They would then note the answers on their forms.

The term 'habitual' was clearly inadequate. It might exclude the many thousands of fluent Gaels who lived and worked in English-speaking environments, as well as such borderline cases as the Edinburgh undergraduate at his Celtic studies and even the shy bilingual Gael. But it would have to do. The 1881 census results reported that 231,594 people out of a total Scottish population of 3,735,573 declared themselves to be 'habitual' speakers of Gaelic.

Almost all of those people – 88 per cent – lived in the Highland crofting counties of Argyllshire, Inverness-shire, Sutherlandshire and Ross and Cromarty, which between them then incorporated most of the Hebrides. In the mainland peninsula of Applecross all but eight of the

966 inhabitants spoke Gaelic. In the parish of Uig on the west coast of the island of Lewis there were 2256 people, of whom 2208 spoke Gaelic. Of the 4297 people in South Uist, 4127 spoke Gaelic. In some such places the question seemed absurd. The 1881 census of the seventy-seven remaining inhabitants of St Kilda was taken by the resident Free Church of Scotland minister, the Reverend Mr John MacKay. Rather than detail his flock's linguistic habits individually, as the form requested, Reverend MacKay scrawled across the first page of his census return the words: 'All of the inhabitants of St Kilda speak Gaelic habitually.' The same could have been written of a good many other islands and parishes.

Campaigners continued to protest that both the question and the method of asking it had been flawed, and that the total number of Gaelic speakers in 1881 was closer to 300,000. The number of Gaels in Glasgow, for instance, was enumerated as only 6085 out of half a million people. Given the traditional Highland domination of the Lowland constabulary, in 1881 there were probably 6000 Gaelic-speaking policemen alone in Glasgow. The Gaelic societies had reason to believe that the true total figure of Clydeside Gaels was closer to 50,000 and that the census takers had managed after all to confuse actual native speakers in exile with 'habitual' speakers back in the Gaidhealtachd, as the Gaelic-speaking north and west was known. The same confusion would have explained the absurdly low numbers of Gaels declared in other Anglophone environments such as Edinburgh (supposedly only 2142 in a total population of 389,164) and Aberdeen (607 among 267,990). In such places, not even the most fluent Gael was a habitual user of his or her native language. The north-eastern fishing port of Fraserburgh recorded in 1881 just four Gaelic speakers in a total population of 7596. Fraserburgh was not a Gaelic-speaking community, but it was close to the Gaidhealtachd and it seems certain that more than four Gaels – who were famous fishermen and herring-girls – lived and worked there in 1881. They simply did not use their language 'habitually' among an English-speaking majority.

Ten years later, in 1891, the question was refined by a new Registrar General, Stair Agnew. In May 1890 the MP for Sutherlandshire, Angus Sutherland, asked in the House of Commons 'whether the attention of the Secretary for Scotland has been called to the desirability, in taking the Census of the Gaelic-speaking population, of having two columns on the subject in the Schedule issued to house-holders: (1) for the enumeration of such as can speak Gaelic only; and (2) for the enumeration of such as can speak both English and Gaelic?' He was told that the matter was under consideration, and his request was agreed. Henceforth the enumerators were told on their printed forms to 'Write "Gaelic" opposite the name of each person who speaks Gaelic only, and "G & E" opposite the name of each person who speaks both Gaelic and English.'

The number of self-confessed Gaels in Scotland duly rose to 254,415. The number in Fraserburgh jumped suddenly to thirty people. Just over one-sixth, or 43,738 people in that total of 254,415, spoke Gaelic and no other language. The total Scottish population in 1891 was just over 4 million. It was the last time but one that a national census would record a rise in the number of Gaelic speakers in Scotland. A century later people would look back at those statistics and wonder what the late-Victorian Gaelic Society of Inverness had to worry about.

There were suspicions in both Ireland and Scotland that the census commissioners, the Registrars General and some of the enumerators were either indifferent or hostile to the well-being of Gaeilge and Gaelic. Those suspicions were understandable. The Education (Scotland) Act of 1872 had, like its 1870 predecessor in England and Wales, established compulsory state schooling throughout the country for all children between the ages of five and thirteen (which was extended to fourteen in 1883).

As education was a devolved matter, the 1872 Scottish Education Act was drafted by the Scotch Education Board in Edinburgh, a body which like so many others was dominated by the great and the good of Lowland society. Gaelic, the native language of at least a quarter of a million people in the north of Scotland – a fact previously recognised by Highland Gaelic-medium church schools, Gaelic Society schools and hedge schools – was entirely excluded from the 1872 Education Act, and therefore from all Scottish education, which would thereafter be conducted, even in St Kilda, solely in English. As in Ireland following that country's 1831 Education Act, administrators in the capital city seemed determined to extirpate the surviving indigenous Celtic language.

It may be the case that some of the Dublin census takers were happy to include Irish Gaeilge in their survey of 1851 in order to monitor the language's decline, and with it the unfortunate 'ignorance' of the peasantry. It was the case that such Edinburgh gentry as William Pitt Dundas, Stair Agnew and the members of the Scotch Education Board stood somewhere on an attitudinal spectrum between nonchalance and disdain for 'Erse' in their nation, despite the efforts in their midst of passionate Gaelic revivalists. But neither Irish nor Scottish Gaels were confronted by such shameless bigotry as that displayed by Registrar General Sir Brydges Henniker towards the Welsh.

After Irish Gaeilge and Scottish Gaelic had been included in the census, it was inevitable that space must also be found for the Welsh language. Wales was distinguished from its Celtic cousins in Ireland and the north-west of Scotland in having experienced during the nineteenth century no famine, no clearances, no mass emigrations to North America and the 'white' colonies, no population decline, and consequently less justified paranoia about the erosion of its native culture.

On the contrary, the population of Wales rose commensurately with that of England. It doubled from 541,546 in the first, 1801 census to 1,188,914 in 1851, and it would be almost 2.5 million at the beginning of the twentieth century. Nor was there any great influx from across the English border – in 1851 no less than 88 per cent of the population of Wales had been born in Wales. There was population flux, but as in England it was chiefly internal, from the country to the industrial centres, and also as in England the Welsh rural communities adapted and survived.

As coal mining and industrialisation changed the faces of Cardiff, Swansea, Rhondda and Merthyr, Wales experienced a familiar shift from countryside to city. Welsh remained dominant in the rural regions and many of the towns, but at least one of the new urban centres took pride in its modernism, which meant the popular adoption of English. Cardiff, reported the *Western Mail* in 1891, was 'a town where the monoglot Welshman is practically unknown'. It was true that there were only 3125 monoglot Welsh speakers and 13,395 bilingual Welsh and English

speakers among Cardiff's late-nineteenth-century population of 138,275 people. But Cardiff was exceptional even in
industrialised Glamorganshire, where the county's 693,072
people contained a total of 320,071 Welsh speakers.

Welsh was, as it would remain, the most robust of the old
British languages. That fact had been implicitly admitted
since 1831 when John Rickman, in a combined celebration
of British linguistic diversity and display of his own polyma-
thy, had included in the census report a sizeable glossary of
Welsh landscape features and place names. 'Aber', Members
of Parliament were informed by Rickman, indicated a
'Confluence of Rivers, Mouth of River'. 'Hen' meant old.
'Garth' was a promontory. 'Ty' was a house. It was confirmed in 1851 when George Graham and William Farr
had printed census forms in the Welsh language, without
actually knowing the true number of Welsh speakers.

The 1891 census showed that despite the example of
Cardiff, in a total Welsh population of 1,776,405, more
than half, a substantial majority of 910,289, could still speak
Welsh, and that no fewer than 508,036, or almost one-third
of the entire country, could speak only Welsh. In parts of
central and western 'Welsh' Wales the means of discourse
had barely changed in 2000 years. Fifty miles along the
coast from Cardiff, the 52,382 people of the town of Llanelli
included 43,000 Welsh speakers, 25,326 of whom could
speak no other language. In Cardigan, Carmarthen and
Aberystwyth, monoglot Welsh speakers formed a majority
of the population. In Anglesey just 327 people spoke English
alone.

Those facts were bemusing to some. The bemused included
the Registrar General, Sir Brydges Powell Henniker. It
did not take much to bemuse Brydges Henniker. An Essex

baronet and an undistinguished product of Eton and the Horse Guards, Henniker had succeeded George Graham in 1880. His was an ill-starred period of office. It began in minor controversy. When Graham made clear his intention to retire, William Farr regarded himself as the natural successor. In terms of achievement and qualification, he was justified. But in 1880 Farr was seventy-two years old and in poor health (he would die just three years later, in 1883). His age and infirmity may have been sufficient reasons for the Home Secretary to give the job to somebody else, although William Gladstone, the leader of the opposition in 1879 and incoming prime minister in 1880, was only two years younger than Farr. Or, as Farr himself suspected, his advanced years could just have presented the government with the ideal excuse to overlook the son of a labourer in favour of yet another aristocrat. Believing the latter, the offended Farr resigned from the General Register Office as soon as he was informed that the top job would go to Brydges Powell Henniker.

Henniker held the post for twenty years and conducted two censuses. He was widely regarded even in his lifetime as the least competent and most unimaginative head of the General Register Office in its history. Following his death in 1906 he was, uniquely for a Registrar General of England and Wales, considered unfit for obituary in both *The Times* and the *Journal of the Royal Statistical Society* and he remains absent from the *Dictionary of National Biography*.

None of those posthumous slights was widely regretted in Wales. Brydges Henniker's reports to Parliament would be described as losing 'much of the vivacity and pugnacity of the heyday of the Graham administration'. On at least one subject, however, Registrar General Henniker was extraordinarily pugnacious. That subject was the Welsh language.

Simply put, Henniker thought that in order to inflate the figures, a lot of Welsh people were untruthful both on their census forms and to the enumerators about their own and their children's fluency in Welsh. Rather than sensibly keeping those suspicions to himself, Henniker stated them in his 1891 census report to Parliament:

> The Census Act enacted for the first time that inquiry should be made as to each person living in Wales or in Monmouthshire, where 'such person speaks Welsh only, or both Welsh and English' ...
>
> This instruction seems clear enough. Nevertheless abundant evidence was received by us that it was either misunderstood or set at naught by a large number of Welshmen who could speak both languages, and that the word 'Welsh' was very often returned, when the proper entry would have been 'Both [English and Welsh]'; on the ground, it may be presumed, that Welsh was the language spoken habitually or preferentially.
>
> Indeed, so desirous do many householders appear to have been to add to the number of monoglot Welshmen, that they not only returned themselves as speaking Welsh, that is, Welsh only, but made similar returns as to infants who were only a few months or even only a few days old.

As a result of what he considered to be cynical distortion of the census returns, Henniker had taken the precaution of deleting from his final figures the linguistic abilities of all Welsh children under the age of two. Parliament need not therefore be overly concerned about Welsh mendacities, 'excepting that they furnish good grounds for regarding with much suspicion the trustworthiness of the statements as to persons of riper years ... Under these circumstances,' the Registrar General concluded, 'we do not think that much value can be attached to the figures which are given in our tables, as to the number of monoglot Welsh people ...'

In other words, up to 500,000 residents of Wales had either lied or been misrepresented on their census forms, according to the Registrar General – who proceeded to add insult to his injury of Welsh pride by seeming to take satisfaction from the fact that as two-thirds of the country spoke at least some English, 'Whichever way the figures are put, the English language clearly predominated not inconsiderably over the Welsh.'

The more interesting fact was ignored by Henniker. It was that at the end of the nineteenth century, in a country far closer than Ireland or the Scottish Highlands to Anglophone central and southern England and its seats of power, an ancient Celtic tongue which had long ago ceased to be the language of government, education or the popular printed media was still spoken by the majority of the population. Unlike Gaelic Ireland and Scotland, Wales had suffered no famine, no clearances and no mass emigration. It had also experienced its own, internal industrial revolution which did not necessarily enforce a linguistic shift to English.

Slate and stone quarries – and therefore Welsh-speaking quarrymen – were abundant in the intensely Welsh-speaking counties of Caernarvonshire and Merionethshire. Scottish Gaels certainly travelled to work in the coal mines of the Scottish Lowlands but Gaelic was hardly ever heard in their Fife and Lanarkshire shafts. What industry was to be found in Ireland was chiefly confined to the English-speaking cities of Belfast and Dublin. In Scotland and in

Ireland a move to the modern industrial world also necessitated an abrupt change of language and culture.

In the Welsh county of Glamorgan in 1891, however, 39-year-old Evan James and his fourteen- and thirteen-year-old sons John and David all laboured underground at a colliery in Merthyr Tydfil, and all three of them spoke nothing but Welsh. They were surrounded at home and at work by women and men who either spoke Welsh as well as English or who also spoke only Welsh. The James family had no urgent requirement to learn English. Within most of Wales outside the port of Cardiff, rather than discarding it, the industrial revolution had in large part been obliged to accommodate the indigenous language.

When Welsh MPs raised in the House of Commons the matter of the Registrar General calling their constituents frauds and liars, Brydges Henniker made a qualified and slightly deceitful apology. He wrote to the secretary of the Local Government Board:

> I understand that some Welsh Members of Parliament complain that, in a paragraph of my Report on the Census Returns of 1891, I imputed to the Welsh people untruthfulness, and charged them with having attempted to increase the numbers of those entered as speaking Welsh only, by fraudulently filling up their schedules ...
>
> I had no intention whatever to accuse the Welsh people of untruthfulness, or of a deliberate intention to make false returns ... What I did intend to convey ... was this: that the people in certain districts in Wales had wrongly understood the requirements of the schedule in the census as meaning that when they spoke Welsh preferentially or habitually, but could also speak English

more or less, they were justified in returning themselves as speaking Welsh only. It was intended that such cases should be regarded as bi-lingual, and entered as speaking both Welsh and English. I am quite aware that it is difficult to lay down any definite standard as to the degree of proficiency in speaking English which would warrant the entry under this head, and hence, no doubt, there has been misunderstanding.

One of those critical MPs was a solicitor in his late twenties who had recently been elected as Member of Parliament for Carnarvon Boroughs. David Lloyd George had been raised as a Welsh speaker in a Welsh-speaking family. In 1891 both he and his wife Margaret, a Carnarvon woman, registered themselves as speaking both Welsh and English. But as their two-year-old son Richard spoke only Welsh – and squeaked narrowly past the Registrar General's prohibition on linguistic returns from the under-twos – their home was clearly an almost monoglot Welsh environment.

In 1916 Lloyd George became not only the first – and so far the only – Welsh politician to become prime minister of the United Kingdom, but also the only prime minister, the only leader of the British Isles in modern times, to have been a native speaker of one of the islands' original Celtic languages.

Others came close. In 1851 the census showed, living at 29 Regent Street in Cambridge, a 36-year-old (he was actually thirty-seven) Scottish Gael named Daniel Macmillan. He was born in 1813 as Dòmhnall MacMhaolain to a Gaelic-speaking tenant farmer named Duncan in the southern Hebridean island of Arran. Duncan Macmillan was an elder of the Church of Scotland who read the Gaelic Bible out loud to his sons. When he was three years old Daniel's family moved to the Ayrshire mainland, where his younger brother Alexander (Alasdair MacMhaolain) was born. When both brothers were in their twenties they migrated to the south of England. Daniel got a job with a Cambridge bookseller and shortly afterwards he and his brother opened their own bookstore. In 1843 they established the imprint Macmillan & Co and began to publish books as well as sell them.

Daniel married Frances Orridge, the daughter of a Cambridge chemist. Their son Maurice duly took over the Macmillan publishing house and prospered. A 1901 census enumerator found him, at the age of forty-seven, living in Chelsea's Cadogan Square with his American wife Nellie Artie Belles, their five-year-old son Maurice Harold Macmillan, a nurse, a cook, a kitchenmaid, a parlourmaid and two housemaids.

Three years later, eight-year-old Maurice Harold was taken for the first time from London to Arran to be made familiar with his origins. He was also fully aware of his grandfather's cradle language: in 1904 half of the 4600 people of Arran, which lies on a line of latitude south of the city of Glasgow, still spoke Gaelic. As an adult Maurice Harold Macmillan would make the same ancestral pilgrimage with his own children and grandchildren. He would also drop his father's forename, and as plain Harailt MacMhaolain the grandson of Dòmhnall MacMhaolain and great-grandson of Donnchadh MacMhaolain of Arran became prime minister of the United Kingdom in 1957, serving until 1963.

In 1901 enumerators in the Isle of Man were asked to register speakers of Gaelg or Manx, the local dialect of the Irish/

Scottish Goidelic Gaelic language group. They discovered in the old sheading of Rushen in the far south of the island a farming family comprised of 39-year-old John Kinvig, his wife Sage and their five young children. John, Sage and their oldest child, a seven-year-old also named John, could speak both Manx and English. John's four younger siblings could speak only English. Caught in a census snapshot in that first year of the twentieth century, the Kinvig family was a small manifestation of an internationally familiar watershed in language decline: the ridge beyond which, usually for reasons of education and social ambition, parents consciously ceased to pass their first language on to the younger of their own children.

John, Sage and young John were among the 4419 remaining speakers of Manx Gaelg in 1901, most of whom were to be found in their small rural district, in a total Manx population of 54,752 people. Sage Kinvig outlived her husband, her oldest son and all of their adult neighbours from 1901; ninety-two years old when she died in 1962, she was then the last fully native speaker of Gaelg.

An 83-year-old former sailor and fisherman named Edward Maddrell was still alive in 1962. Maddrell had spoken English first as an infant, but had been taught Gaelg by a great-aunt in Rushen, where in the 1870s and 1880s 'unless you had the Manx you were a deaf and dumb man and no good to anybody'. Ned Maddrell died in 1974 at the age of ninety-seven, and was widely mourned as the last Manx speaker.

Strictly speaking, he was not. The census of 1911 showed 2382 Manx speakers. There were still 531 in 1931. Those were mainly the last of the older generations of cradle speakers. The numbers bottomed out in the census of 1961, which of course included both Ned Maddrell and Sage Kinvig – but also included another 163 folk who claimed fluency in Manx. By 1971, when Kinvig had died and Maddrell had just three years to live, that number had strangely risen to 284. In 2011, no fewer than 1823 people claimed to be able to speak, read and/or write Manx Gaelg.

They were, from the 1950s and 1960s onwards, almost all revivalists. Unlike Kinvig and Maddrell, who had learned the language as a matter of necessity from their immersion in Manx-speaking families and communities, the revivalists were initially English-speaking adults who took the trouble to teach themselves and each other Manx to a certain degree of fluency in order to preserve the language, and with it a mainstay of their island's cultural identity. Their numbers were boosted in the 1990s and 2000s by the establishment of Manx classes in schools and Manx pre-school playgroups, which were as likely to be in the capital of Douglas as in the traditional southern rural heartland of Rushen.

Some of the ancient tongues unique to the islands would reach the census forms only at an extremely late stage. In 1881 a 66-year-old widower and retired farmer named John Davy was living with his daughter, her husband and their four children on a ten-acre holding in the Cornish village of Boswednack on the isolated northern coast of the far western tip of Cornwall. John Davy would die in January 1891, but in 1890 the local historian John Hobson Matthews sought him out and wrote that Davy 'had some traditional knowledge of Cornish, knew the meanings of the place-names in the neighbourhood' and 'could converse on a few simple topics in the ancient language'.

Davy had been born in St Just, a short walk from Boswednack along the north-western seaboard, in 1816. Almost twenty years later, in 1834, a boy called John Mann was born in Boswednack. During his childhood on his father's farm an old lady of the parish named Ann Berryman, born in 1776, lodged with the Mann family. Ann Berryman certainly spoke Cornish, and in his own old age in 1914 John Mann recalled that as a youngster in Boswednack 'he and several other children always conversed in Cornish while at play together'.

Cornish, or Kernowek, was not included in any nineteenth- or twentieth-century census. In 1700 Cornish was reported to be in decline but still spoken 'from the Land's End to the [St Michael's] Mount and towards St Ives and Redruth, and again from the Lizard to Helston and towards Falmouth'. A hundred years later, at the end of the eighteenth century and the beginning of the nineteenth, there were several disparate accounts of individuals who spoke Cornish.

Cornish probably ceased to be a default conversational medium between a remaining handful of elderly people early in the nineteenth century. But languages do not die abruptly. The historian of and proselytist for the indigenous British Celtic languages, Henry Jenner, was born in St Columb Major in central Cornwall in 1848. As a small boy in the early 1850s 'he heard at the table some talk between his father and a guest that made him prick up his ears, and no doubt brought sparkles to his eyes which anyone who told him something will remember. They were speaking of a Cornish language. At the first pause in their talk he put his query . . . "But is there really a Cornish Language?" and on being assured that at least there had been one, he said

"Then I'm Cornish – that's mine!'" Jenner wrote in 1904, of the remaining Cornish speakers:

> there were probably several ... 'last living men' going on at once, and certainly John Tremathack, who died in 1852 at the age of eighty-seven, must have known a good deal of Cornish, some words of which he taught to his daughter, Mrs Kelynack of Newlyn, who was still living in 1875. There was also George Badcock, the grandfather of Bernard Victor of Mousehole, who taught a certain amount of Cornish to his grandson, who was living in 1875, when the present writer saw him.
>
> Then it is considered that Cornish, as a spoken language, died out. The process was gradual, though perhaps rather rapid at the last ... Words and sentences, and even such things as the Creed [and] Lord's Prayer were handed on, some of them to our own day. The mother-in-law of the present writer, Mrs W.J. Rawlings (nee Hambly) of Hayle, who died in 1879 at the age of fifty-seven, had learnt to repeat the Lord's Prayer and Creed in Cornish when she was a child in Penzance, but unluckily had quite forgotten them in later life ... Mr Hobson Matthews ... gives reasons for supposing that the language survived in St Ives, Zennor and Trowednack even longer than in Mounts Bay ...

The reality was that by the second half of the nineteenth century, when other Celtic languages were being enumerated, there existed only a very small handful of speakers of Kernowek, most of them in or around the hamlet of Boswednack, and none of them ready or able to sustain a fluent dialogue with any other. Yet revival would also be undertaken in Cornwall. In acknowledgement of that initiative the census of 2011 asked for the first time for the 'main language' of English and Welsh residents. In response 557 people, 464 of whom lived in Cornwall, wrote 'Kernowek'. Those small numbers would have delivered disproportionate joy to the heart of Henry Jenner.

At opposite ends of the nation, a thousand miles apart, the languages of other nations, fossils from a time when their archipelagos were the properties of foreign countries, also survived into the nineteenth century in differing degrees of bad health. The Channel Islands, an inheritance of the Norman Conquest of England in 1066, have more or less continuously been undisputed if autonomous possessions of the English and then the British crown for almost a thousand years. The largest Channel island of Jersey is nonetheless only fifteen miles off the coast of France and 100 miles from the south coast of England. The Channel Islands are an ancestral home of Norman French. The extent of that language's survival was not assessed by the British census until the first enumeration of the twenty-first century.

John Rickman had included a headcount of the population of the Channel Islands in 1821. He discovered then the population to be 'In the Island of Guernsey (and its dependent Islets) 20,827 – In the Island of Jersey, 28,600'. Almost all of those 49,500 people were habitual native speakers of *le dgernesiais* or its sibling, *le jerriais*. They were the last repositories of the language which had been the mother tongue of English monarchs between 1066 and 1413, when Henry V became the first king who both wrote and spoke in English rather than in Anglo-Norman French.

The Channel Islanders' insular linguistic redoubt was first broken in the decades following the Battle of Waterloo. In a post-war exercise in both Anglicisation, the precautionary disciplining of this Francophone crown territory, and as a prophylactic against insurgency, some 15,000 British Napoleonic War veterans and their families were granted land and homes within sight of the French coastline in Jersey and Guernsey. Many of the new settlers were ex-army officers on half pay, which meant that they were obliged to stand ready for recall to active service. They are to be found there in the 1841 census: hundreds of Englishmen and women of 'independent means' in such parishes as Saint Saviour. Families named Philips and Holloway and Telford suddenly lived beside, and in some districts outnumbered, their Jersey-born Gosselin, de la Hayes and Ducheaume neighbours.

The 1841 census consequently showed that the population of Jersey had risen to 47,544, of whom 14,547 had not been born in the Channel Islands, and the combined population of Guernsey, Alderney, Sark and the smaller islands had risen to 28,521, of whom almost 7000 had been born elsewhere. Thirteen of the twenty-five inhabitants of little Herm were not native Channel Islanders.

That represented an unprecedented dilution of the Norman-French community. The majority of those 21,500 incomers – numbering 14,600 – came from England and Wales, and 1800 came from Ireland. Whatever languages they spoke, they did not speak *le jerriais* and they did not intend to learn.

In the words of the Welsh academic Meic Stephens, 'The result of this immigration was predictable. Shop-keepers and servants had to learn English. Newspapers in English were launched. By the end of the [nineteenth] century, in the towns at least, English had ousted French as the medium of everyday intercourse.' French remained the official language of government in the Channel Islands until as late as 1946, but Stephens noted that 'Tombstones erected before 1900 are usually in French, while those erected after 1914 are in English.' When Stephens visited the islands in the early 1970s he found 'little hope among them that the Norman-French dialects, now spoken only by the older generation, will survive for more than a few more decades'.

When the national census finally enumerated speakers of *le jerriais* in 2001 it discovered that among an island population of 87,186, just 2874 spoke the old tongue 'occasionally or sometimes', although another 13,000 claimed some understanding of the language. Exactly the same proportions obtained to *le dgernesiais* among the 60,000 people of Guernsey and its populated satellite islets.

Meanwhile, as George Graham and William Farr wrote in their 1851 census report:

> The greater part of the islands, and of points on the coast terminating in ey, ay, a (island), ness (promontory), holm, as well as others, bear names which the Northmen gave them; and were seized, partly for the purposes of commerce, but more commonly as naval stations, from which they could harry and tax the coasts and inland country.
>
> An island was a market, a warehouse, and a castle to these Northmen; who, bred round the sinuosities of the Danish peninsula, in the recesses of the Baltic, and the Fjords of Norway, practised their arts as udal farmers, fishermen, and merchants – forged anchors – built ships

that lived in the Atlantic – fought incessantly along their own coast, from the Elbe to the Naze, to Drontheim, Lofoden Islands, Cape North – and in the eighth century and the centuries following, sailed in fleets, at one time down the east and west coasts of Great Britain, – at another either round France, Portugal and Spain into the Mediterranean, or to Iceland and the coasts of North America.

Those were the builders of the Norse empire, branches of which had by the end of the eleventh century arguably conquered almost all of Great Britain, and which did not formally relinquish its last colonial outpost in the British Isles until Orkney and Shetland were annexed by the crown of Scotland in 1471.

'As the organization of the great nations on the mainland advanced,' continued Graham and Farr, 'the relative power of the Northmen declined; and it was impossible that the inhabitants of the small islands round Britain could long resist the power of even the Gaelic population – little given to the sea as it always has been – which gradually recovered its ground, and diffused its language over the Hebrides and the Isle of Man.

'In Caithness, the Orkneys, and the Shetlands, the Norse language, as well as the men, held its ground, and has latterly given way to pure English ... '

Graham and Farr spoke a few decades too soon. In 1897 the Faroese scholar Jakup Jacobsen published in Danish his doctoral thesis *det norrøne sprog på Shetland* ('The Norn Language in Shetland'). Four hundred years earlier their insular Norn dialect of Norwegian had been the everyday language of Orkney and Shetland. In 1851 Graham and Farr had good reason to believe Norn, as they believed Cornish, to be extinct and therefore of no interest to a census taker. It was popularly rumoured that the last speaker of Norn was one Walter Sutherland. A sixty-year-old fisherman, Sutherland was to be found in 1841 living with the family of the fisherman and weaver Magnus Monat at Skaw in the Shetland island of Unst, the most northerly settlement in the most northerly island in the United Kingdom. Skaw is twice as far from Glasgow as it is from Bergen in Norway.

In the absence of census records Walter Sutherland's place in history remains uncertain. If he was indeed the last native speaker of Norn, then the language was effectively dead before his own death, as he had nobody else with whom to converse. But Jakup Jacobsen cast his net wider and discovered, perfectly feasibly, among the 240 isolated inhabitants of the most remote westerly Shetland island of Foula 'many continuous pieces of Shetland Norn as late as the 1890s'. In Jacobsen's own words, 'The last man in Unst who is said to have been able to speak Norn [Walter Sutherland] ... died about 1850. In Foula, on the other hand, men who were living much later than the middle of the present [nineteenth] century are said to have been able to speak Norn.'

As he implied, Jacobsen did not encounter any of those men. The best that he could uncover was what linguists refer to as 'semi-speakers', much as John Davy was a semi-speaker of Kernowek at the same time in the Cornish village of Boswednack. But there would be no Norn revival. The language was pronounced irretrievable in the twentieth century. Alone among the tapestry of different native languages which still illuminated the British Isles in the lifetimes of George Graham and William Farr, Norn would never be included in the national census.

Others would however be introduced to the census forms long after their function in community discourse had evaporated. Following its inclusion in the European Charter for Regional or Minority Languages, speakers of Kernowek were asked to declare themselves to the census of 2011. The same census recognised as languages two forms of communication which had hitherto been regarded as regional dialects. As a quid pro quo for reinstating Irish Gaeilge in the census of Northern Ireland, those who considered themselves to speak 'Ulster Scots' were also canvassed. Almost 35,000 people in Northern Ireland claimed fluency, while another 185,000 admitted to 'some knowledge' of Ulster Scots.

In the same year over 1.5 million Scottish patriots, almost 30 per cent of the Scottish people, claimed to speak the 'Scots language', while contrarily 93 per cent of Scots reported that they used only English at home. The 7 per cent of Scottish residents who did not speak English at home could be connected to the fact that in 2011 7 per cent of the Scottish population had been born outside the United Kingdom. In 2011 the number of speakers of Scottish Gaelic, virtually all of whom had been born in Scotland and used their language at home, had stabilised at around 59,000. What had once been the predominant language of the court and its subjects in Scotland, a tongue which was spoken by the Scotii, the people who gave the country its name, was familiar in the twenty-first century to just over 1 per cent of the population.

9

A Nation of Emigrants

'There were,' reported the Registrar General of the 1881 census, 'according to the returns received by us, 3,959,899 natives of the United Kingdom living out of the country at the date of the Census ...

Of the 3,959,899 natives of the United Kingdom who were abroad, 89,798 were in India, and 988,934 were in some other of our colonies or dependencies, while the remaining 2,881,167 were in the dominions of foreign powers. Of these 2,881,167 persons, the great bulk, namely 2,772,169, were in the United States, and consisted of 745,978 natives of England and Wales, 170,136 natives of Scotland, and 1,854,571 natives of Ireland, while the precise nationality of the remaining 1,484 was not specified.

The natives of England and Wales enumerated in the United States had increased in the interval between 1870 and 1880 by 19.3 per cent, and the natives of Scotland by 20.8 per cent ... As compared with the contingent furnished by the United Kingdom to the United States, the number of our fellow countrymen in any other foreign state, or in all other foreign states together, was quite insignificant. There were in all but 108,998 of these, of whom 36,447 were in France, 11,139 in the German Empire, 7,230 in Italy, and 5,007 in Russia, these four countries being those in which the British-born sojourners were most numerous.

In the second half of the nineteenth century the English were an emigrant people. Between 1853 and 1905 6 million ordinary Britons arrived in the United States of America alone, having abandoned their homes and hopes in London, Glamorgan, Cork, Inverness-shire and County Durham.

They accounted for almost 30 per cent of new arrivals to the USA at that time. The Irish, from their small native population, constituted a disproportionately large fraction of American immigrants from Great Britain. But in blunt numerical quantities, as many English and Welsh citizens as Irish men and women travelled to the USA. In the quarter-century between 1871 and 1895, 1,334,000 English and Welsh people crossed the Atlantic to the USA, almost exactly the same number as travelled from Ireland. Between them, in that period the English, Irish, Scottish and Welsh accounted for 29 per cent of all American immigrants.

As individuals they signified little. As part of a monumental movement they represented a great deal. The population of the whole of Great Britain in 1881 was 35 million. The 6 million people who went from Britain to the United States alone in the last fifty years of the nineteenth century (another 3 million went to Australia, Canada and elsewhere between 1853 and 1905) were equivalent to one-fifth of the average total population of Britain in their time.

Fully half of them were English. The General Register Office established that in each calendar year of the single decade between 1881 and 1890, one out of every 400 English citizens left his or her native country for the United States. They travelled not to the other white colonies or far-flung countries favoured by British rule but to the free former colony which was the USA. By the time the 1880s were done, English emigrants to the United States alone had totalled in those ten years almost a further million people. They were deserters from the heartland of the largest economy, the greatest military and political power and the most expansive empire in the world.

According to the national census, at the start of the decade in 1881 the pit cottage named 27 Burnhope Colliery in County Durham was home to 61-year-old William Robson, his wife Elizabeth, aged sixty, their youngest son, fifteen-year-old Thomas, who was working with his father in Burnhope Colliery, and a daughter.

That daughter, seventeen-year-old Rosina, having left school, helped her mother at home. Despite the colliery's 'all-pervasive odour of gas and fumes', she still lived in part the rural life of her childhood. She collected wild berries and rhubarb in season. She would have shared with a contemporary and memoirist, Angus Watson, ten miles away, the 'bright moonlit winter nights, when we skated on the "Gut" on the Willows ... there were Guisers, when we blacked our faces and "dressed up", and sang carols at the doors of neighbours' houses. We possessed little lanterns, with red and green glasses, when we played "I spy light" as we hid in Week's Dene ... '

Domestically, Rosina nurtured the hens in the yard. She

worked on the vegetable patch. She cooked and preserved foods. She baked bread. She helped with the weekly wash every Monday, and she cleaned the rooms. She kept the fire in and heated the water for her father's and brother's after-shift hip-baths (in which they would scrupulously clean every part of their bodies but their backs, which were left dirty for fear of weakening the spine).

Rosina was in fact the youngest of William and Elizabeth Robson's eight daughters. Her sisters could have accepted most of those household chores, along with helping to raise the younger children, as a traditional and an inevitable part of their lot. But Rosina had been for seventeen years the baby of seven older sisters. In her teenage years, Rosina's attitude to helping her sixty-year-old mother around the house was probably nuanced. She was certainly restless.

One by one, in the years since her infancy, she had watched her sisters marry and leave home. Ann, who was twenty-one years older, had done so before Rosina was even conceived. The others – Elizabeth, Margaret, Sarah, Mary and Rachel – had subsequently grown into adulthood and deserted her at regular intervals. At the very least Rosina anticipated, in some near future, the adventure of her own adult life. She visualised her own suitor and marriage and children and tied colliery home. She imagined an escape. Her imagination must have worked overtime after the last sister to leave, Catherine, married the coal miner Tom Wilkinson. That was a wholly unexpected development. Neither Catherine nor her family had dared to hope for such a departure.

Catherine was different. Known to her family as Kate, Catherine had throughout Rosina's childhood worked assiduously, mostly indoors, at whatever she was able to do. This had once involved caring as best she was able for her two younger sisters. When they became old enough to take care of themselves, she had undertaken all or most of the family's knitting. Few other tasks were easily available to her, for Kate was among the 1 per cent of the Victorian British population who had been born or had become almost completely blind.

In the summer of 1858, forty miles away, a long day's hike to the south-west of Brandon Colliery, a two-year-old boy was learning to walk through the rough lanes of a tiny hamlet lost in the north Yorkshire Dales.

Miles Hutchinson had never known a world much beyond the huddled greystone cottages of Thwaite. People walked and carts were hauled down the paved track of Cloggerby Rigg, on the route from the market towns of Kirkby Stephen in the west to Reeth in the east, through the outskirts of Thwaite, but little Thwaite detained them not at all. Travellers and traders entered the margins of the village, crossed the hump-backed bridge that spanned a bubbling tributary of the River Swale, and were gone again in minutes.

From all the narrow sides of Thwaite the immense bare shoulders of Swaledale rose towards the sky, enveloping and diminishing the modest settlement at their feet. Miles's miniature universe of village lanes, meadows, river and bridge was circumscribed by those hills, but they also represented an intriguing future, which became with each infant birthday steadily more comprehensible. On most of the mornings since Miles had been born in November 1855, his father and other men of Thwaite had climbed those hills, to earn at least part of their living mining for lead.

Miners they all were, but the people who dug lead in Swaledale were different from those who cut coal in County Durham. They were different in conditions of work and quality of life, different in tradition and history, different perhaps in character, and different certainly in expectation.

The nineteenth-century Durham mining community was mostly new, transient and volatile. The Swaledale mining community had been at work in its lonely valleys for at least a thousand years. The name Thwaite means a piece of claimed agricultural land and probably originated before the Norman Conquest, in the Anglo-Saxon word *thweoten* – 'to clear away trees'.

The work itself was different. Some lead mining took place underground (although never so far underground as coal shafts), but much of it was done in the open air. Seams of lead were traditionally exposed at the surface by 'hushing', the sudden release of a dammed stream along a hilltop vale, causing a flash flood which stripped away the topsoil and exposed the mineral deposits. Those deposits were then hacked out of the ground like tree stumps, by men who knew all about removing tree stumps, and carted off to the nearby smelt.

The Durham mining community lived in farmland and among farmers; the Swaledale miners were often farmers themselves. Durham coal miners had been imported to the collieries by entrepreneurs on unfavourable terms of employment. Many Swaledale miners had been accustomed for centuries to exploiting their lead reserves communally, in their own time and on their own terms. When the industrial revolution reached Swaledale and capitalised companies moved into the area, lead miners insisted on retaining a degree of autonomy. While Rosina Robson's father William was working a twelve-hour shift as a bonded labourer in a Durham coal mine, Miles Hutchinson's father John, and all of John's colleagues, would adamantly refuse to put in more than eight hours a day at any seam of Swaledale lead.

They had other things to do. The Durham miners were largely unpropertied and asset-free; expendable pawns on the vast, crowded board of the labour market. Swaledale lead miners also sometimes occupied tied housing, but they were often settled agriculturalists with their own homes, smallholdings and stock. Miles's great-uncle William Hutchinson proudly declared to the national census enumerators that he was occupied both as a lead miner and a farmer. Not as a farm labourer, but as a farmer – an important distinction.

The lead-mining companies which employed William and John and Miles Hutchinson could be quite clear: they were taking on in Swaledale not potential bondsmen, not peripatetic casual labourers, but men of substance, property and a strong sense of individual worth; men whose families had, come to that, been living in Thwaite and taking lead from the neighbouring hills for a lot longer than the directors and agents of the Kisdon Mining Company Limited. Most of the working families of Swaledale could not, however, have survived there without the lead.

Two miles down the dale from Thwaite, invisible among folds in the escarpment, but a mere half-hour's walk away, stood the much larger settlement of Muker. Thwaite looked to Muker: to its school, to its shops, to its church, to its market and its fair. Many a Thwaite person would, in the future, describe themselves actually as hailing from the parish of Muker. People had heard of Muker; no one had heard of Thwaite. Miles Hutchinson may not, as a boy, have known much of the world outside Thwaite, but he certainly knew the bustling streets of Muker.

In 1823 a man called Edward Baines visited the Muker which was familiar to Miles's father and grandfather. Baines discovered there a busy working population of 1425 people. There was 'a Grammar school for the education of six poor children ... and also a subscription library, established in 1819.

'The market, which has been established by custom, is held on Wednesday, and is well supplied with the necessaries of life. There is likewise an annual fair for sheep and general merchandise, held on the Wednesday next before Old Christmas Day. The north side of the Dale abounds with lead mines ...'

Edward Baines listed the professionals and tradesmen of Muker in 1823. The township had a surgeon and a curate. There were several shopkeepers, a shoemaker, and a victualler with a premises called the King's Head. There was a carrier and a carpenter. There was a mining agent. Baines mentioned, in all, sixteen such professional adults. The other 600 or so working people of Muker, whom he did not describe, were largely agricultural labourers and lead miners.

And so were, as they had been for generations past, the working people of neighbouring Thwaite. Miles's grandfather and great-grandfather, Miles and Jonathan Hutchinson, had been the village blacksmiths. But in the 1850s, the decade of Miles's birth, of the 165 residents of the farming community of Thwaite, among the few property owners and professionals, and all of their servants and their farm labourers, nineteen men were still lead miners. Those nineteen included every male teenage and adult member of the Hutchinson family.

So it was as a 25-year-old lead miner that John Hutchinson married twenty-year-old Alice Alderson, the daughter of another Thwaite family, in the spring of 1855. It was therefore as the son of a lead miner that Miles Hutchinson was born in November that year. Not for five years would Alice Hutchinson raise another child past infancy. To John and Alice Hutchinson, Miles would have been a treasured asset. His young brother Thomas came along in 1860, and at first Thomas also seemed likely to escape the lethal ambushes of a nineteenth-century babyhood.

Six years passed between John and Alice's country wedding in 1855 and the spring day in 1861 when the national census enumerator arrived, with his pencil and papers, to record this young family in its stone cottage in the isolated Swaledale hamlet of Thwaite. Those six years were both professionally and personally a period of unusual calm and security in the troubled life of John Hutchinson, and consequently of his oldest son Miles. There followed two decades of death, redundancy and loss.

Their 26-year-old wife and mother Alice may already have been mortally ill when the census enumerator called on 7 April. Her death certificate recorded that she had been unwell for six weeks when she died, in the presence of her husband John, on 19 May 1861. She had suffered from a 'disease of the brain'. Perhaps she had a stroke, and lingered on for over a month. Or she may have had a tumour that manifested in its later stages as epilepsy or blindness. An infection may have 'gone to the brain', causing encephalitis . . .

Eighteen months later Alice was followed to the graveyard by two-year-old Thomas, who died of pneumonia in the relentlessly wet October of 1862, in the arms of a child-less middle-aged neighbour called Margaret Kearton. The cottage at 68 Thwaite was suddenly a quiet and empty place. At the age of thirty-two John Hutchinson was a widower and a single parent. Six-year-old Miles had lost, within a year and a half, his mother and his younger brother. The lead miner and his son were alone.

That was not only regrettable; it was, in 1862, an unsustainable situation. At the age of six, Miles did not attend school: in adulthood he would be incapable of writing his own name. He could not be watched over and fed by kindly neighbours while his father worked for each and every day of the remaining six, seven or eight years of his childhood, even in the friendly lanes and fields of Thwaite. And John Hutchinson was quite young enough to attract another bride.

He did so within eight months. Hutchinson met, and married in May 1863, a 25-year-old woman from Wensleydale, the next glacial valley south of Swaledale. Ellen Routh, born in Aysgarth, was working as a servant for a manufacturer in Hawes when John swooped to carry her north, over the high watershed to Thwaite.

Ellen lived for only another year. In September 1864 she died while giving birth to a son. This infant survived, and was named Christopher. As he buried his second spouse in two years, John Hutchinson, his troubles doubled, may have despaired of his ability to keep a wife alive. Miles, now eight, could be forgiven for concluding that mothers were a transient blessing.

This battered family of three males faced another threat, of which only John Hutchinson might have been fully aware. He stood likely to lose his job.

The lead mines and smelts of upper Swaledale had been in serious decline for forty years. Their contribution to the new industrial British economy had peaked in the 1820s, when Edward Baines discovered such a busy community in Muker. Since the end of the Napoleonic Wars, cheaper imports from abroad, chiefly from Spain, had steadily undercut the industry.

The danger was alarming as early as 1830, when the people of Arkengarthdale sent a 'Petition against Importation of Lead' to the House of Commons. The petitioners begged leave 'to represent to the House, that in their humble opinion the present distress of that and other mining districts is much increased by the almost unrestricted importation of Lead and Lead Ore; and praying the House to take the distressed situation of that parish into consideration, and grant such relief either by imposing a sufficient protecting Duty upon Foreign Lead and Lead Ore, or by such other means as the House may think proper'.

Their plea went unanswered. No duty was imposed on Spanish lead. By the 1860s there was evidence before John Hutchinson's eyes that the decline might be worse than serious. It might be terminal. Shafts had been closing, and men made unemployed, at a steady rate throughout the 1840s and 1850s. Lead miners' earnings had in some cases halved in thirty years. The population of Muker had fallen from almost 1500 in 1821 to fewer than a thousand in 1861.

Throughout his youth and early married life, John Hutchinson had watched his neighbours leave. Some decided to join what they could not beat, and went to work the fertile lead mines near Grenada in southern Spain. The only substantial work of fiction based on the lead mining industry in the Yorkshire Dales, *Adam Brunskill* by Thomas

Armstrong, is set in the early 1880s. Significantly, its narrative begins at a substantial expatriate British lead mining community in the shadow of the Sierra Morena mountain range in Andalusia. When young Adam Brunskill returns from Spain to the land of his father, back home in 'Skewdale' the villages are almost as silent and empty as the mine shafts and smelts.

Some went to lead mines elsewhere in Britain. Some mined other minerals in other parts of Britain. And a great number went from Swaledale across the Girt Dub, as they knew the Atlantic Ocean, to the United States of America.

Both John and Miles Hutchinson were accustomed in Thwaite and Muker to stories and rumours of new lives in the New World. In 1839, when John was nine years old, William Harker Calvert had left Thwaite for the American Midwest in the company of ten other local men, all of whom pledged to stick together until they reached their destination. Calvert's band was not the last.

Many of them went to Dubuque, west of the Mississippi River, where rich veins of lead had been uncovered and mined. There, in places such as English Hollow on the Fever River, they settled in the land of promise. 'We have no crown,' wrote Jonathan Alderson from the Fever River to his relatives back in Arkengarthdale, 'no duty, no bishops, nor yet have I seen a beggar running from door to door nor anything like an overseer gathering rates.

'We sit in our humble little cot free of rent, we can turn on the prairie horses or cows free and, by humbly asking leave to mow, we can have as much hay as we please. No gamekeepers, we work as we please, we play when we please, we have no Stuarts to bow to, one is as independent as another but we never forget our native land.'

Those were tempting tales of ordinary freedom. They were leavened with such exotica as the legend of John Harker from Muker, who made his way to the republic of Colombia in South America, married a glamorous young Colombiana named Mercedes Mutis and became director of the Zipaquira lead mines. (Harker never returned, but his grandson Simon was sent from Colombia in the 1880s to be educated at a Catholic college in the north of England.)

If John Harker found a wife in South America, the North American dalesmen were generally less lucky. There was an insufficiency of eligible young women on the banks of the Fever River. So in 1848, after nine years in the Mississippi basin, William Harker Calvert returned to Thwaite with money in his pocket. He married Jane Alton in Muker parish church and in 1849 the couple sailed back to New Orleans and took a Mississippi steamboat up to Fever River, where they proceeded to enjoy a long and distinguished life as stalwarts of the pioneer community.

John Hutchinson was, of course, nineteen years old, single and working as an underpaid lead miner when William Calvert returned to Thwaite to display his prosperity, win his girl and whisk her back across the Atlantic Ocean to a place without crowned heads, taxes, bishops or gamekeepers. When his second wife Ellen died in 1864, leaving him with two young sons, Hutchinson was working the seam on Kisdon Hill, a mile above Thwaite. He was an employee of the Kisdon Mining Company, an enterprise established in 1858 by Sir George Denys of Draycott Hall near Reeth in lower Swaledale. Sir George worked his way through a number of partnerships with men of Thwaite and Muker, and the Kisdon Company worked its way through even more unproductive veins of lead, before stuttering towards closure in the late 1860s and suspending operations in 1870.

Having lost two wives and a son, in his late thirties John Hutchinson's concerns about the longevity of his employment were realised. As he had feared, he also lost his job. He packed his things, prepared his surviving sons and left Thwaite for the last time. He moved over the county border into Durham, and took a twelve-month bond at a coal mine in the Tyne and Wear field.

Given his longer working day, more hazardous conditions and crowded industrial environment, it was even more unthinkable for a Durham coal miner's than a Thwaite lead miner's children to have no mother. Hutchinson remarried almost immediately. Louisa Mole was the nineteen-year-old daughter of a carpet weaver when she took her vows with 39-year-old John at the register office in Auckland, County Durham, in March 1869. Within nine years she had presented him with three more sons and two daughters. They would all survive. Equally to the point, so would she.

In 1869 John and Louisa Hutchinson, Miles and Christopher set up home in a colliery cottage in Billy Row, a small Durham mining village a short walk north of the township of Crook. Almost immediately, the teenage Miles followed his father down the Lucy Pit of Pease's West Colliery at Billy Row. Almost immediately after that, the cottage at Crook-with-Billy-Row grew too small to contain Hutchinson's third family. In 1870 and 1871, the birth of Fred was quickly followed by the arrival of young John. In 1873 baby Hannah was born. William appeared in 1875. It was time for nineteen-year-old Miles to strike out on his own.

He had grown into a handsome adult. Of medium height – perhaps slightly taller than the average nineteenth-century coal miner – Miles was lean and muscular and rangy, with an erect stance and a head of rich black hair. His face was proud and stubborn; his nose was straight, his chin was firm, and his eyes commanded attention. They belonged to a man who was determined to stare down a dangerous world.

Miles took with him out of Billy Row his eleven-year-old brother Christopher, his remaining human connection with his abandoned rustic childhood. Miles and Christopher, two strong young men like so many others from the rural hinterlands, moved tracklessly through the seething central Durham coalfield. They climbed the steep terraced main street of Billy Row, strode by the village's pasturelands and walked for half-a-dozen miles due north across the high moor before descending to the recently opened pit at Cornsay Colliery. They took lodgings there with an ageing coal miner and began their independent adult working lives underground.

In 1878, three years after leaving Billy Row, they received word from home that their stepmother Louisa had given birth to another baby girl, who was christened Louisa Jane. Just one year later, in 1879, their father John Hutchinson died of a 'suffocating virus'. He was forty-nine years old. He had outlived two wives and been survived by a third. It was the turn of Louisa and her five young children to be left alone. Her 69-year-old widowed mother, Jane Mole, moved into the Billy Row cottage to help with her daughter's fatherless family.

For their part, six miles away at Cornsay Colliery, at the ages of twenty-three and fifteen, Miles and Christopher had lost their last blood link to Thwaite and the farming, smithing, lead mining Hutchinsons of Swaledale.

They did not at first know it, but when Miles and Christopher Hutchinson turned in to their rented beds at Cornsay they were only four miles south-west of where young Rosina Robson lived with her elderly parents at 27 Burnhope Colliery. When the connections were eventually made, the results would be disruptive.

If Miles's first two decades had been turbulent and Rosina's relatively calm, the youngest daughter of the Robson family was about to overcompensate. Within three short years she would turn inside out her own life, Miles's life, the lives of their immediate families and neighbours and those of one or two accidental passers-by. Before the age of twenty, Rosina had taken her settled world in both hands and convulsed it so thoroughly that she and those in her immediate orbit had little choice but to set course for a new one.

Rosina had known a boy called George Hall since she was eight or nine years old. In the early 1870s, when she was still a schoolgirl, her older sister Sarah had at the age of twenty-one met, courted, married and settled down to raise a family with a man from Billy Row named Thomas Hall.

Billy Row was the same small industrial suburb of Crook-with-Billy-Row that was still in the early 1870s the home of the teenage Miles Hutchinson and would remain the address of Miles's stepmother Louisa and his five half-brothers and sisters. Like Miles, like almost every other working male of the district, Thomas Hall was a coal miner and the son and the brother of coal miners. 'There were two Robson sisters married two Hall brothers,' their twentieth-century grandchildren would say. 'One of the Halls was a good man. The other was a waster.' The noun could have meant several things, none of them flattering. At bottom, it signified that its subject was a waste of time, a man who preferred idleness or drink or violence, or all three, to an ordinary, useful life.

The older brother, Thomas, was not a waster. He made a home for Sarah and their daughter Elizabeth, who was named in typical tribute to Sarah's and Rosina's mother, at 185 Billy Row. Next door, at no. 186, Sarah's and Rosina's older brother William Robson lived with his family: his wife, Harriet, who was all the way from Cornwall in the far south-west of England, and their infant son and daughter. The conjunction of brother William's and sister Sarah's married homes was neither unusual nor coincidental. Members of the same family often lodged in neighbouring or adjacent pit cottages. It was an arrangement with which most colliery managers sympathised and which they consequently facilitated.

For almost ten years, as she progressed from girlhood into her teens, Rosina Robson could travel nine miles from the parental home at Burnhope to visit both her sister Sarah and her brother William in the same street at Billy Row. In the course of that time she inevitably met and got to know her sister's husband's own Billy Row family. That family included a younger brother named George. George Hall was five years older than Rosina Robson, but he may have been merely a thirteen-year-old schoolboy when the little Robson girl first came to call.

They grew up, their age difference notwithstanding, in tandem; sharing during Rosina's visits to Billy Row the shadow of their older siblings' married lives. That they became close, a certain kind of close, is obvious. The character of their short youthful relationship will remain obscure. Only one result of it would be as visible as visible can be.

Rosina Robson, this pretty, assertive girl, made extra-marital love with 23-year-old George Hall, probably in the vicinity of Billy Row, certainly in the spring of 1882, a few months after her eighteenth birthday. 'Made love', that is, in the wholly physical twenty-first-century meaning, rather than the nineteenth-century expression of polite flirtation. This was not so unusual as later generations might have imagined. A survey carried out in the 1950s by the psychiatrist and social reformer Dr Eustace Chesser reported that almost one in five British women born in the last decades of the nineteenth century admitted to having engaged in premarital sex.

George Hall had by then been working in the local pit for almost ten years. He was unmarried and still lived with his mother and father. Rosina Robson returned the nine miles home to her parents' cottage in Burnhope, and woke up one morning in the summer of 1882 to the knowledge that she was pregnant.

She had been carrying their child for eight months before she and George Hall married in November 1882. The shotgun service was held at St Thomas's Church on a hillside overlooking Billy Row. None of George's family attended the wedding. Rosina's mother Elizabeth served as her witness before vicar Joseph Roscamp. George's best man was an illiterate 52-year-old neighbour and workmate from Billy Row named John Stoker.

The newlyweds walked out of the vestibule of St Thomas's under a Norman archway. A country lane ran past the church. At the other side of the lane stood a low drystone wall broken by a stout wooden stile. The nineteen-year-old bride in her tight wedding dress may have been helped over that stile by her husband. From its topmost step

Rosina could have gazed forever across the gentle folds of southern County Durham.

It was a Saturday. The fields and woodland would have been shrouded at regular intervals by the steam, dust and smoke of working coal mines. If she did not pause to consider those familiar scenes, she may have glanced briefly down into the nearest houses of Billy Row. From the church, from the wall and the stile, Rosina could also see her married home. She stepped onto a footpath which traversed a large meadow, downhill for a few hundred yards from the church and the stile to West Terrace in Billy Row, where she and George would set up house in a two-up, two-down corner cottage.

George and Rosina Hall's life together in that end terrace in Billy Row lasted for no more than ten weeks. On Christmas Eve 1882, a month and a half after her wedding, Rosina gave birth in West Terrace to a baby boy. She christened him William, after her own father. At about the same time she finally decided that the other male in the house, the boy she had known since girlhood, the man who had become her lover, her husband and the father of her child, was a waster.

The meteorological office in the city of Durham, nine miles from Billy Row, recorded the December of 1882 and January of 1883 as being unusually wet, windy and cold. It was roughly twice as cold, twice as windy and a third again as wet as an average nineteenth-century Durham winter, and the average Durham winter is not temperate. In the closing days of December 1882 or the first weeks of January 1883, the nineteen-year-old mother pulled together her few belongings and clothes, took her infant son in her arms and walked away from George Hall and Billy Row.

She did not go very far. She walked north, up through the wide sloping meadow, over the stile and past St Thomas's Church. She walked through the winter's day across one of the highest and most exposed heaths in County Durham. For most of her journey she unwittingly followed the path taken away from their own Billy Row home seven years earlier by Miles and Christopher Hutchinson.

But after two miles on the blasted open moor Rosina Hall diverged from the Hutchinsons' route. She turned west and walked abruptly downhill into a sheltered and isolated valley named Hedley Hill, where another cluster of cottages surrounded yet another coal mine. She entered the warmth of 49 Hedley Hill. There she and baby William found temporary comfort and refuge with her older sister Mary, Mary's coal-miner husband James Allison and their only child Betsy.

That part of rural County Durham is a landscape of hollows and crests, with the human settlements mostly in the hollows and therefore mostly invisible to each other. Billy Row, from where Rosina had fled, was just four miles from Hedley Hill, yet was as far out of sight as Madagascar.

There were exceptions to this rule. On almost every day she passed in Hedley Hill during 1883 Rosina could look down the short, flat, cultivated floor of the dale and see clearly, just half an hour's slow walk away, another, larger mining settlement. She could see the terraces, shops and looming works of Cornsay Colliery, where 27-year-old Miles Hutchinson was still employed, where he still lodged, and where he was still unmarried.

What are the chances that Miles had known Rosina's older brother and fellow coal miner William Robson a decade earlier in Billy Row? They are good. What are the chances that Miles had also known the Hall family into which Rosina had been obliged to marry? They are equally good. In the early 1870s there were 200 colliers in Billy Row. They mined the same shafts and lived in the same cluster of terraces. Anybody who lived and worked as a coal miner in Billy Row for six years between 1869 and 1875, as Miles Hutchinson had done, was likely to know at least by sight most of his colleagues and neighbours.

What are the odds that, while he was still living there in the early 1870s, Miles had seen, or even met, the young Rosina Robson when she visited her sister and brother in Billy Row? They are impossible to quantify, but are less good. Miles was then a teenage working coal miner; Rosina was almost half his age. He was one miner among many; she was just another schoolgirl on holiday. Without a family connection, there was no obvious reason for either of them to take notice of the other.

In 1883 and 1884, in Hedley Hill and Cornsay, they quickly and enthusiastically made up for their earlier indifference. If they had met before, or noticed one another before, as young working man and schoolgirl, the preliminaries would have been easy. If not, there were plenty of reasons to notice each other now. Miles was twenty-seven years old, leaner and more handsome than ever, but fortuitously still unmarried. Rosina was at the age of nineteen already a woman with a past, but motherhood had turned her prettiness into some-thing approaching beauty. To the rootless, wandering Miles Hutchinson, she was irresistible. Exactly how irresistible is best demonstrated by what they did next.

Fairly quickly they agreed to marry. But before she could legally marry Miles Hutchinson, Rosina must divorce, or be divorced by, George Hall.

She could not do that. The reasons must have been Hall's rather than Rosina's. Throughout 1883 and into 1884 he did one of three things. He rejected outright her petition for divorce. Or he procrastinated and refused to discuss the matter. Or he temporarily disappeared.

The result was the same. By the beginning of 1884, a year after leaving him, Rosina was still legally bound to the absent father of her son, with no realistic possibility of untying the knot. This would have been profoundly annoying to any ordinary young woman. To Rosina Robson-Hall it was unbearable. She had a baby son in need of a real father, and a man with whom she had fallen in love was anxious to fill that vacancy. But unless George Hall agreed to a divorce, or until he had been unjustifiably absent from her life for at least seven years, she could not legitimately marry Miles Hutchinson.

She decided to marry him anyway.

It was a dangerous step to take. Bigamy had been frowned upon by English criminal law for centuries. Until 1828, just fifty-six years earlier, convicted bigamists were routinely executed. The penalty had been moderated during the nineteenth century. Between 1828 and 1861 (when Miles Hutchinson was five years old) any person who, 'being married, shall marry any other person during the life of the former husband or wife', was liable to transportation 'beyond the Seas for the Term of Seven years'. In short, had they attempted this felony two decades earlier, Rosina Robson-Hall-Hutchinson would have been looking at the possibility of a new life, or death, in a convict settlement on the fatal shore of Botany Bay in Australia.

In 1861 the Bigamy Act was repealed. Its replacement, which was still on the statute books in the early 1880s, substituted for transportation a maximum sentence of seven years' penal servitude and a minimum, mandatory sentence of three. The quid pro quo was straightforward. If Rosina and Miles Hutchinson were caught getting married in 1883 and 1884, she would face at least thirty-six months in Durham gaol. They were probably persuaded to go ahead and take the risk by another momentous family event; one which both motivated Miles and Rosina and offered them an escape from the possible consequences of her bigamy.

In the last days of December 1883, a year after she had given birth to baby William and then walked away from George Hall, three of Rosina's older sisters emigrated to the United States of America. They sailed from Liverpool shortly after Christmas and arrived in the USA on 10 January 1884, to start a new life in a new country in the New Year. Thirty-one-year-old Sarah, 25-year-old Kate and 22-year-old Rachel boarded the *British Crown* at Mersey docks in the company of two of their husbands and two of their children. Sarah travelled with her husband Tom Hall and daughter Elizabeth from Billy Row. Rachel, whose husband James McCormack was already waiting for them on the western side of the Atlantic Ocean, brought her three-year-old girl Eliza. And their blind and childless sister Kate took ship with her husband Tom Wilkinson.

Rosina and Miles would surely have preferred to travel with them. But until her marital situation was somehow resolved, Rosina could not properly plan a new life. Miles in his turn may not have wished to run away with another man's wife and child. So for the moment they stayed behind, hoping and failing to wring a voluntary divorce out of George Hall. In the early summer of 1884, seventeen months after Rosina had walked away from Hall and five months after her sisters had emigrated to the United States, they ran out of patience.

If they were to marry bigamously, they must do so in a place far enough from Cornsay and Hedley Hill and Billy Row that nobody – especially, perhaps, the vicar – would object to the reading of their wedding banns at services on three consecutive Sundays before the nuptial tie. They settled on St John's Church in the parish of Brandon. This establishment stood ten straight miles away from their homes. It was close enough for Rosina and Miles to travel there in a day, and for another of Rosina's older married sisters, Elizabeth Watson, to attend the ceremony with her husband William and act as witnesses. And it was far enough away, this cluttered little township of Brandon, for the nervous couple to hope for anonymity, to assume with some confidence that neither the vicar nor any of his congregation would be aware that Miles Hutchinson's fiancée was already a married woman. As it turned out, that was a fair assumption.

Rosina nonetheless took care to disguise her identity. She described herself to Reverend Lawson of St John's Church, and in the banns which he duly announced, as a spinster whose name was Rosina Hall. That was half a lie. Rosina Hall she was; a spinster she was not.

She then gave her father's name, for obvious reasons, as William Hall instead of William Robson. Her sister Elizabeth, her brother-in-law William and her bridegroom Miles all signed up to these deceits on the marriage certificate. When the three walked out of St John's Church, Brandon, on 14 June 1884 they were vulnerable to charges of aiding and abetting a felony. When Rosina walked out with them she was both a fraud and a bigamist. But she also walked out as Rosina Hutchinson, and she would cleave to that name up to and beyond the grave.

Elizabeth and William Watson returned home to their working lives in the County Durham coalfield. Miles and Rosina Hutchinson picked up young William and the few possessions they could carry. Miles took his nineteen-year-old half-brother Christopher out of Cornsay Colliery and the group of four set off on foot for Liverpool. They were all of them – Miles and Rosina and Christopher Hutchinson, Sarah and Tom Hall, Kate and Tom Wilkinson and Rachel McCormack – moved in those few months of 1884 by great coincidences. Their reasons for leaving Britain were as diverse and individual as the motives of every one of the 23 million Europeans who emigrated to the United States of America between 1880 and 1930.

They were economic migrants, certainly. But Miles and Rosina Hutchinson were also fleeing a prison sentence for bigamy. Rosina had clearly been disowned or disinherited by her parents following her extra-marital pregnancy, her short-lived first marriage and her illegal second wedding. Miles, the restless, motherless young itinerant from Swaledale, had no parents left alive to disinherit him.

Miles and Christopher and the two Toms were also extracting themselves from serious industrial disputes in the Durham coalfield, which would lead to a series of long and painful strikes. Although they knew, as did every coal miner in every coalfield in Britain, that the newly opened underground workings of Pennsylvania and Virginia were desperate for imported pitmen, they may have hoped to be able in the land of the free to cut themselves and their children loose from the hereditary occupation of mining.

All four men – Tom Hall, Miles Hutchinson, Christopher

Hutchinson and Tom Wilkinson – were the sons of miners and had worked in collieries since their early teens. But in passage to the USA, each of the first three registered their occupations as 'labourer'; optimistically, poignantly, Tom Wilkinson claimed to be a 'farmer'. He was travelling to America. Why not dream?

Miles, Rosina and William Hutchinson stayed in the United States of America, chiefly in the multinational coal patches around Pittsburgh, for six years. There, in 1889, Rosina gave birth to a son. He was christened Thomas, clearly after Kate Wilkinson's husband. As soon as Rosina felt that baby Thomas was ready to travel they retraced their journey across the eastern continental divide to Philadelphia. And there, back on Delaware Wharves, they boarded a ship and steamed across the Atlantic Ocean to Liverpool.

It may have been a heavy-hearted homecoming. But if they wanted consolation, Rosina and Kate and Miles and Tom could have gained some from the realisation that they were very far from being the only emigrants to give up on the New World and return to the Old. The ships going home contained almost a third of the emigrants who had earlier crossed the Atlantic Ocean in a westerly direction.

Fifty years earlier Charles Dickens had encountered such 'return emigrants' upon his own return from New York to England. As he wrote in *American Notes*:

We carried in the steerage nearly a hundred passengers, a little world of poverty: and as we came to know individuals among them by sight, from looking down upon the deck where they took the air in the daytime, and cooked their food, and very often ate it too, we became curious to know their histories, and with what expectations they had gone out to America, and on what errands they were going home, and what their circumstances were . . .

Some of them had been in America but three days, some but three months, and some had gone out in the last voyage of that very ship in which they were now returning home. Others had sold their clothes to raise the passage-money, and had hardly rags to cover them; others had no food, and lived upon the charity of the rest . . .

The history of every family we had on board was pretty much the same. After hoarding up, and borrowing, and begging, and selling everything to pay the passage, they had gone out to New York, expecting to find its streets paved with gold; and had found them paved with very hard and very real stones. Enterprise was dull; labourers were not wanted; jobs of work were to be got, but the payment was not.

They were coming back, even poorer than they went. One of them was carrying an open letter from a young English artisan, who had been in New York a fortnight, to a friend near Manchester, whom he strongly urged to follow him. One of the officers brought it to me as a curiosity. 'This is the country, Jem,' said the writer. 'I like America. There is no despotism here; that's the great thing. Employment of all sorts is going a-begging, and wages are capital. You have only to choose a trade, Jem, and be it. I haven't made choice of one yet, but I shall soon. At present I haven't quite made up my mind whether to be a carpenter – or a tailor.'

They returned in their millions, for as many different reasons as they had left. Members of some ethnic, religious, national or cultural groups went home again in great numbers; those of others barely went home at all. Hardly a single Amish man or woman, for instance, returned to Switzerland or Alsace from Pennsylvania or anywhere else in the New World. Similarly, as few as 5 per cent of the Jewish peoples of Europe who crossed the Atlantic in the late nineteenth and early twentieth centuries ever went back to face pogrom and later holocaust.

The Irish who fled their own famine in the mid-nineteenth century had nothing to return to but starvation; understandably, only a small proportion of them ever saw Ireland again. The large numbers of Irish men and women who made their new homes in Boston, Chicago, New York, New Orleans and elsewhere carved out such a substantial livelihood and subculture for themselves in America that they were able to offer hospitality and a degree of security to their compatriots who followed them, with the result that even many years later, into the twentieth century, decades after the end of the Great Famine, no more than 10 or 11 per cent of Irish men and women who emigrated to the USA ever went back to live permanently in Cork, Killarney or Dublin.

Comparatively small numbers of Welsh and Scottish people left on the emigrant ships, but once in the United States between 80 and 90 per cent of them also tended to settle. They were usually (although not always) English speakers, which gave them a linguistic pass onto the higher slopes of the US economy. In the cases of the Welsh and the Scots, it can be difficult to distinguish in the statistics between those who emigrated with a new beginning in their hearts but then gave up and straggled home, and those who travelled to and from the United States only for a long holiday or to visit relatives, but never had any intention of settling there.

There is a similar dichotomy in the figures for workers from eastern and southern Europe. Large numbers of Greeks, Italians, Poles and Croats undoubtedly went to the USA to find work. It is equally beyond doubt that large numbers of them – more than half – subsequently went back to Greece, Italy, Poland and Croatia. What is in doubt is how many of that 50, 60 or (in the cases of Serbs and Bulgarians) 90 per cent of migrant workers were driven from the USA back to Europe by the financial and other exploitations to which an untrained, illiterate and incomprehensible peasant workforce was prone, and how many of them ever actually intended to resettle in the United States for good – how many of them, in short, only crossed the Atlantic to raise quick cash to improve their standing when, not if, they returned home to southern and eastern Europe.

There had been within Europe a long tradition of migrant workforces travelling for seasonal work from the poor lands to the richer industrial or rural economies of France and Germany. Italians spent their summers harvesting grapes in Burgundy and grain in Provence; Swedes and Poles travelled in their tens of thousands to earn marks in the factories of Prussia. Very few of them ever intended to stay in France or Germany. Their purpose was to take enough money home to support their families, or to improve the size of their family's holdings, or to establish themselves as prospective family men back in Italy, Sweden or Poland.

When steamships made the transatlantic crossing quick, cheap and dependable, many such Europeans simply substituted the USA for France and Germany. In the first years of the twentieth century the Italian prime minister Giuseppe Zanardelli was greeted by the mayor of a southern Italian village with the words: 'I welcome you in the name of the five thousand inhabitants of this town, three thousand of whom are in America and the other two thousand preparing to go.'

The mayor did not add – neither he nor Signor Zanardelli at that point may have known – that almost two-thirds of their thousands of citizens in the United States would return to the Mezzogiorno. Millions of southern Italians travelled across the Atlantic in the fifty years of the Golden Age between 1870 and 1920. At least 60 per cent of them sooner or later went back to Italy.

Italians, especially from the south, had few if any industrial skills and little English, were consequently unable to command substantial wages, and were often the subjects of racial and religious hostility within the USA. Their homelands were certainly poor, but they had not run away from genocidal famines or pogroms. They had something to return to, and the majority of them reached the opinion that they would sooner grow old and die in Italy than in Manhattan.

The English had all the advantages that the Italians lacked. They spoke English. They were often literate. They usually possessed the skills necessary to a developing economy. They were generally white, Anglo-Saxon and Protestant. But for all those silver tickets into North American prosperity, a fifth of English emigrants returned home from the USA. Out of the 3 million English men, women and children who emigrated to the United States, some 600,000 looked around and then went back again. They had not fled famines or pogroms. They had something to return to. They decided that they would rather grow old in County Durham than in Pennsylvania.

Perhaps something fundamental propelled them onto the ship back to Liverpool at Delaware Wharves. Perhaps it was at heart nothing more or less than the lure of green fields and black pitheads, mild summers, North Country accents, reliable food, the laughter of family and old friends. They had been to see the elephant jump the fence, and it had jumped. It had jumped quite high enough for six lifetimes. They never wandered again.

A decade later, in the spring of 1901, a census enumerator was making his way along the doorsteps of the village of Ryton in County Durham on the south bank of the River Tyne. The old market cross still stood, surrounded by the twelfth-century Norman church, the two venerable country inns, the Squire's Hall, the Manor House and the Home Farm with its 'hay-ricks, its clucking fowls, and flock of turkeys'.

Just a mile to the west of this bucolic scene, still within the parish of Ryton, the census enumerator walked with his forms and his pencils into 'a huddle of little houses built in rows'. He had entered the pit village of Addison Colliery. It was an expanding enterprise in 1901. Just five years earlier only 240 miners had been employed by the Stella Coal Company at Addison. By 1901 almost 500 men were working there underground.

The enumerator was told that three people lived at the terraced pit cottage 108 Addison Colliery in the spring of 1901. They were a 45-year-old man named Thomas Wilkinson, his 43-year-old wife Catherine, and Catherine's eighty-year-old widowed mother, Elizabeth Robson. Thomas was occupied as a coal miner.

If there were no children in the cottage, next door made

up for it. At no. 109 lived 45-year-old Miles Hutchinson and his 37-year-old wife Rosina. Miles was employed as a 'coal miner hewer'.

There were also seven youngsters in the cottage. Eighteen-year-old William was employed as a 'coal miner putter'. His younger brother Thomas, aged twelve, was at school, as were nine-year-old John and seven-year-old Rosin. Five-year-old Alice, two-year-old Miles and Rachel, born just a month before, were playing and crawling and being dandled around the two cottages, receiving – the enumerator might have noticed – considerable practised attention from the middle-aged Catherine and the elderly Elizabeth at no. 108.

William still did not know that Miles Hutchinson was not his genetic father, and that his six younger siblings were his half-brothers and half-sisters. On the morning of William's wedding three years later to a girl called Mary, Miles would take his adopted son to one side and tell him the truth about William Hall and Rosina and Miles himself. 'Well,' said William stoically, 'if it's all right with you, I've always been a Hutchinson and a Hutchinson I'll remain.'

The census enumerator recorded in his careful copper-plate the birthplaces of all the members of the household. Miles had been born in Swaledale, in the county of Yorkshire; Rosina and all her children but one in County Durham. The exception was twelve-year-old Thomas. Although born in America, he was, Rosina Hutchinson insisted, a British citizen. Thomas Hutchinson was a very small manifestation of that large but disregarded British social phenomenon: the emigrants who returned.

10

Aliens

Early in the twenty-first century the British journalist and author David Aaronovitch began searching for his immigrant grandparents in the 1911 census returns. David had been told by his father that Morris and Kate (Moishe and Gitel) Aaronovitch had arrived in London from a Jewish hamlet outside Vilnius in Lithuania 'in about 1903 or 1904'. Genealogists and experienced family historians will be unsurprised to learn from Aaronovitch that 'I could find no sign of any Aaronovitches at all in the 1911 census.'

Finally Aaronovitch's half-sister went to his aid. Armed with the knowledge that Morris and Kate could speak very little English, let alone write the language, she 'solved the mystery of my grandparents' missing years.

Realising that customs officers and census takers had sometimes been a little hasty when dealing with incomprehensible foreigners, she entered a whole series of variants on 'Aaronovitch' into the census database. She found the family – parents, Uncle Joe and my aunt Rachel . . . entered under the name 'Aronofitch'.

In 1911 they were living at 4, St George's Square in the Stepney parish of St George's in the east. The square (which later became Swedenborg Square but has now disappeared into council estates) had been built for the well-off tradesmen who had supplied the masted ships of the nineteenth century. By the time Kate and Morris moved there it was a run-down area of largely Jewish immigrants subletting rooms in its once-commodious houses. It was just as well they were there.

Had the Aaronovitches not arrived in Britain before 1906 it's more likely that they would either be pushing up pine needles in some mass grave in a Lithuanian forest, or that some version of me would be writing this on the Upper West Side from the library of his $20 million penthouse. But arrive they did, and went to live in a teeming, filthy-bricked house on one of London's most notorious thoroughfares, Cable Street, where my father Sam was born, and from where my grandfather went out to work as a needleman in the rag trade.

Even before it was confirmed, David Aaronovitch was reasonably certain that his father had been right and that Morris and Kate had arrived in the United Kingdom at least six years before the 1911 census, because in 1905 the Aliens Act went through the Houses of Commons and Lords.

The Aliens Act, which Aaronovitch correctly describes as 'the first proper legislation in Britain aimed at limiting immigration', was specifically designed to exclude Jews and was the result of several decades of popular anti-semitism. It was also, however unintentionally, enabled by the national census.

Throughout the nineteenth century the British authorities,

and therefore their census, had not been much concerned about the origins of citizens. Since 1841 an English person in Ireland or a Scottish person in England had been asked to state the country of their birth when it was different from the country in which they were enumerated. Anybody born outside the British Isles, which included a large number of children of British imperial administrators, diplomats and entrepreneurs as well as other returned emigrants from the colonies or the United States, would simply write 'Germany', 'India' or 'Ceylon' in the box marked 'Foreign Parts', and that was that.

Following the census of 1861, Registrar General George Graham reported without prejudice:

In the midst of 19,982,623 British subjects [in England and Wales] lived 84,090 subjects of Foreign States. They are of all ages; but there is a great excess of men between the ages of 20 and 40. 9,502 of the subjects of Foreign States belonged to America, 518 to Africa, 358 to Asia, and 73,434 to Europe; 40,909 of them are in London, and the rest are distributed all over England . . .

Of the subjects of France, 12,989 are reckoned, including teachers of languages, governesses, cooks, servants, merchants, clerks, seamen (1,532), tailors, bootmakers, dressmakers, and smaller numbers in a great variety of occupations.

Italy sends us musicians, artists, priests, figure and image makers, looking-glass makers, and merchants. 667 Italian seamen were in our ports. Germany, with Austria and Prussia, besides seamen (4624), supplies us with a large number of musicians, teachers of the German language, servants, merchants, factors, and commercial clerks, watch and clock makers (965), engine and machine makers, tailors, shoemakers; with many bakers, and a large colony of sugar refiners (1345).

The cities, and especially the metropolis, are the principal seats of foreign residents. London in 1851 contained 30,057 persons born in Foreign Parts; and in 1861 it contained 48,390 foreigners by birth.

Ten years later in 1871 Graham would report with pride that 'the country contains representatives of nearly all the civilized nations, who have voluntarily sought these shores for the sake of trade, or have been driven at various times by persecutions to a land which has ever been, the sacred asylum and the inviolable home of freedom'.

The census had, to the relief and then the pride of the British people, indicated that their numbers were swelling rapidly. This was almost universally regarded as a good thing and left little room for theories of racial purity. Before the introduction of passports and immigration controls in the twentieth century, anybody could move to Great Britain from anywhere else in the world. If, like Ringo Starr and his ancestors, they kept their heads down and stayed out of trouble, few people would notice them.

The numbers of English, Welsh or Scottish people resident in Ireland bothered nobody outside Ireland. Such internal dispersals within the United Kingdom were fondly regarded as the beneficial introduction of diligent Protestants to an obdurately Catholic island. Irish people who moved to England and Scotland had become the objects of racial discrimination. But as they had been made part of the same state as recently as 1801, without being consulted or asked permission and in many cases against their expressed will, it was difficult for any patriotic British unionist to argue that the movement of Irish people elsewhere in the British Isles should be restricted. They were instead reluctantly allowed across the Irish Sea and then mocked, assaulted, denied decent jobs and crowded into slums out of sight and mind.

They would not be the last to be treated in such a fashion. Towards the end of the nineteenth century the Irish were joined in those slums by a substantial number of people who also adhered to a different faith, who were not the children of the colonies but who had undeniably been born in 'Foreign Parts'.

In April 1891 the *Yorkshire Post* published an account by an 'Assistant Enumerator' of helping to take the census of that year in the 'courts, alleys and yards' of a large town which was unnamed but may have been Leeds. He offered the readership a description of being guided by an experienced enumerator through the urban jungle of a late-Victorian slum in the north of England: 'The twistings and turnings through which he took me: the steps up and the steps down where he led the way: the curvings and sinuosities from which we emerged safely: the tenements he found swarming with women and children, where I could see nothing but projecting corners, or pigeon-holes, or unsuggestive attics ... soon I followed him with unquestioning faith, knowing that no hole would escape him, and that he would unearth human beings from spots where existence seemed to me impossible.'

In those warrens the assistant enumerator discovered 'a few English in the worst quarters, more Irish, and still more Jews, the elders of whom entered themselves as born

in Russia, with the exception of three or four whose birthplace was somewhat widely given as "America"'. That
Jewish population 'within the last few years have made their
way into a certain town in the West Riding in hundreds if
not thousands'. The enumerator's account continued:

> My first two hours were spent in a narrow back street –
> a street so narrow that it was necessary to step into the
> middle of it, throw your head right back, and bring your
> eyes to the perpendicular before you could see its own
> little patch of grey sky: and a street so hideously ugly in its
> grotesque piles of bricks and mortar as to defy my modest
> powers of description.
>
> There, in and out, up steps and down steps, in rooms
> low, unventilated, and often filthy, amid surroundings
> that are an abomination, and where all sanitary con-
> veniences and laws are at defiance, is a considerable
> population, and a proportion of children such as made
> one's heart ache to look at. Here and in other parts of the
> district are many families of Russian Jews ... I could not
> converse with them, for they were as ignorant of English
> as I of their language ...

('To the end of her life in a hospital ward in Dalston in 1969,'
wrote David Aaronovitch, 'my grandmother spoke almost
nothing but Yiddish.')

> Singularly, their papers were all filled up, and the work
> was carefully done and the writing generally good.
>
> But in one respect those Russian or Polish Jews are
> unique. Without exception the stench that greeted one at
> their open doors was overwhelming. The only occasion

when the Enumerator and his assistant came into collision was when, having incautiously advanced a few steps into one of those abodes, they by a common and simultaneous impulse ran against each other in their haste to reach the comparatively fresh air of the street. Hitherto the most villainous smells had always been associated by me with Irish cabins or a 'slum' tenement occupied by an Irish family in one of our large towns; but yesterday my opinion was changed. The Irish must make way for the Russian and Polish Jew in this respect.

What a pleasure it was to come upon, right in the centre of the block, a really clean and well-furnished house, occupied by a Yorkshirewoman and her husband, with a canary trilling as happily as though he were enjoying the sunshine in a suburban villa.

The absence of a common language; the insanitary conditions which were inescapable in substandard housing; the strange smell of foreign cooking: the assistant enumerator listed in Yorkshire in 1891 many of the ingredients which would fuel racism in Britain in the twentieth and twenty-first centuries.

To his particular mix could be added endemic European anti-semitism. In the last two decades of the nineteenth century more than 2 million Jews fled persecution in Tsarist Russia and elsewhere in eastern Europe. Most of them went to the United States but it is estimated that 100,000 Russian Jews, including the grandparents of David Aaronovitch, arrived in the United Kingdom. Once in London or Leeds they experienced, at best, the haughty distaste of the Yorkshire assistant enumerator. 'There is a lower depth than the Irish in some of our large towns,' he concluded in April

1891, 'and that lower depth comprises the recently arrived Jews from Russia.'

There were certainly lower depths to be plumbed in British responses to those recently arrived Jews. Right-wing populists denounced an 'alien invasion' which was apparently taking British jobs from British workers. Ratepayers were, according to the Manchester *Evening Chronicle*, being bilked of excessive poor relief for 'the dirty, destitute, diseased, verminous and criminal foreigner who dumps himself on our soil and rates simultaneously'. An extreme anti-immigration party, the British Brothers' League, was established; it marched, held rallies, and served as the grandfather of other such movements until events on the European continent between 1933 and 1945 made anti-semitism briefly unfashionable.

While the assistant enumerator was making his appalled tour of Jewish households in urban Yorkshire in 1891, another enumerator listed Michael Marks, whose age was given as thirty, living in the terrace of Great George Street in Wigan with his wife 'Anna' (she was actually Hannah) and their infant children Simon and Rebecca. Michael and Hannah Marks each submitted their birthplace as 'Russian Poland'. Simon and Rebecca had been born in 'Yorkshire Leeds'. Michael recorded his profession or occupation as 'smallware dealer'.

Michael Marks was part of the late-Victorian alien invasion which so agitated the British Brothers' League. Born Michal, he had left Belarus a little less than ten years earlier and made his way to Leeds where he knew that work was available to Jewish immigrants. When he arrived in the West Riding of Yorkshire as a young man, he did not speak English. In 1886, by then known as Michael, he married his fellow Russian émigrée Hannah Cohen at the Great Synagogue in Leeds.

In 1891 Marks was in the process of establishing a string of market stalls in Yorkshire and Lancashire. Even though he had left them behind, he was familiar with the inhabitants of such ghettos as described by 'Assistant Enumerator' in the *Yorkshire Post*: his first stall had been a celebrated Penny Bazaar in Leeds covered market.

With the help of the capital investment and accountancy skills of the Yorkshireman Thomas Spencer, throughout the 1890s Marks opened at breathtaking speed a chain of thirty-six stores across the north of England, in Cardiff, Swansea and at seven different sites in London. By 1901 Michael and Hannah Marks and their young family had moved again, to a large house with two servants in the centre of Manchester. Marks then described himself as 'Hardware, Software, Toy Dealer, Employer'.

In 1903, shortly after Marks & Spencer became a limited company, Spencer retired with a large return from his initial investment. Michael Marks himself died in 1907. Despite the entry in the 1891 census, his age remained uncertain. His naturalisation papers stated that he had been born in 1859 in the city of Slonim in the former Polish–Lithuanian Commonwealth, which was by the nineteenth century part of the Russian empire and would become the country of Belarus. That would have made Marks around forty-eight when he died. But the date of birth offered on his marriage certificate lost half a decade and would have made his life span forty-three years. The 1891 census was told that he was thirty years old, the 1901 census that he was thirty-eight, which made his age at death either forty-six or forty-four. It can only be said with certainty that by the time of his passing in his forties, after spending just twenty-five years in the country to which he had emigrated knowing not a word of any of its native languages, Michael Marks had achieved more than most British octogenarians.

Young Simon took over the business. In 1928 he introduced the brand name 'St Michael' to the company's goods in honour of his father. The St Michael logo was deliberately established to represent to the British consumer the best of British produce. In 1998 Marks & Spencer PLC, the achievement of a foreigner who in the early 1880s had travelled from a Russian stetl and dumped himself 'on our soil and rates simultaneously', became the first British retail business to make a pre-tax profit of over £1 billion.

Those destitute Jews who found themselves fighting to stay alive and healthy among 'grotesque piles of bricks and mortar' were of course mere drops in the ocean of the British population. Even if their presence had been a burden – and the subsequent social, economic, scientific, political and cultural achievements of twentieth-century British Jews suggested the exact opposite – it was a tiny weight to bear.

Following the retirement in 1900 of Brydges Henniker, the centennial English and Welsh census of 1901 was conducted and collated by two Scots. Reginald MacLeod's father Norman, twenty-fifth chief of the Clan MacLeod, had in the middle of the nineteenth century left his ancestral home at Dunvegan Castle on the island of Skye to seek a new life and career in London. His second son Reginald, who would succeed to the clan chieftaincy upon the death of his older brother in 1929, was educated at Harrow School and Cambridge University and married Lady Agnes Northcote, the daughter of Sir Stafford Northcote, a late-nineteenth-century Conservative Chancellor of the Exchequer and Foreign Secretary.

Reginald MacLeod was rejected by his tenants and other crofters when he stood for Inverness-shire in the Conservative interest in 1885. He was compensated by an office in the Court of the Exchequer, and then in 1900 by the post of Registrar General for England and Wales. He did the job for just two years before becoming permanent under-secretary of state for Scotland. MacLeod therefore organised the 1901 census, becoming the first registrar to employ women as clerks – not least because they were cheaper than men – but his successor after 1902, a Scottish baronet named William Cospatrick Dunbar, collated most of the information and wrote the reports.

Dunbar discovered from MacLeod's census that in a total English and Welsh population of 32,527,843, just over 1 per cent, 339,436, had been born in 'Foreign Countries'. Those countries excluded 'persons born in the British Colonies and Dependencies', who numbered 136,092, but included substantial numbers born in the United States of America, France, Germany and 'Russia (including Poland)'.

The one-third of a million foreign-born people then living in the United Kingdom was twice as many as twenty years earlier. In 1881, 174,374 non-colonial foreigners had been counted. There was no doubt that the extra 165,000 immigrants between 1881 and 1901 included substantial numbers of Jewish refugees. The number of 'natives of Russia' living in England and Wales had risen in those two decades from 3789 to 61,789. Among them were Michael Marks, Hannah Cohen and their fellow escapees from murder, assault, theft, pogrom and discrimination in eastern Europe.

Although Jewish immigrants plainly constituted a minority of the 1 per cent of the population born outside Great Britain and its empire, their presence attracted a disproportionate level of fear and loathing. Between 1871 and 1901 the number of Italians living in Britain increased fourfold, from 5000 to 20,000. The Italians were equally foreign, equally unfamiliar with the English language and equally impecunious. Unlike the eastern European Jews they were mainly economic migrants who had escaped from rural penury rather than religious persecution. But their presence attracted almost no criticism.

The numbers of Jewish immigrants were hugely exaggerated even in the respectable national press. When the 1881 and 1891 censuses showed their numbers to be comparatively small, it was claimed that Jews had simply dodged the enumerators. Registrar General Reginald MacLeod attempted to appease such paranoia; as his successor William Dunbar reported in 1903:

> Previous to the taking of the Census, it was thought that many of the Jewish aliens in the East End of London, apprehensive of conscription abroad, of special taxation or of police espionage, might object to fill up the Census Schedule, or through inability to understand the form, might fill it up incorrectly.
>
> The Jewish Board of Guardians were therefore asked, as on former occasions, to prepare a Circular in Yiddish and German stating the objects of the Census and the desirability of making accurate returns. This Circular, on the back of which was printed a translation of the Census Schedule in Yiddish, was distributed with the Census Schedule to the foreign Jews resident in the East

of London and in parts of the City of Manchester; the Chief Rabbi also courteously arranged for the nature and objects of the Census to be explained from the pulpits of the Synagogues.

In addition to these precautions, the foreign Jewish quarter in the East End of London was mapped out into small districts, and the houses in each district were visited by a Member of a Committee of ladies and gentlemen, who gave assistance where required by explaining, and if necessary by filling up, the Schedule. It is confidently believed that these measures had the effect of obtaining approximately accurate returns from this class of the population in the East End of London.

That 'courteous' intervention by rabbis also helps to explain the surprised discovery by the 'Assistant Enumerator' in an impoverished, Yiddish-speaking quarter of the West Riding of Yorkshire that 'their papers were all filled up, and the work was carefully done and the writing generally good'.

When all the statistics were assembled it was announced that in 1901 only thirteen towns and cities in the whole of England and Wales contained a foreign-born population of more than 1 per cent. Outside London, 2.2 per cent of Mancunians were foreigners, while just over 2 per cent of the people of Tynemouth had been born abroad. They were followed by 'Cardiff, South Shields, Leeds, Grimsby, Kingston-upon-Hull, Liverpool and Bournemouth, with proportions ranging from 18 to 13 per 1,000, while Hornsey, Swansea and Willesden had proportions a little above 10 per 1,000'.

The industrial powerhouse of Manchester, which was by 1901 the home of Michael and Hannah Marks, had an established Jewish population. The same applied in a smaller degree to Leeds, where Michael Marks and Hannah Cohen had first arrived from Russia, where they had married and produced their first two children. Tynemouth, South Shields, Cardiff, Swansea, Grimsby, Hull and Liverpool were all busy ports, four of which looked across the North Sea or the English Channel directly to continental Europe. As ports, they were also harbours for the merchant navy. In 1901 there were 15,755 'European Foreign Sailors' working in the British mercantile marine. If their ship happened to be in a British port on census night, the entire crew was duly counted as being in Britain, no matter where they really called home.

Bournemouth was, following the opening of a railway line, a booming resort whose population had increased from 17,000 in 1881 to 60,000 in 1901; many of the incomers were immigrants working in the service industries. Hornsey and Willesden were already home to small English Jewish communities and therefore attracted other continental Jews at their time of crisis late in the nineteenth century. One of them, Solomon Barnett, born in Russian Poland in about 1845, married a Devonshire woman, raised a large family and was noted for a lifetime spent developing the roads and infrastructure of much of suburbia and for founding and helping to fund the Brondesbury Synagogue, which opened in 1905 to serve Jews who settled in Cricklewood, Willesden and Brondesbury.

The huge exception to those modest numbers of provincial immigrants was the East End of London, and in particular the Borough of Stepney where David Aaronovitch's grandparents Moishe and Gitel would settle a few years later. In 1901 a remarkable 40 per cent of the inhabitants of Stepney had been born in foreign countries, and 77 per cent of them – 30 per cent of the total population – came from Russia and Russian Poland. Those numbers were not enough to push the total of foreigners in the whole of London above 3 per cent, but it represented a substantial Jewish enclave.

Immigration was nothing new to Stepney. The borough's cheap housing and proximity to the London docks had attracted earlier influxes of French Huguenots and Irish emigrants, and would later in the twentieth century become home to Bangladeshis and other Asians escaping conflict and famine in their home countries. The pattern established in preceding centuries was for the immigrant populations to use Stepney, and other neighbouring East End boroughs, as footholds. They settled uncomfortably in the inexpensive slums before their children and grandchildren hauled themselves up the social and economic ladder and moved out to more salubrious neighbourhoods or dissolved into the general population.

The same would be true of Stepney's late-Victorian Jews. One of the better, if least remarked, services of the 1901 census report was to dismiss through incontrovertible statistics the myth that such immigrants dumped themselves 'on our soil and rates simultaneously'.

'It has often been stated,' wrote William Dunbar, 'that the Alien Immigrants in this Country largely help to fill our Workhouses, Infirmaries, and Lunatic Asylums. In order to ascertain what measure of truth there is in such a general assertion, an examination has been made of the birth-places of the pauper inmates of the workhouse establishments belonging to the Parishes or Unions of Shoreditch, Bethnal Green, Whitechapel, St. George in the East, Stepney, Mile End Old Town and Poplar.'

The results of that examination were dramatic. In 1901 those combined East End parishes contained '715,739 persons, of whom 62,843 were European Foreigners, mostly living under the poorest conditions. In the Workhouse establishments serving these areas, there were, at the date of the Census, 10,820 pauper inmates, of whom only 109 were European Foreigners. The proportions of indoor Paupers among the general population and among the European Foreigners were 15.1 and 1.7 per 1,000 respectively.'

In other words, recent immigrants from the European continent, most of whom were Jewish, comprised almost 9 per cent of the population of the East End of London. But they made up only 1 per cent of the population of the workhouses, which were subsidised by ratepayers. One and a half per cent of the mainly native British population of the East End was categorised as 'indoor paupers', who were drawing poor relief from the rates. Fewer than one-tenth – as little as 0.17 per cent of the immigrant population – of those were 'European Foreigners'.

What was more, the European immigrants were dragging themselves out of poverty at a disproportionately rapid rate. Just ten years earlier in 1891, reported William Dunbar, the relative figures concerning indoor paupers had been 1.3 per cent of the general population and 0.3 per cent of foreigners. Between 1891 and 1901, therefore, the already minuscule percentage of immigrants entitled to poor relief had more than halved.

According to his grandson, following his arrival in Stepney early in the 1900s Moishe Aaronovitch changed his name to Morris and 'went out to work as a needleman in the rag trade'.

He was far from untypical. The Registrar General helpfully supplied a summary of the different occupations which engaged 'European Foreigners' in Britain in 1901. Almost 25,000 immigrants from Russia (Jewish), Russian Poland (Jewish), Germany (mainly Jewish) and the Austro-Hungarian Habsburg Empire (mainly Jewish) were employed as 'Tailors, Clothiers' or 'Tailoresses'. A further 5400 were 'Cabinet Makers, Upholsterers, Furniture Dealers, French Polishers'. Just over 5000 immigrants from Russia, Poland and Germany were 'Boot, Shoe and Slipper Makers and Dealers'. Three thousand were hairdressers or wigmakers. Stereotypically, almost 2000 of the 20,000 Italians were waiters, 600 were cooks, 2600 of them were 'Costermongers, Hawkers, Street Sellers' and, as had been the case forty years earlier, a whopping 1800 worked as 'Musicians, Music Masters, Singers and Art, Music, Theatre Service'.

So far from being disease-ridden criminals who scrounged on the ratepayers, those immigrant communities were clearly industrious and vital additions to the commerce and gaiety of the nation. 'It is clear then,' concluded Registrar General Dunbar, referring to the claim that the workhouses were full of immigrants, 'that the Census Returns do not sustain the above allegation.'

William Dunbar's findings and his sober words were not enough to prevent the Aliens Act from being passed in 1905. By the standards of later legislation it was far from draconian. The Act gave the Home Secretary, through government inspectors, 'the power to exclude paupers, unless they could prove that they were entering the country solely to avoid persecution or punishment on religious or political grounds or for an offence of a political nature'. It was leniently exercised and resulted in very few exclusions. But the Aliens Act was both a fertile precedent and, as William Dunbar recognised with discomfort, a sharp break with the past and with George Graham's 'land which has ever been, the sacred asylum and the inviolable home of freedom'.

By 1905 the British public had forgotten that its national census had been established a century earlier to reassure a worried polity that its population was increasing rather than disappearing. The delighted conclusion of Simon Gray that his friend John Rickman had confirmed 'the real and pleasing effects of a rapid increase of population' belonged to another era. From 1905 onwards the British would not particularly object to population increase. But they became increasingly choosy as to who increased the population, and concurrently intolerant of those 'dirty, destitute, diseased, verminous and criminal' foreigners. The Aliens Act did not of course introduce anti-semitism and racism to the white British population. It did, however, for the first time in the archipelago's history, institutionalise and lend the authority of government to prejudicial notions of racial purity.

The irony early in the twentieth century was to be found chiefly in the fact that a noisy section of British society could get hot and bothered about the presence in the country of a few hundred thousand foreigners, while simultaneously delighting in their jurisdiction over countless millions of other foreigners elsewhere in the world. That contradiction would come home to roost.

11

Empire

The census had originally been taken to ascertain the strength of Great Britain during the Napoleonic Wars, to assess how many men could be raised to arms and how many British people required to be fed. As the nineteenth century progressed the census became established as a routine and widely accepted survey of the British condition. 'I should say,' wrote the assistant enumerator in Yorkshire in 1891, 'that the taking of the Census is becoming a very commonplace matter. People, even the lowest in education, better understand its object, and there is none of the reticence to give information that there once was, and the racy encounters between enumerator and occupant are things of the past.'

The Yorkshire assistant enumerator's colleagues in Ireland and parts of Scotland might not all have agreed. In that same census enumeration of 1891 disturbances were reported from Dundee, where some forms were delivered late on a Saturday night. 'One old woman on being knocked up out of her bed demanded to know the object of her disturber. On his replying that he had come with her census paper, she decisively replied, "I want nae assessment paper here. Gan awa' wi' ye.'" Others refused to open their doors, and damaging rumours were later spread that some census papers had actually been delivered after midnight on Saturday, thereby breaking the Tayside Sabbath.

But, broadly speaking, by the beginning of the twentieth century the job within the British Isles was considered to be complete. In the course of the post-Napoleonic nineteenth century, however, the United Kingdom's naval power had succeeded in amassing and consolidating under one form or another of British rule a vast overseas empire. Inevitably the eyes of the General Register Office turned to such places as the Caribbean and British India. Shortly before he joined the Register Office, as a young man in 1837 William Farr had after all helped John Ramsey McCulloch to compile his independent 'A Statistical Account of the British Empire'.

The problems facing any Victorian assessor of the empire were manifold, but that empire was impossible to ignore. Imperial influence was evident even in the most far-flung corners of the British Isles. In 1857 an Edinburgh writer named Alexander Smith married into a landed family on the island of Skye, which had during his lifetime a population of just 20,000. In that small place he discovered more than a taste of the Orient. In the north of Skye Smith befriended a landowner named Lachlan MacDonald who had raised a small fortune in the Indian Raj. The result was an extraordinary cultural blend. MacDonald, wrote Smith, 'had spent the best part of his life in India, was more familiar with huts of ryots, topes of palms, tanks in which the indigo plant was steeping, than with the houses of Skye cotters and the processes of sheep-farming.

He knew the streets of Benares or Delhi better than he knew the streets of London; and, when he first came home, Hindostanee would occasionally jostle Gaelic on his tongue. The Landlord too, was rich, would have been considered a rich man even in the southern cities; he was owner of many a mile of moorland, and the tides of more than one far-winding Loch rose and rippled on shores that called him master.

In my friend the Landlord there was a sort of contrariety, a sort of mixture or blending of opposite elements which was not without its fascination. He was in some respects a resident in two worlds. He liked motion; he had a magnificent scorn of distance: to him the world seemed comparatively small; and he would start from Skye to India with as much composure as other men would take the night train to London. He paid taxes in India and he paid taxes in Skye.

His name was as powerful in the markets of Calcutta as it was at the Muir of Ord. He read the Hurkaru and the Inverness Courier. . . . You made the overland route twenty times a day. Now you heard the bagpipe, now the monotonous beat of the tom-tom and the keen clash of silver cymbals. You were continually passing backwards and forwards, as I have said. You were in the West with your half-glass of bitters in the morning, you were in the East with the curry at dinner . . .

Contemporaneously, the owner of a further 35,000 acres of northern Skye was Sir John MacPherson MacLeod. He had been one of the first students to attend Haileybury College, a school established in Hertfordshire in 1806 by the East India Company specifically to train young men as 'writers', or administrators, in the Raj; his professor of political economy at Haileybury was John Rickman's old adversary, Thomas Malthus.

Following Haileybury, MacLeod went straight to Madras, and in 1832 he became commissioner for the government of Mysore. By the early 1850s, when he added almost all of the large estate of Glendale to his property portfolio, sixty-year-old MacLeod was living with a butler, a footman, a ladies' maid, a cook, a housemaid and his wife Catherine – an Edinburgh woman from an elevated social background – in an elegant town house in Stanhope Street, close to Hyde Park in west London. He was semi-detached from the East India Company and would soon retire from service. In recognition of his Highland background and interests he had been made an Inverness-shire magistrate and would shortly be raised to Deputy Lord Lieutenant of the county. He was knighted by Queen Victoria in 1866, and sworn into the Privy Council at Windsor Castle in 1871.

To compound the eastern flavour of the upper social circle of this small offshore island, the local sheriff, Peter Alexander Speirs, had been born in 1842 in Cawnpore in British India. He was sent back to Britain when he was five years old, which almost certainly saved his life. Young Speirs returned first to Stirling in Scotland, where he was raised and tutored at home by five maiden aunts – his father's sisters – before qualifying as an advocate and eventually becoming sheriff-substitute in Skye. If fifteen-year-old Peter Speirs had still been in Cawnpore in the summer of 1857 he would not have survived the year, let alone lived to marry a woman from Newcastle upon Tyne and be employed as sheriff-substitute in Portree. Cawnpore had been a bloodbath during the Indian Rebellion, which Speirs, MacLeod and MacDonald knew as the Indian Mutiny, of 1857. All but seven of 1200 British soldiers and civilians, including women and children, in Cawnpore were massacred by rebel sepoy troops and irregulars.

The empire was huge, globally scattered and constantly expanding – it would not reach its zenith until the 1920s, after which decade it was dismantled much more speedily than it had been assembled. In the middle of the nineteenth century, far from being efficiently administered, many of its component parts were unexplored and uncharted by Europeans. A simple headcount of the imperial population was a daunting challenge; a thorough census on the model of the British survey was clearly impossible. Was there any way to count those countless millions?

In 1861 Graham and Farr made a stab at it. As Graham wrote:

It is desirable on many grounds that the population of the Queen's dominions should be enumerated simulta-neously. And accordingly the Census of all the Australian Colonies was taken on the same day (April 8th) as the Census of England, and on the same plan ...

The population of nearly all the colonies and depend-encies was enumerated in 1861, except India ... The Government of India has always been too weak to procure an accurate enumeration of the population, notwithstand-ing the remarkable and partial success in taking the Census of certain provinces under able administrators.

The Registrar General then announced that in 1861 British 'European Possessions' such as Gibraltar, Malta, Heligoland (a cluster of islands 'against the mouth of the Elbe, with 1,913 inhabitants' which were British between 1814 and 1890) and the Greek Ionian Islands (British protectorates between 1815 and 1864) contained a total of 397,746 people. The North American colonies, which amounted mainly to Canada, had 3,333,507 inhabitants. There were 1,114,508 people in the British West Indies, just over a million in British Africa, 7426 in such South Atlantic islands as the Falklands and Saint Helena, 2,363,767 in the Indian Ocean and Hong Kong and 1,322,937 in Australia and New Zealand.

'The population we give of India must,' continued Graham, 'be considered as only a rough approximation, available for some purposes, until the results of an accurate enumeration are obtained by the present Government of India. The area of British India is 933,722 square miles, and the population 135,571,351 by estimate ... '

As a result of those calculations, in 1861 Graham felt himself able to announce that while the population of the home islands of the United Kingdom stood at a heartening but still modest 29,321,288 people, 'the area of the British Empire [is] 4,420,600 square miles, and the population 174,389,308'.

Ten years later, in 1871, Graham and Farr offered a more thorough assessment of an imperium which had apparently grown by around 40 per cent in the previous decade. They viewed it with some astonishment, writing:

It is not for us here to tell how this Empire subsists or has been built up. Yet the Census will show its essential parts in their relations to each other, constituted not only for continuance but for growth.

For it is growing, increasing, and multiplying still. And this development of the nation is the characteristic of its life. How a few shiploads of hardy adventurers from the other side of the North Sea, settling among and mingling with a scanty population of Celts and Gaels, multiplied, and became seven millions in the year 1600, sixteen millions in 1801, and thirty-two millions in 1871, is the problem, to the solution of which the series of facts in the Census must essentially contribute. For the evolution of such a nation is not the result of chance; and although it cannot be traced to the policy or the genius of one man it will be found to be the result of an elaborate and skilful organization acting under constant forces regulated by wiser, diviner laws than Plato gave his commonwealth.

Their report continued:

The Empire is divisible into three portions: (1) the United Kingdom; (2) colonies in the proper sense of the word – plantations – in congenial climates, where the English race can take root and multiply indefinitely until the unpeopled land is occupied, as in North America, the Cape, Australia, or New Zealand; and (3) Ceylon and India, which are inhabited largely by Aryan or Semitic stocks that have given abundant evidence of courage, culture, skill, and industry. The military and naval stations, the factories for commerce, as they were first called, and the fertile tropical islands and settlements of the West Indies and Central America, which have been cultivated by English planters, employing black and Creole labour, might be thrown into a class apart; but as it is difficult to draw the line, or to foresee their future, they may for the present be classed with the colonies ...

The Empire possesses 7,769,449 square miles of territory: the United Kingdom Area 121,608 square miles, the colonies 6,685,021, India and Ceylon 962,820 square miles.

There are 30 persons to a square mile in the Empire; 260 in the United Kingdom; 201 in India; 1.41 in the colonies.

While there are 14 acres to a household in the United Kingdom, and 17 acres in India, there are 2,534 acres to a household in the colonies.

The colonies differ to an indefinable extent in capacity as fields of labour and sources of produce. Thousands of miles of water, of intractable moors, of marshes, of ice-bound earth, of barren mountains, are intermingled with fat pastures and fertile soil, widely distributed, nearly equivalent in their expanse to a tract of 4,000 miles in length and nearly 2,000 miles in breadth.

England, the most highly cultivated centre of the Empire, has only three fourths of its area under crops of any kind, and can so deal with little more profitably. But after every reduction has been made for waste in the colonies, there will remain open to enterprise a vast extent of pasture and of arable land, besides inexhaustible stores of mineral wealth. The young plantations will one day be mighty forests, shedding their leaves and seeds over the ages to come.

The population of the Empire, nearly all enumerated, is 234,762,593, of whom 31,629,299 inhabit the United Kingdom, 9,420,937 inhabit the colonies, and 193,712,357 inhabit Ceylon and India.

The human unit differs as much as the unit of land; but it is always human. In the old language of statistics, the Queen's sceptre extends over two hundred and thirty-four million subjects; her Government has charge of two hundred and thirty-four million souls.

Following that lyrical appraisal the next two censuses, which were conducted by George Graham and Brydges Henniker, stepped back from the task of assessing the comparative population densities and unexploited resources of Canada, India and New South Wales. In the approach to the turn of the century, which had in the eyes of most of the world been a British century, the subject was open to re-examination. Reginald MacLeod's General Register Office was tasked by the Secretary of State for the Colonies, Joseph Chamberlain, to mark the occasion of the tenth national census in 1901 by compiling as a separate volume a complete Census of the British Empire.

The clerks, and MacLeod's successor William Dunbar, rose to the challenge. As if the project was not already difficult enough, it was hindered by the fact that between 1899 and 1902 the United Kingdom was at war in southern Africa with the white Afrikaans-speaking settlers of Transvaal and the Orange Free State. The 379 pages of the *Census of the British Empire, 1901* was not delivered until December 1905.

It was a remarkable document: a sketch of the British Empire in its pomp, when it encompassed about a fifth of the surface of the earth. The Register Office conceded:

it was found impracticable, owing to the varying conditions of life in different parts of the Empire, and to the want of uniformity in the methods of construction and tabulation of the Colonial Censuses, to prepare a Report on the precise lines of the English Census Report ...

In some of our East Indian and in certain of our African Possessions, as well as in a few of the West Indian Islands, the Authorities were, for financial or other reasons, unable to take a complete Census. The best available estimates of such populations have, however, been inserted in the Tables, but these populations amounted to less than one-tenth part of the total for the British Empire, which numbered in the aggregate nearly 400 millions ...

Those 400 million subjects of the Queen-Empress Victoria were unevenly scattered. The British Empire was usually compared favourably with the Roman Empire, which at its zenith had also governed an estimated one-quarter of the population of the earth as it was known to the imperialists. During the millennial census of Caesar Augustus the Roman Empire was comprised of more than 2 million square miles and contained between 5 million and 12 million inhabitants, depending upon whether only Joseph and his fellow adult males had been counted, or if Mary and the baby Jesus were also included – something of which scholars are still uncertain. At its height the Roman Empire contained between 50 million and 60 million people of both genders. The 10 million square miles and 400 million inhabitants of Caesar's early twentieth-century British successor formed, by any measure, a larger imperium.

It was a comparison with which the British delighted to flatter themselves. When Thomas Thornycroft's bronze statue of Boudica, the Celtic queen who led a fierce revolt against Roman rule in the south of England in about AD 61, was erected on the Thames Embankment in 1902, the self-satisfied inscription chosen to be carved beneath Thornycroft's gloriously fantasised regal female chariot-eer was a quotation from an ode to the resistant queen by William Cowper which read 'Regions Caesar never knew, Thy posterity shall sway'.

But there were marked differences between the two empires. With the minor interruptions of such narrow straits of sea as the English Channel and the Dardanelles, the Roman Empire had been one contiguous land mass, from Clydeside to Africa and from Syria to Spain. The British Empire had been acquired more by sea power than land armies. As such its character, if not its vast expanse, had more in common with the scattered, frequently insular north Atlantic Norse empire of the ninth to thirteenth centuries and the Mediterranean Venetian empire of the second millennium AD.

In the words of Ferdinand Mount, 'The language of "imperialism" suggests a single driving force, to be compared with the force that fuelled the expansion of the Roman Empire. But the British version was created out of such a mixture of motives – the protection of trade, the migratory itch, strategic paranoia, unvarnished greed, missionary zeal, scientific inquiry, dishing the French (or the Russians) – and the forms it took were too hopelessly various to fit a single model.' At its peak the British Empire was therefore composed of a great many coaling stations, trading posts, strategic islands and ports which not only had no shared borders and no long straight roads between them; they were also unconnected by anything other than the facts that they flew the union flag above their administrative offices and were coloured red on British maps.

There were huge continental exceptions, such as the supposed 'white dominions' of Australasia and North America, large and growing swathes of Africa (an unusual increase in the imperial population between 1881 and 1891, noted the Registrar General matter-of-factly, was mainly due to the acquisition in that single decade 'of Nigeria, East Africa Protectorate, Uganda, British Central Africa, Rhodesia,

&c.') and the Indian subcontinent. They comprised the bulk of the land mass of the empire and, in the case of India, most of its population. But the unprecedented geographical reach of the British Empire from one corner of the earth to its polar opposite, from the 2263 people of the Falkland Islands to the 297,212 inhabitants of Hong Kong, were both a result and an expression of naval supremacy.

'The distribution, in 1901,' reported William Dunbar, 'of the population of the Empire in the several Continents was as follows: In Asia there were more than 300 millions, in Africa about 43 millions, in America 7½ millions, in Australasia more than 5 millions, in our Mediterranean Possessions nearly half a million, and in the Islands in the British Seas 150,000; while the remaining 41½ millions were enumerated within the limits of the United Kingdom.' Most of those properties continued to bloom, but some were less predictable – 'for the whole Empire the aggregate rate of increase of population showed a great decline in the last decennium; this was mainly due to the fall in the rate of increase of the population of the Indian Empire, in the Native States and Agencies of which there was an actual decrease of 5.5 per cent. The comparatively small increase in the Indian population between the Censuses of 1891 and 1901 was in great part due to famine and plague – these disasters, with their attendant mortality, having also adversely affected the birth-rate.'

By 1901 the 'white dominions' and India were following the mother country in its example of urbanisation. In 1901 over 71 per cent of the people of the United Kingdom lived in towns or cities, 'the proportion of urban dwellers in the three divisions of the Kingdom being 31 per cent, in Ireland, 70 per cent, in Scotland, and 77 per cent, in England and Wales'.

Throughout the entire empire, it was discovered, there were 187 cities or towns whose populations exceeded 50,000 persons. Eighty-seven of them were situated in the United Kingdom, seventy-eight were in India, seven in Australasia, five in Canada, two in the West Indies, two in the Straits Settlements, and one apiece in the Colonies of Hong Kong, Ceylon, Mauritius, Cape of Good Hope, Natal and the Transvaal.

Urbanisation, after the model of the Mother Country, was identified as evidence of progress. 'Excluding London,' noted the Registrar General with some pride, 'the most populous City in the British Empire at the present time is Calcutta, the population of which in 1710 was about ten or twelve thousand; thence it grew rapidly, and by the middle of the eighteenth century was estimated to have exceeded 100,000; by the year 1850 it was at least 400,000; the Census of 1872 showed a population of 633,000, which, after a slight fall in 1881, rose to 682,000 in 1891, and further rose to nearly 848,000 in 1901.

'The City of Bombay, which passed from Portuguese to English rule in 1661 by the Treaty on the occasion of the marriage between Charles II and the Infanta of Portugal, rapidly developed in the next fourteen years from a town of 10,000 to one of 60,000 inhabitants. In 1780 the population had risen to 100,000, in 1836 to 236,000, and in 1872 to 644,000, or more by 11,000 than that of Calcutta at the same date. In 1891 the population stood at 821,764; for the next five years the city doubtless continued to grow, but since then the plague, which first appeared in September, 1896, has struck a severe blow at its prosperity, the result being that, instead of a further increase being recorded at the last Census, the population had declined to 776,000.

'The growth of the two chief Cities of Australia has been remarkable. In 1841 the population of Sydney numbered about 30,000, and that of Melbourne was less than 5,000. In the space of 20 years the population of Sydney had increased to nearly 96,000, while that of Melbourne had shown even greater progress, the population in 1861 numbering nearly 140,000 – this remarkable advance being due to the discovery of gold in Victoria in the 'fifties.' At the Census of 1881, 225,000 persons were enumerated in Sydney, and 283,000 in Melbourne, and at the last Census (1901) the population in each City had increased to little short of half a million, the exact numbers enumerated being 487,932 in Sydney and 496,079 in Melbourne.'

Better yet, the expansion of the cities could be cited as evidence of the superiority of British over French governance. 'Montreal, the largest City in British North America,' noted Dunbar, 'was founded in the year 1642, and was transferred from the French to the British Government in 1760. The population in 1815 numbered about 15,000, since which year the growth of the City has been extraordinary; in 1851 the population had increased to over 57,000 . . . and at the last Census it had further risen to nearly 268,000. Of the population enumerated at the last Census, about 43 per cent were stated to be of French descent.'

As well as those cities, 'it will be found that the rate of increase in the last intercensal period exceeded 50 per cent in the following Towns, in which the population ranged from 25,000 to 78,000 at the date of the last Census, viz.: Cape Town, East London, Durban (white population only),

Vancouver, Winnipeg, Perth (Western Australia), Port of Spain, and Kuala Lumpur in the Malay States.'

In three colonies there was a striking gender imbalance in favour of men. Hong Kong was apparently 72.6 per cent male. The Federated Malay States were 72 per cent male, and the Straits Settlements of Penang, Malacca, Dinding, Christmas Island, the Cocos Islands and Singapore were two-thirds male. Those anomalies excited the curiosity of the Register Office clerks, who determined that:

For the Straits Settlements it is impossible, owing to the absence of complete Birth-place statistics, to determine precisely the effect of immigration on the sex proportions.

It may be seen, however, that it is solely among the alien races that the excess of males obtains; among the Malay and other native races of the Archipelago the proportions of each sex are practically equal, while among the other races, the proportion per cent of males is 66.9 among Europeans and Americans, 73.9 among Indians, and 77.8 among Chinese. The Chinese amount to almost half of the total population, and, excluding Christmas Island, comprise 219,204 males and only 62,729 females, of whom 21,639 males and 22,383 females were said to be 'Straits-born.' It follows, therefore, that in the Straits Settlements the disparity between the numbers of the two sexes is mainly due to the large volume of Chinese male immigrants.

Without going into great detail, it may be stated that in the Federated Malay States the high proportion of males (72.0 per cent) is due to the numbers of Chinese attracted thereto by the development of the tin-mining industry; while in Hong Kong the 72.6 per cent of males in the population consists principally of Chinese from the mainland.

Tin mining in the Federated Malay States occupied 157,000 men, or more than 32 per cent of the male population.

According to the bare statistics, the longest life expectancy in the empire was to be found in Ireland, where more than 6 per cent of the population was aged over sixty-five, and the shortest in Hong Kong, where less than 1 per cent of men were in that age group. Dunbar pointed out that those figures, too, owed as much to immigration and emigration as to good health:

> The effect of migration on the age constitution of a population is considerable.
>
> For example, the low proportion of children and the high proportion of old people enumerated in Ireland are mainly accounted for by excessive emigration. During the 50 years 1851–1901 no fewer than 3,846,393 Irish persons left the country with the intention of settling elsewhere; and in the decennium 1891–1900, the ages of 91 per cent of the emigrants were returned as between 10 and 45 years. On the other hand, the effect of immigration on the age constitution of a population is well illustrated in such Colonies as Hong Kong ... where the proportions of males aged 25-45 years were abnormally high, ranging from 32 to 46 per cent of the total male population.

The clerks took a deep collective breath before launching themselves into a survey of the occupations of the 400 million imperial subjects, 'as the number of distinct manufactures and industries in all civilised Countries has greatly increased, and moreover most of these manufactures and industries are continually tending towards greater subdivision. It is very doubtful whether completely satisfactory returns of Occupations can at any time be obtained except by means of specially qualified Enumerators who would personally ascertain the precise information required and enter the particulars on the Census Schedule.'

In the meantime, they did their best. They were able to suggest that India and Ceylon had more clerks per head of population than any other dominion or colony. England, Scotland and Wales had more lawyers, and Australia and New Zealand had more doctors, nurses and teachers, most members of the last two vocations being women.

The most agricultural countries were Ireland, India and the Cape and Orange River colonies in southern Africa. The Orange River Colony was the former Afrikaaner territory of the Orange Free State. The Boer War, which had been contested on and over its veldt and had delayed the Census of the British Empire, had only recently been decided in Britain's favour. The Afrikaaners promptly found that martial injury to be compounded by the insult of their inclusion in a British imperial survey, which declared, doubtless accurately, that over 40 per cent of the Orange River Colony's population made its living on the land. The same proportion of Indian and Irish people worked in agriculture, while Scotland, England and Wales were at the bottom of that table.

After the extraordinary numbers of tin miners in the Malay States, the highest proportion of miners in the empire were to be found in Scotland, where 6 per cent of men dug for coal. Scotland also had more metalworkers than anywhere else, as well as more builders, masons, navvies and roadworkers than anywhere in the empire except England and Wales.

Numbering the indigenous population of the empire, let alone describing its occupations, was, as the Registrar General conceded, all but impossible. While William Dunbar concluded by recommending that an imperial census should in future be taken every ten years, he admitted:

> The difficulties encountered in the preparation of this report and of the annexed tables have been neither few in number nor trivial in kind: and the task of surmounting them has been rendered more arduous by reason of the insufficiency of the clerical staff available for the extra duty required of them . . .
>
> . . . the present is the first serious attempt that has been made by this Department to prepare anything like a full and comparative resume of the results of the Census, as far as available, of the entire British Empire. We accordingly present this volume with considerable diffidence, whilst we venture to hope that, notwithstanding its many imperfections, it will at all events awaken renewed interest in Census Statistics, promote greater uniformity of action in the future, and create a fresh link of sympathy between the Census Authorities of the Mother Country and those of her Colonies and Dependencies.

There would never be another census of the British Empire. Other, larger concerns were soon to engage the British government, following which the empire itself rather quickly dissolved.

Dunbar and his assistants had arrived at the round figure of a total imperial population of 400 million chiefly by estimating that over 295 millions were either Natives of India or descendants of Indian Emigrants, 3½ millions were Natives of Ceylon, and a further 2½ millions were Natives of other East Indian possessions. Natives of the West African Colonies numbered nearly 29 millions; the South African Colonies contained over 5½ millions of Coloured persons, other African possessions over 7 millions, and our West Indian possessions, about 1½ millions. The Coloured population enumerated in the Dominion of Canada numbered over 167,000, in the Australian Commonwealth 120,000, and in Polynesia and British New Guinea about 500,000.

The 'Coloured' populations were not however entirely comprised of pre-imperial settled peoples. Natives of India in particular had transplanted themselves widely across the empire, from Africa to the Caribbean, where they found themselves listed as 'Coloured' beside Bantus and former slaves. The west coast of Canada contained 20,000 'Coloured' Chinese and Japanese immigrants.

The problems lay in the vast interiors of India, Australia, Africa and Canada, where some settled peoples had never seen a European, let alone a census enumerator, while others were at least partly nomadic and were therefore difficult to pin down. So it was relatively straightforward to announce that in Canada,

The majority of persons of Irish descent were enumerated in Ontario, no fewer than 624,332 residing there, while 114,842 were enumerated in Quebec and 83,384 in New Brunswick.

The number of persons of Scotch descent was greatest

in Ontario, 399,530 being there enumerated, while next in importance came Nova Scotia with 143,382, and Quebec with 60,068.

Of other persons of European origin, 1,649,371, or 30.7 per cent of the total population of the Dominion were returned as of French descent, the majority of these, viz: 1,322,115, being resident in Quebec.

But it was questionable to add that in Canada 'there were enumerated 34,473 Half-breeds [and] 93,459 Indians', when the authorities were as likely to have missed as many 'Red Indians' as they counted.

The same applied to Australia. 'In the Australian Commonwealth,' according to the imperial census, 'the aboriginal population numbered about 65,000 persons (including an estimate of 20,000 nomadic aborigines in Queensland). South Australia contained the largest number of aborigines – 27,123, or over 40 per cent being there enumerated; and next in order came Queensland, Western Australia, New South Wales and Victoria with 26,670, 6,212, 4,287 and 652 respectively.' How did they know?

Although it was safe to agree that Hinduism, with its 208,342,276 adherents, was comfortably the largest religion in the empire, the precise number of 8,910,826 who were 'Primitive Animistic, Pagan' (three times as many as there were declared Christians in India) was surely guesswork unless British administrators had spent a good deal of their time with pencils and sheets of paper in the forests surrounding the upper reaches of the Gambia and Niger rivers. As well as the more orthodox and recognisable confessions, the census acknowledged that within the British Empire smaller numbers of people, chiefly citizens of the United Kingdom itself, also identified themselves as Alexandrian, Altruist, Ambrosian, Antinomian, Assembly, Astronomical, Believer, Brotherhood, Calathumpian, Canopist, Cosmosophist, Eclectic, Ethicist, Faithist, Gentile, Hoke, Hylozoist, Idealist, Millennial Dawnite, Monotheist, Morrisonian, Mosaic, Pelagian, Re-Incarnationist, Separatist, Sung Quong, Thesian, Tipon, Universalist and Utopian.

And so the number crunching continued. The highest level of literacy in the empire was found in Australia and New Zealand, where around 78 per cent of the population could read and write, and the lowest among the 300 million people of India, only 5 per cent of whom were literate. Within India, none of the female animists who were surveyed could read or write. The unhealthiest colony by far was Gambia, where almost 1 per cent of the population was returned as blind, deaf and dumb, lunatic, imbecilic or leprous. There were however only eleven registered lepers among the country's small population. There were almost 100,000 in India.

The *Census of the British Empire* was published in the same year, 1905, that the Aliens Act passed through Parliament, and shortly after the arrival of Morris and Kate Aaronovitch in London. The imperial census showed conclusively that the United Kingdom was itself more an emigrant than an immigrant nation – there were far more natives of the British Isles who lived elsewhere in the empire than there were foreigners who lived in the British Isles.

Within England, Scotland and Wales 150,000 people, or less than 0.5 per cent of the population, had been born in overseas parts of the British Empire; 300,000, or 1 per cent, had been born in foreign, mainly other European, countries. In contrast, between them India, Canada, Australia and New Zealand alone were home in 1901 to almost 1.5 million people born in the British Isles. Even little Trinidad and Tobago had 1385 British-born immigrants. Those numbers excluded second- and third-generation immigrants, the children and grandchildren of British families born in the colonies but who mostly regarded themselves as native Britons. People of English or Scottish, Welsh or Irish descent, along with emigrants to British imperial possessions from other European nations, made up in 1901 the 50 million or so 'white' newcomers who lived among the 350 million 'Coloured' natives of the empire.

The comparison was hardly made, because to most British people in the first decade of the twentieth century it would have seemed absurd. The British, and to a lesser extent other Europeans, were not only entitled to relocate to their global acquisitions; according to the precepts of empire they had a duty to do so. They were required in Calcutta, Montreal and New South Wales as administrators, as keepers of the peace and guardians of the faith, and most of all as the bearers of the flame of western civilisation. The notion that the natives of Calcutta, or the Iroquoian tribes of Montreal, or the aboriginal Wiradjuri of New South Wales might have thought differently – might, indeed, have been entitled to their own versions of the British Brothers' League – was unworthy of consideration.

The Aaronovitches could, from that counter-perspective, have been regarded as positive replenishments of the families who had abandoned England for sunnier climates and broader pastures. The contributions of their own offspring, as well as of the offspring of Michael and Hannah Marks, to British society suggested that the United Kingdom got the better part of the exchange.

12

Great War

For four years between 4 August 1914 and 11 November 1918, the United Kingdom of Great Britain and Ireland was involved in a great intercontinental war with other imperial powers. By the time the Armistice was signed, everything had changed, at home as much as abroad.

The 1921 census of England and Wales was chiefly the work of Sylvanus Percival Vivian. A formidable organiser and a ruthless careerist, Vivian was a son of the metropolis and a product of the 400-year-old St Paul's private school in London and of Oxford University. Following a steady rise up the ranks of the civil service, 39-year-old Vivian was appointed deputy Registrar General at the end of 1919. He was briefed 'to examine the organisation of the department' and report directly to the government, bypassing his superior. Registrar General Bernard Mallett, who had succeeded William Dunbar in 1909, just in time to face the suffragettes' subversion of the 1911 census, was only to be kept 'informed of all proposals and developments'.

Mallett was infuriated by the insult and resigned in 1920.

Vivian stepped calmly into his shoes, serving as Registrar General for the following twenty-five years.

Vivian's first national census did not run smoothly. The 1921 census, like most of its predecessors, was scheduled to be taken in April. On the first day of that month the coal mining industry, which had been taken under government control during the Great War, was re-privatised. Coal owners instantly threatened wage cuts and the Triple Alliance of miners', transport workers' and railwaymen's unions seemed likely to call a strike which would paralyse the country and, as an incidental side effect, make census-taking all but impossible.

Vivian therefore postponed the census until 19 June, printing and distributing an amendment slip which gave notice of the delay. In order to subsidise the slip, he had the bright idea of selling advertising space on its blank side. He ill-advisedly sold the space to a weekly publication called the *Sunday Illustrated*, a short-lived creation of the rabble-rousing independent Member of Parliament Horatio Bottomley. Following a string of court appearances in 1921 and 1922 Bottomley was convicted of a series of frauds, sentenced to seven years' imprisonment and evicted from the House of Commons. Commercial advertising space was never again sold on census material.

While Horatio Bottomley languished first in Wormwood Scrubs and then in Maidstone prison, Sylvanus Vivian addressed the sombre task of assessing the material effect on the British Isles of the Great War. He would neglect the great 'social survey' nature of the Registrar General's census report to Parliament, which had found its fullest expression in the mid-nineteenth century era of Graham and Farr. From the turn of the twentieth century onwards the

General Register Office would content itself with presenting the statistics and would leave others to draw conclusions about the state of the nation.

But the occasion of Vivian's first census demanded some comment. He began his preliminary report in August 1921:

> The great events of the decennium thus concluded cannot fail to impress a character of uncommon significance upon the results of this Census, whether regarded as vestigial records of the passage of the War itself or as a source of enlightenment upon the many problems which the War has bequeathed to us.
>
> For such enlightenment, at the very time when it is most sorely needed, the country has been unusually at a loss, since there are but few questions today upon which guidance can be sought of the last Census across the great gulf of War which lies between. It is thus with a full sense of the heavy and responsible burden of service which this Census will be called upon to render that the operations now completed have been planned and carried out.

The first and most striking observation was that the loss of almost a million men between 1914 and 1918 had resulted in the smallest decennial increase in the populations of England, Scotland and Wales since the period between the first census of 1801 and the second of 1811. 'Proportionately,' wrote Vivian, '[the increase] is far lower than any hitherto recorded.'

At every census since 1841 the population of Great Britain, excluding Ireland, had risen by more than 2 million. Between 1901 and 1911 it rose by 3,780,000, or 11 per cent; between 1911 and 1921 it rose by 1,937,500, or 5 per cent. In Scotland the rate of increase was just 2.5 per cent. Only two towns in the entire country recorded population increases of more than 50 per cent between 1911 and 1921. They were Blackpool and Southend on Sea, which at the time of the delayed enumeration on 19 June were swollen by their summer holiday crowds. To a lesser extent, the same artificial seasonal increase was reported from Ayrshire and the island of Bute in Scotland.

Killing large numbers of people was not the only means by which war slowed down the rate of population increase. In wartime the birth rate diminished. That was partly due to the absence of men serving overseas and partly to the uncertainty people felt about bringing infants into a world at war. In the pre-war years of 1901 to 1910 about 930,000 babies were born each year in England and Wales. The number 'thereafter diminished at a much greater pace to 1918, when a minimum of between 662,000 and 663,000 [births per annum] was registered'. While births fell, deaths rose inexorably – 'the peace-time average of 507,000 registered in 1911–13 rose to between 600,000 and 700,000 in each of the years 1915–17, and probably reached 750,000 in 1918 owing to the further imposition of the severe influenza mortality experienced towards the end of that year'.

Rural areas suffered disproportionately. In England and Wales the highest losses were experienced in agricultural East Sussex; the lowest occurred in County Durham, where a majority of men were engaged in the essential, reserved heavy industries of coal mining, iron and steel manufacture and shipbuilding.

One big rural region of the kingdom reported a persistent, increasing decline which had been appallingly exaggerated by the losses of the Great War. Due chiefly to the disproportionately large numbers of their young men in the army and navy reserve, communities in the north of Scotland suffered up to three times more casualties per head of population than the rest of Britain.

The results of that carnage were diligently relayed to the Scottish Secretary of State by the Registrar General in Edinburgh, Dr James Craufurd Dunlop. In the Gaidhealtachd of the north-west, reported Dunlop, which had suffered steady decline through forced and voluntary emigration since 1841, the picture was bleak:

In 1911 the population of the County of Inverness was ascertained to be 87,272; it is now found to be 82,446, of whom 39,490 are males and 42,956 are females.

The total population shows a decrease of 4,826 or 5.5 per cent, the male population one of 2,950, and the female population one of 1,876. The burghal population of the county is found to have fallen from 25,389 to 24,052, a decrease of 1,337 or 5.3 per cent, and the extraburghal portion of the population is found to have fallen from 61,883 to 58,394, a decrease of 3,489 or 5.6 per cent.

The Burgh of Inverness is found to have a population of 20,937 which is 1,279 or 6.8 per cent less than in 1911 . . .

Of the eight county districts all, Badenoch excepted, show decreases of population, the largest decreases being 12.9 per cent in Skye District, 12.3 per cent in North Uist District, and 11.1 per cent in Inverness District . . . those showing the larger decreases are Ardersier, Inverness and Bona, Duirinish, North Uist, and South Uist. The insular parishes of the county are found to have a total population of 27,919, which figure shows a loss of population of 2,925 or 9.5 per cent. All the parishes in the insular portion, with the exception of Small Isles, individually show a loss of population.

The population of the neighbouring county of Ross and Cromarty 'is found to be 70,790, which is 6,574 or 8.5 per cent less than in 1911. The male population numbers 33,668, and the female 37,122, the former showing a decrease of 5,095, and, the latter one of 1,479.' Essentially, the population of almost all of north and west Scotland had fallen by between 10 and 40 per cent.

Those results, reported Dr Dunlop, had profound cultural implications:

The total number in Scotland of . . . those able to speak Gaelic but not English, amounts to 10,314, and the total number of . . . those able to speak both Gaelic and English, 151,159. Compared with the numbers at the time of the previous Census, those speaking Gaelic only are 8,086 fewer, and those speaking Gaelic as well as English 32,839 fewer . . . The number of persons speaking Gaelic and English in 1891 was 210,677; in 1901 it had fallen to 202,700; in 1911 to 183,998, and it is now 151,159. In 1891 6.3 per cent of the total population of Scotland were able to talk Gaelic, the corresponding figure is now 3.3 per cent.

The post-Great War statistical returns also reflected the beginning of an east–west divide in Scotland. In common with its English equivalent, the north–south divide, it was a twentieth-century phenomenon which was ignored or denied until it was too firmly established to be removed. It applied from one end of the country to the other. Glasgow, the only major city in the west of Scotland, lost two-thirds of its population in the seventy years before 2011. It fell from being three times bigger than Edinburgh to almost the same size as the capital, but measurably poorer. A study by think tank Demos in the twenty-first century reported that families in the western city of Glasgow had the highest prevalence of 'multiple disadvantage' in Scotland, while families in the eastern cities of Edinburgh, Aberdeen and Inverness had the lowest. The north-eastern islands of Shetland were among the most affluent communities in Britain, while the Western Isles were among the poorest. The populations of Galloway and Ayrshire in the south-west fell during the later twentieth century, while those of their eastern equivalents, Perthshire and East Lothian, rose by a third.

Despite a decline in its oil industry, Aberdeen, on the far eastern coast of Scotland, was by 2011 by a couple of measures the wealthiest place in the United Kingdom. In the twenty-first century the city contained more million-aires than anywhere in the UK outside London. It also had more multi-millionaires (that is, people worth £20 million or more) per head of population than any other city in Britain. Aberdeen had proportionately more super-rich citizens than London or Cheltenham, and a lot more than Edinburgh.

The population of Aberdeen had grown by a third in the past 100 years and was still rising. The average age of men and women in Aberdeen was below the Scottish average, which means the number of young families was above the national average. Aberdeen stands at latitude 57° north. Following that line westwards a crow would arrive first in the fields, towns and villages of rural Aberdeenshire. Over the next quarter-century from 2011, if trends continued as before, that thriving region was predicted by the Scottish General Register Office to have a net population increase of 25 per cent, the third largest projected rural growth in Scotland. It would be bettered only by East Lothian and Perthshire, further south on the east coast, whose rural populations were predicted to rise by a third before 2035.

Over 60 per cent of the increased population of Aberdeenshire, Perthshire and East Lothian, according to the Edinburgh census statisticians, would be immigrants from the rest of the UK, and most of those immigrants would come from elsewhere in Scotland. Further along the 57th parallel in Aviemore, heavy investment in tourism had led to a slight population increase before 2011. Aviemore was a watershed, in the central, marginal lands. Loch Ness-side had been stabilised by its proximity to the growing east coast city of Inverness.

After Loch Ness the line of latitude passes through Kinloch Hourn, which early in the twentieth century was a busy fishing village and in 2011 was deserted. The line skims the shores of Arnisdale, once the home of 600 people but with just thirty year-round residents in 2011. The crow flies over Canna, which supported sixty people in the 1930s but whose population in 2011 was in single figures and was set fair to become the next evacuated Hebridean island. That hooded, northern crow arrives finally at its most westerly destination: the island of South Uist, the ninth biggest of 100 populated Hebridean islands. But in the same few decades that the population of Aberdeen had increased by 33 per cent, that of South Uist had halved from 3500 to 1800. In the same period that the number of people in rural

Aberdeenshire was predicted to grow by 25 per cent, the number in South Uist was predicted to fall by between 18 and 25 per cent.

South Uist has the lowest average household income of any sizeable Scottish island, and no recorded multi-millionaires. The average age of an inhabitant of South Uist was well above the Scottish median age of thirty-seven for men and thirty-nine for women. Many if not most of the island's young people had left. By the time they reached the Scottish median age they were living in places like Inverness, Aberdeen, Perthshire and Edinburgh.

Then again, there was Ireland, most of which by June 1921 was lost forever to the United Kingdom. The Irish census of 1911 had reported that, far from recovering from the post-famine total of 5,764,543 which had so agitated Commissioner William Donnelly in Dublin Castle in 1861, the population of the island had continued to collapse to 4,381,951 – half the number counted in 1841 and probably the lowest population in 200 years. While the rest of the British Isles had largely thrived in the Edwardian late summer sun, Ireland had watched itself disappear. The population of England, Scotland and Wales rose by 11 per cent in the decade between 1901 and 1911; that of the westerly Irish province of Connaught fell by almost 6 per cent. The number of people in Connaught had therefore fallen from 1,421,000 in 1841 to 610,000 in 1911, the number of speakers of Irish Gaeilge from 1,524,205 in 1851 to 582,446 in 1911.

Unlike the outraged William Donnelly fifty years earlier, the commissioners in Dublin in 1911 had given up trying to explain, and probably also trying to understand the malaise. They simply rehearsed the numbing statistics.

The number of people emigrating from Ireland in the ten years before March 1911 was 345,169, fully 8 per cent of the early twentieth-century population. It also meant that since 1851 a total of 4,191,552 Irish men and women – the rough equivalent of the entire residual population in 1911 – had been recorded as boarding emigrant ships.

More than half of all Irish jobs were still in agriculture, but the number of people working on the land had collapsed by 9 per cent between 1901 and 1911. Roughly half of all adults over the age of twenty were unmarried, which suggested not so much a lack of morals as an absence of hope. The only age group which was increasing in number was those over fifty-five, many of whom, the census commissioners uncharitably opined, had suddenly remembered their actual dates of birth upon the introduction of the old age pension in 1908.

Ireland did not need a Great War to reduce its population and lower its national spirit. It had got one anyway. More than 200,000 Irishmen volunteered to fight for the United Kingdom between 1914 and 1918 and 30,000 of them were killed. Even the most sceptical and reserved of Irish patriots recognised that his compatriots had no dog in that race. 'I know that I shall meet my fate,' wrote the Anglo-Irish Protestant William Butler Yeats of an Irish Great War airman,

> *Somewhere among the clouds above;*
> *Those that I fight I do not hate,*
> *Those that I guard I do not love;*
> *My country is Kiltartan Cross,*
> *My countrymen Kiltartan's poor,*
> *No likely end could bring them loss*
> *Or leave them happier than before.*

In 1911 a young man named Francis Edward Ledwidge was counted by the Royal Irish Constabulary, who still took the census in almost all of rural Ireland, in the settlement of Slane in County Meath, where he lived in poverty with his elderly mother, his older sister and his younger brother. Their father Patrick had died when Francis was five years old. Francis left the local national school at the youngest possible age, when he was thirteen, to take whatever work he could find on the farms, roads and in a nearby copper mine. It was far from an easy task. Slane was a typically depressed community whose population fell from 3433 to 2858 in the first twenty years of Francis Ledwidge's life. Ledwidge nonetheless continued to take whatever paid employment he could find, became involved in trade union activity (which cost him his job in the copper mine) and nationalist politics, and educated himself to the extent that he was able to publish a book of poems, *Songs of the Fields*, while still in his twenties.

Ledwidge became a member of the nationalist Irish Volunteers. In that group he met and befriended Thomas MacDonagh, a teacher and poet. MacDonagh in his turn was a good friend of Patrick Pearse, at whose Dublin school he taught before becoming a lecturer in English at the city's University College.

At the outbreak of the Great War Ledwidge overcame his considerable doubts and enlisted in the Royal Inniskilling Fusiliers, seeing action in the Dardanelles and in Serbia. 'I joined the British Army,' he would tell such colleagues in the Irish Volunteers as MacDonagh, 'because she stood between Ireland and an enemy of civilisation and I would not have her say that she defended us while we did nothing but pass resolutions.'

In April 1916 Ledwidge was home on leave. Easter Monday fell that year on 24 April. On the same day a coalition of Irish republicans, including members of the Irish Volunteers, attacked and occupied important buildings in Dublin and elsewhere, including the post office and the barracks of the Royal Irish Constabulary at Ashbourne, just to the south of Ledwidge's home village of Slane. In Dublin the rebels proclaimed the provisional government of an independent Irish Republic. They held out at the city's general post office for six days before unconditionally surrendering to the British Army 'In order to prevent the further slaughter of Dublin citizens, and in the hope of saving the lives of our followers now surrounded and hopelessly outnumbered . . . '

Notwithstanding their surrender, following courts-martial fifteen men were executed by firing squad at Dublin's Kilmainham Gaol between 3 and 12 May 1916. One of the first to be killed was Thomas MacDonagh, the friend and mentor of Francis Ledwidge. MacDonagh's death would be memorialised by W.B. Yeats:

> *I write it out in a verse –*
> *MacDonagh and MacBride*
> *And Connolly and Pearse*
> *Now and in time to be,*
> *Wherever green is worn,*
> *Are changed, changed utterly:*
> *A terrible beauty is born.*

The response of his protégé Francis Ledwidge would illustrate how much things had 'changed, changed utterly'.

Ledwidge, who had played no part in the Easter Rising,

was devastated. He went on a bender, overstayed his leave from the Royal Inniskilling Fusiliers and finally reported back drunk, for which he lost his corporal's stripes. He could hardly have cared less. 'If someone were to tell me now,' he wrote later in 1916, 'that the Germans were coming in over our back wall, I wouldn't lift a finger to stop them. They could come!'

He returned to the front, preoccupied by death. 'For mine,' he would write of the martyrs of 1916, 'are all the dead men's dreams.' Death arrived. On the last day of July 1917, during the Third Battle of Ypres, Ledwidge and some of his comrades in the Royal Inniskilling Fusiliers were hit by fragments of a German shell. The Catholic chaplain who arrived on the scene noted 'Ledwidge killed, blown to bits'. He was twenty-nine years old.

Francis Ledwidge was therefore not alive to see his Irish Volunteers merge into the Irish Republican Army, or to experience the guerrilla war for independence which was halted only by a truce in July 1921, or the Anglo-Irish Treaty which later that year conceded dominion status to the southern and western provinces of Ireland while leaving six of its former nine counties in the north-eastern province of Ulster within the United Kingdom.

Even if he had survived, Ledwidge would not have been enumerated in the 1921 census of the British Isles. It was not conducted in Ireland because the island was convulsed first by that guerrilla war and then by civil war, before the eventual ratification of an Irish Free State.

Even without the Irish wars, the 1921 census was a delicate subject. Until then, every survey since 1801 had been enabled by its own separate Act of Parliament, passed in the previous year. In 1920 it was agreed that the census had become so thoroughly accepted by the British public that it could confidently be legislated for every future decade, or if the government wished, every five years, in perpetuity.

That was a significant measure. The government was anxious that it should not be derailed at the outset by events in Ireland or anywhere else. They were warned. In August 1920 the Member for Kingston upon Hull, Joseph Kenworthy, a Liberal anti-imperialist who later joined the Labour Party, told the House of Commons:

If things go on as they are in Ireland the census will be a farce, because the great aim of about three-fourths of the people of Ireland to-day is to defy this Government in every possible way they can, and the greatest delight of every Irishman to-day is to say he has done something the Government does not want him to do or has not done something the Government want him to do.

This census, if it is taken next year in Ireland, will give a Heaven-sent chance to all these people at no large risk to themselves, because you cannot prosecute 500,000 or 600,000 people who refuse to fill up the forms, and the thing will be a farce. In fact the White Paper that hon. Members have says the reason why the cost of taking the census has gone up from £19,000 to £90,000 is that in past years the members of the Royal Irish Constabulary and the Dublin Metropolitan Police were appointed as enumerators, and they did not get any special remuneration. It was part of their duty to enumerate the people. Now apparently it is anticipated that special enumerators will have to be appointed and will have to be paid for their services. If you cannot even use the police to go round and collect the forms in the morning which have been filled up on the night appointed by Parliament, what is the good of proceeding with the thing at all?

The whole thing will be a farce if things in Ireland next year are as they are now. If, on the other hand, the Irish, as we all say we hope, have got some broad measure of self-government, it is their business to take the census of their people, and this is just the sort of domestic legislation that ought to be left to the Irish Parliament or Constituent Assembly, or whatever you have.

Kenworthy continued presciently, 'I want to make a prophecy. The hon and learned Gentleman has told us that he thinks the census will be taken. I say that it will not be taken by this Government at all, but will be taken as a matter of propaganda and as a way of showing their authority by the Sinn Fein Government. If Sinn Fein can hold courts in spite of the efforts of the police and military to suppress them, and can keep order on racecourses and stop illicit stilling, it will take a census. Sinn Feiners will do it as a matter of pride, and they will pay for it.'

As late as February 1921 the Lord Privy Seal, Andrew Bonar Law, was still asserting that the British census would be taken in Ireland that year. But just two months later, in April, the Attorney General and MP for Londonderry South, Denis Henry, told the House of Commons that he had 'received a report from the Census Commissioners in Ireland recommending that in view of the disturbed state of the country and of the impossibility of procuring accurately the necessary information the taking of the Census in Ireland should be postponed'.

It was not so much postponed as cancelled. Thereafter, as Kenworthy had suggested, the Irish Free State held its own census in 1926 and in the middle of every succeeding decade. Ireland had been included in ten British censuses between 1821 and 1911. From 1921 onwards, for reasons fully anticipated in its own surveys and reports, the United Kingdom census would cover only England, Scotland, Wales and Northern Ireland. Within a further hundred years it would find itself in danger of being abandoned by at least another one of those nations.

13

The Fractured Kingdom

Back in the rest of the diminished kingdom, Sylvanus Percival Vivian continued to examine 'the many problems which the War has bequeathed to us'. In 1921 there were almost 2 million more females than males in England and Wales than there had been in 1911. That was not entirely due to the number of young men who lay dead in Flanders. Thanks to 'the members of the fighting forces and mercantile marine temporarily abroad and also the numbers of fishermen absent at sea on the night of the census' there had been more women and girls than men and boys recorded in every census since 1801.

But the discrepancy had never been so great. 'Of the 37,886,699 persons enumerated in England and Wales in 1921,' reported Vivian, '18,075,239 were males and 19,811,460 were females, giving an excess of females of 1,736,221 ... the greatest changes of all are those shown for the age groups between 20 and 45 in 1921, the years covering the ages of the majority of those who fell in the war.'

The number of British men in that active and reproductive age group had fallen from 6,671,000 in 1911 to 6,566,000 in 1921. Simultaneously, the number of their female contemporaries had increased from 7,307,000 to 7,693,000. A traditional small excess of women between twenty and forty-five years of age, which had been decreasing before 1911, rose from 636,000 in that year to 1,127,000 ten years later.

By the time of the 1921 census there had been three years of peace and a baby boom which allowed the population to begin to recover. In 1920, for instance, a record number of 957,782 births was recorded in England and Wales. (That inexplicable natural correction which appears to manifest in such circumstances meant that, unusually, more of the post-war newborns were male than female.) The annual figures tell the wartime story more vividly. In 1914 there were almost 18 million men and boys in England and Wales. In 1918, the last year of the war, there were 14,433,000. The missing 3.5 million were in uniform or dead.

In 1921 there were 1,621,758 widows in England and Wales. There were 730,845 children without a father and 55,245 orphans. 'The most striking feature of these proportions,' commented Vivian, 'is the large excess of fatherless as compared with motherless children, the former outnumbering the latter in a ratio of nearly 3 to 1. Male mortality is markedly higher than the corresponding female mortality at all adult ages, and to this, aggravated in general by the higher average age of the fathers and in respect of this particular experience by the loss of men during the war, part of the excess must be due.'

Then there were the crippled survivors. As a boy in the North Riding of Yorkshire in the 1920s, John Rouse 'saw something that I never understood until later in life. Groups of men congregated on street corners to chat or watch the world go by. Many of these had a leg, an arm or part of a limb missing. They seemed to be everywhere. Some would shuffle along like a child playing trains. Others would stand on the kerb singing, or selling boxes of matches to earn a few pennies. The Great War lived on in these men, scarred for life.'

Even three years after the Armistice, 'the number of persons under treatment in hospitals has grown from nearly 59,000 in 1911 to 80,020 in 1921, more than three-quarters of the increase being in respect of males and presumably due, therefore, to a great extent, to injuries received during the war', reported the Registrar General. More than 41,000 British men had limbs amputated during the war; 272,000 suffered serious injuries in the legs or arms that did not require amputation; 60,500 were wounded in the head or eyes; and 89,000 sustained other serious damage to their bodies. Two decades later in 1939, as a second great war was about to be declared, 639,000 British ex-servicemen and officers were still drawing disability pensions from the 1914–18 war.

The figures included 65,000 men whose disabilities were not physical but mental. 'My mother ran a boarding house,' remembered Daisy Woods of Buckinghamshire, 'and we had two men who lived there all the time. Both of these men had fought in the trenches and one of them, who I remember was called "Chalky", suffered from shell shock. Sometimes, when the hot water pipes banged and rattled in the early morning he would run round the house with no clothes on shouting "The Germans are coming, the Germans are coming." My mother had to calm him down and take him back to his room. He used to cry a lot. I'll never forget Chalky.'

'My father had returned to Scotland after the war,'

recalled Helen Price of Edinburgh, 'following a stay of 2½ years in hospital in Kenilworth suffering from "gastritis". This was likely to have been a cover for the real reason that he was there – he was almost certainly suffering from shell shock. Many men suffered from this during and after the war and the condition was eventually recognised as a genuine illness. This came too late for many of the men and boys who had been shot as deserters as they fled the Front in dazed confusion after seeing friends blown apart before their eyes.

'Men fought in the war on behalf of "a land fit for heroes". They returned as heroes but as the '20s progressed many of these heroes found themselves with no work. They were reduced to begging on the streets with little or no help from the government that had sent them off to war on its behalf. My father had survived, partly due to the decision that he made in 1915. He was asked to go for officer training. My mother begged him not to accept and he decided against becoming an officer. This decision was based largely on the fact that officers "led from the front" in those days, leading to an average life expectancy for an officer at the Front of two weeks.'

The father of Nellie Lucas in Birmingham was not discharged until 1921. 'I didn't really know him because he'd been away so long. I was born in 1912 so I'd only seen him when he came home on leave. The First World War finished in 1918 but dad was still out in France for another three years. I was too young to understand at the time, but later I found out that he'd been kept out there on "jankers".

'Dad was in the gunnery regiment and he looked after the horses that pulled the gun carriages. One night, in 1917, he was on duty guarding the horses when one of his pals asked him to come for a drink. Dad couldn't resist it and went off for an hour or so. When he returned to the stables, he found that one of the horses had got its trace caught around its neck and had hung itself. Horses were considered more valuable than the men at that time – men were easier to replace – and so having a horse kill itself whilst the person guarding it was away, was a serious offence. Dad was court marshalled [sic] and sentenced to work on grave duty. He spent the years after the war digging up the dead bodies of soldiers (from both sides) and reburying them in proper war graves.'

The hundreds of thousands, effectively an entire male generation, who did not return left behind them a physically and psychologically fractured nation. It was, even as their deaths were counted and mourned and as 100,000 war memorials bearing their names were erected in towns and villages throughout the kingdom, a much smaller country. The loss of most of Ireland from the United Kingdom of Great Britain and Ireland reduced the nation's land mass by 25 per cent and its population by 9 per cent, from 45 million to 41 million.

Only the empire continued to grow, due in part to the post-war British annexation of many of Germany's overseas colonies. Despite the departure of Ireland, in 1921 the British Empire contained a quarter of the world's population (458 million people) living on a quarter of the earth's surface (14.2 million square miles). That would be its peak.

As if anointed to carry their fallen comrades' memories into a further century, some of the surviving veterans would prove very hard to kill.

Henry Allingham was born in Clapton in 1896. Following

the premature death of his mother, a widowed laundress, in 1915 nineteen-year-old Allingham enlisted with the Royal Naval Air Service. He subsequently fought at the Battle of Jutland and on the Western Front, where he was shot in the arm. 'The stench of death is sweet,' he said. 'It stays with you always.' Following his demobilisation in 1919 Allingham worked as an engineer in the car industry.

He retired in 1960. Forty years later, in 2001, he was identified at the age of 105 as one of the very few surviving British veterans of the Great War. In 2007 he became the oldest living veteran. Allingham accepted the burden gracefully, although he had tried to forget. 'I dare not think about things too much because I would not be able to control myself. I take a deep breath.' In December 2005 he became the oldest man in Britain, and in November 2006 the oldest man in Europe; in March 2008 he became the oldest British man ever recorded. On 19 June 2009, aged 113 years and 13 days, Allingham became the oldest man in the world. At a civic reception in his adopted town of Eastbourne he attributed his longevity to 'Cigarettes, whisky and wild, wild women – and a good sense of humour.' Henry Allingham died on 18 July 2009 at the age of 113 years and 42 days, ninety-four years after he first saw service in the Great War.

Harry Patch was born into a stonemason's family in the Somerset village of Combe Down in 1898. At the age of eighteen in 1916 he became a private in the Duke of Cornwall's Light Infantry. Injured at the Battle of Passchendaele in September 1917, he was invalided home and was still convalescing in the Isle of Wight when the Armistice was signed in November 1918. He spent his subsequent working life as a plumber in the West Country and refused to talk about the Great War until he reached 100 years of age in 1998. Nine years later in 2007 Patch revisited Flanders and repeated his conviction that 'war isn't worth one life'.

When Henry Allingham died on 18 July 2009, Harry Patch became the oldest man in Europe. He held the position for one week. 'The last fighting Tommy' died at Wells in Somerset seven days later at the age of 111 years and 38 days.

Florence Patterson was born at Edmonton in London in February 1901. In September 1918, when she was seventeen years old, she joined the Women's Royal Air Force. Florence did not serve overseas, but when she died in February 2012 at the age of 110 years and 351 days, she was the last surviving veteran of the Great War from any combatant nation.

The longest-living person to be enumerated in the national census was already thirty-seven years old when war broke out in 1914. Charlotte Milburn worked as a teacher in her native Middlesbrough throughout the Great War and beyond. She retired in 1940 and then married Noel Hughes. Noel predeceased his older wife, dying at the age of eighty-eight in 1979. Charlotte Hughes, who unlike Henry Allingham attributed her longevity to 'a good honest life and adherence to the Ten Commandments', celebrated her 108th birthday at 10 Downing Street, where she told prime minister Margaret Thatcher, 'Don't cuddle me, I'm Labour.' She marked her 110th birthday by flying to New York on Concorde. She followed her husband to the grave in 1993 at the age of 115 years and 228 days; she was then the second oldest person in the world, and the oldest Briton of either gender ever to be recorded.

Centenarians, and to a lesser extent nonagenarians, attracted enduring attention. Not only did they defy the edict of Psalm 90 that 'The days of our years are threescore years and ten', they were also living history. They occasionally offered a form of time travel. Maurice Bowra, the warden of Oxford University's Wadham College between 1938 and 1970 – and himself an infant in China during the Boxer Rebellion of 1900 – would write in his memoirs of older members of Wadham whom he had met in the early 1920s. 'The most astonishing was Frederick Harrison,' recalled Bowra in the 1960s. 'He was ninety-two, and his first question to me was, "When did you come up to Oxford?"

I told him, 'In 1919', and he answered, 'I came up in 1848'. So indeed he had. What is more, he had toured parts of Europe in that year of revolutions and had vivid memories of Paris after the fall of Louis Philippe. He remembered the accession of Queen Victoria when he was seven years old ... Incidentally he provided a link with a still remoter past by a neat chain of circumstances. He had as an undergraduate met [Martin] Routh, President of Magdalen [College], who died in his hundredth year soon afterwards. Routh had in his boyhood met an old lady, who had in her girlhood seen Charles II exercising his spaniels in Magdalen Grove.

In similar vein, in 2015 the historian Adam Smythe would write in the *London Review of Books*:

A friend who teaches in New York told me that the historian Peter Lake told him that J.G.A. Pocock told him that Conrad Russell told him that Bertrand Russell told him that Lord John Russell told him that his father the sixth

Duke of Bedford told him that he had heard William Pitt the Younger speak in Parliament during the Napoleonic Wars, and that Pitt had this curious way of talking, a particular mannerism that the sixth Duke of Bedford had imitated to Lord John Russell who imitated it to Bertrand Russell who imitated it to Conrad Russell who imitated it to J.G.A. Pocock, who could not imitate it to Peter Lake and so my friend never heard it. But all the way down to Pocock was a chain of people who in some sense had actually heard William Pitt the Younger's voice.

In 1821 John Rickman discovered that the highest proportion of centenarians in the kingdom were to be found in the two Scottish Highland counties of Ross and Cromarty and Inverness. Between them those two districts contained almost the whole of the north of Scotland apart from the islands of Orkney and Shetland and the counties of Sutherland and Caithness. They stretched from the Black Isle, the Moray Firth and the towns of Dingwall and Inverness in the north-east to the Outer Hebrides in the far north-west. Apart from collecting seaweed to reduce by fire into alginate, they had almost no industry.

Ross and Cromarty had in 1821 a population of 68,000, of whom 0.045 per cent, or thirty people, claimed to be over 100 years old and 115 people said they were between ninety and ninety-nine years old. Inverness-shire had a population of 92,000, which also included thirty centenarians as well as 110 nonagenarians. The sixty Highlanders born in or before 1721 would have been at least twenty-four years old at the beginning of Charles Edward Stuart's last and most dramatic Jacobite rising, and twenty-five years old when it was crushed at the Battle of Culloden outside Inverness.

In England the highest numbers of people over ninety years old were to be found in the rural hamlets of Herefordshire, Worcestershire and Warwickshire. Those three counties, with their combined population of almost 500,000, contained in the spring of 1821 about eighty people born before 1721 and 200 born before 1731. The one person that John Rickman discovered in 1821 to be over 100 years old in Derbyshire, a man living in the textile town of Wirksworth, would have been an adult when Charles Edward Stuart's army of Highlanders passed by at the end of 1745, on its way to overthrow the Hanoverians in London. He would have been a few weeks older when the army passed by again, this time returning north to its fate at Culloden.

In sharp contrast the county of Middlesex, with London, had a population of 1,167,500. That million included only fifty-five people over the age of 100 – fewer centenarians than in Ross and Cromarty and Inverness-shire, which combined had just one-seventh of its population – and 500 people over the age of ninety. A survey taken of the 'stinking, smoke-laden slum' of Bradford in the twenty-four years between 1841 and 1865, when the average Bradfordian life expectancy at birth was eighteen, revealed among the mills only two centenarians in more than 100,000 citizens, one of whom worked as a weaver in the rural outskirts of Shipley.

In 1821 less than 5 per cent of the population of Middlesex was over sixty years old, compared to between 8 and 10 per cent in the more bucolic English shires and the Scottish Highlands and Islands. London was already a young person's town. The industrial north was already no country for old men or women. The Highlands and the shires were already places in which to spend one's sunset years.

And so, for a while, was Ireland. The 1821 census in Ireland caught a 25-year-old stonemason and travelling Gaelic poet from Connemara named Colm de Bhailís. De Bhailís's verse would become popular throughout nineteenth-century Ireland without making him much money. At the age of 104 in 1900 he retreated to the poorhouse at Oughterarder in Connemara. He was discovered there by the Irish nationalist Patrick Pearse, future leader and martyr of the 1916 Easter Rising in Dublin. Although a Dubliner, Pearse had Irish-speaking relatives who instilled in the young teacher a love and knowledge of the language. He sought out de Bhailís in Oughterarder poorhouse, released the old man and ensured that a collection of his verse was published. Pearse then moved on to higher things and de Bhailís moved back into the poorhouse, where he died in February 1906 at the age of 109. Colm de Bhailís had not only lived in three centuries and probably featured in almost every Irish census in the nineteenth century. For a short time before his twentieth-century death he was one of the few dozen surviving citizens of the United Kingdom to have had personal experience of the eighteenth century.

Intensely rural Connaught, which included Colm de Bhailís's Connemara, in the western Gaeltacht of the country echoed the Gaidhealtachd of the Highlands of Scotland in having most centenarians – 104 men and women among the 1,110,000 Connaught people declared themselves in 1821 to be over the age of 100. In the whole of the British Isles it appeared that Gaelic-speaking agriculturalists, if they survived high levels of infant mortality, could expect to lead the longest lives.

The 1891 census reported that in England and Wales 'The number of persons returned ... as being 100 or more years of age was 146 of whom 104 were women and only 42 were men ... Although it is indisputable that now and then human life is prolonged to over a century, yet this is so rare an occurrence, that it may be doubted whether the age of many of these reputed centenarians would stand the test of rigid investigation.' The 1911 census recorded twenty-four centenarians in Scotland, with the similar qualification that 'These figures, however, are not very reliable, for experience shows that a considerable proportion of old people, probably from ignorance of the facts, overstate their ages.'

Whether that caution was justified or not, it meant that when in 1917 King George V instituted a practice of sending a birthday telegram to each one of his subjects who reached 100 years of age, he dispatched only twenty-four royal greetings across the kingdom. The census report for England and Wales in 1921 stated: 'One hundred and ten persons declared their ages as 100 or over, 30 of them being males and 80 females. The corresponding numbers in 1911 were 128, 36 and 92 respectively, so that at these extreme ages there would appear to have been a decrease in each class. Past experience, however, suggests that there is a measure of unreliability in the statements at these ages due to overstatement, conscious or otherwise, and this probably obscures any real movement at this period of life.'

There would in the following ninety years be considerable 'movement at this period of life'. By the second decade of the twenty-first century there were an undisputed 14,450 centenarians living in the United Kingdom and employees of Queen Elizabeth II were sending cards to everybody who could prove that they were 100, 105, 110 or, as in the single case of Charlotte Hughes, 115 years old.

*

In his thirtieth year, Private William Hatman of the Queen's Royal West Surrey Regiment suffered serious wounds on the Western Front. He was invalided home to south London and died there on 15 March 1916.

With Hatman's death, his family's surname temporarily disappeared from the United Kingdom. It was not the only name to be buried in the Great War. A side effect of the destruction of 800,000 men, most of them young and unmarried, was the end of several family lines. Hatman had been a relatively common British surname since the Middle Ages. It did not derive from the headwear industry but either from Norman French or from the German 'Haddo'. In England, Hatman was a variation of such homophones as Hatton, Hattons, Hattyn, Hattins and Hattans. Several Hatmans emigrated to Ireland and to the United States but in 1851 there were still more than twenty households of Hatmans scattered across England.

They then went into decline. A succession of daughters and childless marriages left the surname Hatman in a parlous position. It could not afford to lose young William Hatman and his promise of an heir. But it did.

Name extinction was a long-standing phenomenon. Just as new names such as Aaronovitch regularly appeared in the United Kingdom, old ones died out. Variable spelling was often to blame. There was nobody left in nineteenth-century Britain who carried the surname of the great fourteenth-century writer Geoffrey Chaucer, although there was a Chauser and three Chocers. The Chauser was an elderly single man and the Chocers were all women, and by 1901 those names also had disappeared.

The 1871 and 1881 censuses recorded two women, Elizabeth Bythewood of Worcester and Emma Pauncefoot of Holborn in London, who were the last bearers of their old surnames in Britain. Bythewood had reflected a medieval trade in carpentry; Pauncefoot, which appears in the Domesday Book as Pauncevolt, was probably a nickname for a person with a fat belly, from the Old French word *pance* or *panch*, meaning 'stomach', and *volt*, meaning 'vaulted' or 'arched'. Since 1881 the surname has survived only in the name of the Somerset village of Compton Pauncefoot. Early in the twenty-first century genealogists estimated that 200,000 surnames had appeared in and then disappeared from the British census, including Chips, Temples, Raynott, Woodbead, Nithercott, Rummage, Southwark, Harred and Jarsdel. In 1901 William was the 374th most common surname in Britain. In 2001 it had fallen to 12,500th position in the chart.

'Whether through misfortune, emigration or a disposition towards having daughters instead of sons,' reported *The Times* in April 2011, 'some of the most colourful surnames in Britain are on the brink of dying out.

A list of the dozen most endangered names suggests that the Relishes, Birdwhistles and Miracles of Britain are unlikely to survive beyond the twenty-first century, despite existing for hundreds of years.

Among the family names with fewer than 20 bearers in Britain, identified by the family research website MyHeritage.com, is Dankworth, one of the last of whom was Sir John Dankworth, the jazz composer and musician, who died last year. He left behind a son and a daughter as well as his widow, Dame Cleo Laine, but the youngest generation is exclusively female.

Jacqui Dankworth, the daughter of the musicians and

a singer in her own right, said that it would be up to her niece Emily, 26, to continue the name: 'The future of the Dankworth name carrying on in this country is up to her,' she said.

The name probably derives from Tancred, an Old German first name, with the English suffix 'worth' meaning a farmstead.

The list also includes Culpepper, an occupational name for a herbalist derived from Middle English, that has fallen below 20 holders in Britain, despite flourishing in America.

Matt Culpepper, one of the survivors, said that his family helped to reintroduce the name to Britain when his grandfather migrated from America, where there have been Culpeppers since the seventeenth century.

A search of Ancestry.com for the appearance of these names in Australia found Judith Relish, who arrived as a convict but married and changed her name. James Birdwhistle also arrived as a convict in the early 1800s, whereas the Dankworth family settled in east Sydney and Parkes, NSW.

Laurence Harris, who managed British genealogy for MyHeritage.com, compiled a list of names that appear to have died out in Britain. They included Bread, for which records survive until the mid-twentieth century, and Puscat, which had evolved from an affectionate medieval nickname. Bythesea and Bytheseashore were last recorded in telephone directories at the end of the twentieth century but no longer survive on public records. 'Other names,' said *The Times*, 'such as Spinster, may have been gratefully discarded.'

Mr Harris said that names that never established themselves widely, such as those linked to local topography, such as hills or streams, were much more vulnerable to sudden declines.

'The Napoleonic conflicts and the First World War saw entire generations of young men wiped out: boys who often bore distinctive surnames relating to the villages or hamlets from which they came,' he said.

'Likewise, migration resulted in already rare names leaving British shores, in some cases enjoying a new lease of life in the Americas or Australasia.'

Some names managed to appear, fade and then reappear. The celebrated medieval surname Baldrick had still half-a-dozen bearers in the twenty-first century. It had gone out of fashion as a Christian name in Britain by the middle of the nineteenth century. Early in the twentieth century Baldrick's Germanic origins led to a couple of Polish immigrants carrying it with them into Northern Ireland, just in time for inclusion in that new province's own chapter of the United Kingdom's national census.

14

Depression

The first census of the Irish Free State was taken on 18 April 1926. The first UK census of the six 'loyalist' counties of Northern Ireland alone was taken on the same day. In 1925 a subsidiary register office had been set up at the politically charged address of Whitehall Buildings in Belfast. Initially just seven male clerks were appointed but the total staff, which included eleven women, rose to forty-three at the office's peak of activity late in 1926. The most overtly political statement made by the 1926 census takers in Northern Ireland, however, was their omission of any enumeration of Irish speakers.

In 1911 there had been 680,245 Irish speakers in the whole of Ireland, making up 13.3 per cent of the total population. In the city of Belfast and the six Ulster counties of Antrim, Armagh, Down, Fermanagh, Londonderry and Tyrone there lived just 26,639 of those 680,000 Irish speakers. Only in County Tyrone did they comprise a little more than 3 per cent of the population.

They were not however dropped from the 1926 Northern Ireland census because of their comparatively small numbers.

They were dropped because the promotion and revival of the Irish language had been, and would remain, central to the nationalist manifesto and was supposed to be a foundation block in the building of the Irish Free State. The explicit intention of many Irish nationalists was to return their island to a Gaeilge-speaking civilisation. The first constitutions of the Irish Free State in 1922 and 1937 confirmed Irish as its 'national language', although English was 'equally recognised'.

That was unacceptable to the unionists in Northern Ireland who by 1926 controlled civic society in their province and composed its census. Omitting Irish speakers from that census, they explained, 'brought [it] more in line with the decennial censuses taken in Great Britain'. Native Irish speakers in Castlederg and Strabane were henceforth to be given the same official recognition as those in Shoreditch and Manchester, which was no recognition at all. Irish speakers did not become non-persons. They were still enumerated; their names and occupations and ages and marital conditions were noted. But as far as the account of the people of Northern Ireland by its government was concerned, their language ceased to exist.

Irish speaking or not, the population of Northern Ireland quickly discovered that it was no more insulated against economic hardship than was the Free State to its south. The next census of the province was taken in 1937. It discovered that the population had risen from 1,256,561 to 1,279,753. 'The increase over the intercensal period of nearly eleven years,' reported Belfast to London, 'is, therefore, 23,192 persons or 1.85 per cent.' That small increase actually represented a decline in 'natural increase', or the healthy growth indicated by birth and death registrations in a stable society.

'The migration loss or net movement outwards,' wrote the Northern Irish commissioners, 'still accounts for a loss of some 70 per cent of what would otherwise appear as the natural increase of the population.'

That was largely because, in common with the rest of the British Isles and the industrialised western world, throughout the 1930s Northern Ireland suffered from the Great Depression.

The 1931 census was the first to enumerate the 'out of work' in its categories of occupation. As the historian Edward Higgs points out, 'almspeople, and persons in the receipt of parish relief' were included in 1851 but dropped from the next two censuses. Higgs writes:

> Unemployment made its first specific appearance in these years since the schedules carried the instruction that, 'Persons ordinarily engaged in some industry, but out of employment on April 2nd, should be so described, as "Coal miner, unemployed", "Printer, unemployed".' Thereafter, with the introduction of columns for employment status, the question regarding unemployment seems to have been dropped. In 1911 the household schedule specifically instructed householders that if the member of the household was out of work 'the usual occupation must be stated'.

The concept of 'unemployment' as it came to be understood in the twentieth century was new and difficult for a nineteenth-century mind to grasp. Throughout earlier history almost everybody but the halt, the lame and the insane had done something to feed and clothe themselves, even if that something was begging or picking pockets or robbing houses, and even if its slim returns made them paupers. Before the industrial revolution most working people were dependent on their own training or initiative to make a living. They would later be described as 'self-employed', but the term is anachronistic. They considered themselves to be free agents, whether they were up for six months' hire as labourers or ploughmen at a Whitsun agricultural fair, or Swaledale smallholders who also hushed for lead, or Durham coal miners who moved from one colliery bond to another, or whether they made shoes or wove cloth in their own homes. There were still a great many such homeworkers: artisans and craftspeople who, often as not, manufactured their earthenware and candle snuffers on their own premises.

In the open market outside government service and the church, the notion of being dependent for life upon one external employer was slow to establish itself, and would prove to be no more than a hiccup in British working history. Lifetime 'job security' might have been comprehensible to most people by the beginning of the twentieth century; 100 years later it had all but disappeared again. Similarly, before the twentieth century there was no state pension and no commonly accepted pensionable age. People worked until they had saved enough for a comfortable retirement, until their children could provide for them, or until they dropped. Higgs explains:

> Part of the problem was the difficulty in making a clear distinction between being in employment, being retired, or being unemployed. When work was very casual and stoppages commonplace, especially for the elderly, the distinction might be very difficult to draw. A dock labourer, for example, would not know if he was to get

work until he arrived at the dock gates. Much work was seasonal in the Victorian period, with periods of customary idleness in between. What was voluntary retirement for the elderly, and what was an involuntary inability to participate in the work force, might also be difficult to distinguish.

By 1931 such distinctions were more easily made and the unemployed were included in the census. It could not have been more timely. Even in the early years of the depression, the 'out of work' formed the largest bloc of employable adults in the country. On 26 April 1931 no fewer than 2,520,113 persons declared themselves on the British census forms to be out of work – a number almost exactly commensurate with those who were registered at Employment Exchanges. It was also a number which continued to rise. Between 1929 and 1933 Britain's world trade halved and its heavy industrial production fell by a third. By the summer of 1932 there were 3.5 million British citizens registered as unemployed.

The census did more than simply report those catastrophes. The General Register Office was asked early in 1931 to alleviate them by ensuring 'that as many of the unemployed as possible are engaged [as enumerators] for the forthcoming census'. Shortly before she and her government were voted out of office in October 1931, the Labour MP for East Ham North and parliamentary secretary Arabella Lawrence reluctantly pointed out that while 'all would agree that the unemployed should have the maximum opportunity of work consistent with success in carrying out the census work', such employment, so far as it entailed enumeration, 'does not last very long'. She continued:

It is a condition of such success that persons recruited as enumerators must be fully qualified for the work, and must also be so situated that they can be relied on to be available for instruction during the necessary interval between their appointment and the census, and to do the work without fail when the day comes.

Therefore, enumerators are required to bind themselves under penalty not to make default. Wholesale recourse to the unemployed in such conditions is not consistent either with their interests or with safety in the census arrangements, since, if offered regular work in the interval, they must refuse the offer or make default. [The government], however, has taken all steps practicable to see that full consideration is given to unemployed persons, with the necessary qualifications, so situated that they can be relied on to do the work efficiently when the time comes. The success of the census enumeration has, however, to be the paramount factor in deciding what can and should be done.

'There was a lot of unemployment and real poverty was a way of life for many people,' recalled Eileen Kelly in Birmingham. 'At the primary school there were children with holes in their shoes and clothes and some of them smelt a lot. I felt very sorry for them shivering in their thin clothes during the very cold winters that we seemed to have then. They were also looked down upon as they had free dinners. Everyone knew because they were given a ticket for dinner. I asked a boy what he had for dinner at the school and he replied, "It's always cheese pie." As I was going home to meat with vegetables and pudding, that didn't sound like a dinner to me. They were also supplied with free boots, paid for out of the police "boot fund", which supplied needy children ...'

The depredations of the depression fell chiefly upon such industries as coal mining, steel manufacture and shipbuilding. The 1931 census, which was taken before the depression reached its nadir, recorded as 'out of work' 213,000 coal miners and 423,000 steel and metalworkers; 220,000 unemployed textile workers, most of whom were women; and 136,000 laid-off transport and communications employees.

That was disproportionately damaging to south Wales, to the central belt of Scotland and to northern England. 'One of the interesting things that was discovered as a result of the last census,' said the Conservative Member for Southport, Robert Hudson, in 1932:

> was the unexpectedly great progress that had been made, without any Government assistance, in the transfer of population ... the perfectly ordinary normal transfer of population has gone on to an extent which no Government could possibly have undertaken. In South Wales in 10 years there was a net loss by migration of 242,000 persons, in Durham and Northumberland a net loss of 207,000 and in Cheshire and Lancashire a net loss of 154,000.

On the other hand, the south-eastern counties, including Greater London, gained during the corresponding period no fewer than 615,000. Similar figures are forthcoming in detail. But the interesting point is that, in spite of that enormous increase of population in London and in the Home Counties, there was not a corresponding increase of unemployment. The average unemployment, for example, in the country today is 22 per cent. I find that the average unemployment in London is only 11 per cent.

Therefore, in spite of the fact that there has been this tremendous internal migration of the population from the distressed areas to the south-east of England, it has not meant that there has been any corresponding increase in unemployment in the south-east of England but that, on the contrary, the experience of the south-east of England has been better than that of the rest of the country.

That early evidence of what would become known as the north/south divide, which afforded Robert Hudson MP some satisfaction, was in part due to the fact that many of the southern light industries were largely unscathed by the depression, while such new industries as motor vehicle manufacture, which was at first largely although not exclusively based in the south-east of England, were booming. The young William Maxton left school in Kent and found an unexpected job 'at Burrill's Garage in London Road [in Bromley] ... as a garage hand ...

Unemployment figures were already beginning to climb, my own trade in the doldrums and my parents and girl-friend expecting me to get on and do something. As it turned out, I was given a month's trial. The motor trade was then in its infancy, most mechanics were army trained and the majority of these were drivers with just sufficient knowledge to do running repairs. There were only two firms established in the district, Soans and Dunn, Ford agents and Anthony's both in Mason's Hill. It would have been useless for me to apply at either of them as they only took apprentices; this was my first stumbling block.

My apprentice years had been wasted, no lad could start his apprenticeship over the age of sixteen, and I was now eighteen, and for years after this was a barrier that kept me out of many a decent job. George Burrill, the boss at the garage, was an ex-coachman. He knew as much about a car as an elephant knows about knitting, yet there was nothing unusual in this; the car was replacing the horse and pair, younger coachmen were drifting into other trades, the older ones just faded out ...

There was a chap who lived opposite who I knew slightly who was in the motor trade working for Paige Motors, an American firm in Grosvenor Road along the Embankment. I met him one day and he said, 'What's the matter with you, you look as if you lost a shilling and found a tanner?'

I said I was browned off hanging around.

'But,' he said, 'you were in that garage in London Road, weren't you?'

I told him I'd had a bust up.

'Look,' he said, 'why don't you try Maxwell Motors in Lupus Street, they're taking on hands.'

'Well,' I said, 'I've only been in the trade about a year.'

'That doesn't matter,' he said. 'Tell them you've been in it for four years.'

'All right, I will.'

I felt it would be a waste of time though. I found Lupus Street in the heart of Pimlico, just off Grosvenor Road: Maxwells were at the top end from Vauxhall Bridge Road, the entrance was through a passage just about wide enough for a car or small lorry to get through. The first thing to catch the eye was a large board with 'Maxwell Motors, Experimental Station' in gilt lettering. That I thought has just about put the kibosh on it. It was obvious this wasn't just nuts and bolts, but for people with wide experience.

However, I got an interview and was started as an improver at 1/5d or 7p per hour, on the following Wednesday.

Similar opportunities were offered to young men in, for instance, Coventry. An early centre of the British motor trade, the city's population rose by 50 per cent, from 176,303 to 260,685, between 1931 and 1951.

Robert Hudson might have been contented to note that economic migrants from the north could get on their bikes and find work in the Midlands or the south. Others were less convinced. 'Would it not be possible for the Government to press on farther with the policy of decentralisation?' asked the historian and Labour peer Baron Godfrey Elton in 1936.

It looks as if London were becoming almost dangerously the Capital of the country, not only because of the industries which it attracts, but also because of the enormous proportion of the country's talent and earning power in the higher grades which is attracted there. Cobbett – I have never been able to understand exactly why – used to refer to London, you will remember, as "the Wen"; and if that metaphor was meant to represent the exaggerated growth of the head of the country in proportion to the rest of the body, I think we are beginning to see its force to-day. I believe there are very few salary-earners earning over £1,000 a year in public employ outside London – relatively extraordinarily few.

Now an example of decentralisation was begun by the Post Office not long ago, and decentralisation is being undertaken to a very considerable extent, I understand, by the British Broadcasting Corporation. These are devolving more responsibility on their regions, and are sending out there highly-paid, responsible officials, who not only bring earning power into other parts of the country but also give a lead in civic enterprise. That example has also been set by a number of industries, and I hope that His Majesty's Government will find it possible, when they are planning not only the increase of armaments but other Government enterprises, to bear in mind the necessity of decentralisation.

If the south-east of England remained comparatively undamaged by the depression, while south Wales, Northern Ireland and some northern counties of England were gravely affected, Scotland's census returns of 1931 offered the most dramatic headlines. For the first time in recorded history, between 1921 and 1931 the country's population fell.

'The population of Scotland on Census day, 26th April, is found to be 4,842,554, of whom 2,325,867 are males and 2,516,687 are females. At the Census of 1921 the total population was 4,882,497, of whom 2,347,642 were males and 2,534,855 females,' reported the Scottish Registrar General, a blacksmith's son from Lanarkshire named Andrew Froude. He continued:

The 1931 population is thus 39,943 less than that ascertained at the 1921 Census, the decrease of males being 21,775 and that of females 18,168. The intercensal decrease of the total population is equivalent to 0.8 per cent. of the

1921 population, that of males being 0.9 per cent. of the male population in 1921, and that of females 0.7 per cent. of the female population in 1921.

It was the first Scottish census to record a fall in the nation's population. As Froude hinted, the decline was in part due to the continuing effects of high Scottish mortality during the Great War. The presence of fewer men had resulted in fewer marriages and consequently in the birth of fewer children. But despite those losses, between 1921 and 1931 there had been 352,386 more births than deaths in Scotland, 'and as a decrease of 39,943 is found in the population, 392,329 may be taken as a measure of the population lost by migration'.

Despite declines in shipbuilding and the steel and coal industries, with the consequent high emigration from the central belt and south of Scotland, it was chiefly a rural phenomenon. The four main cities of Edinburgh, Glasgow, Dundee and Aberdeen, which between them contained almost 37 per cent of the Scottish populace, had actually increased in population by an average of 4 per cent between 1921 and 1931. Fifteen of the twenty-four larger Scottish burghs, or towns, had also grown in size.

However, wrote Froude, 'in the landward areas' which in 1921 had still been home to over 30 per cent of Scots 'the decrease is general, the principal percentage decreases being 9.5 in Orkney, 9.7 in Sutherland, 9.8 in Kincardine, 11.5 in Caithness, 12.0 in Ross and Cromarty, and 17.1 in Zetland [Shetland] . . . It will be observed that the increases and the smaller decreases are generally in those counties in which the landward areas are to some extent of an urban or semi-urban character, and that the larger decreases are in those counties, chiefly in the North and North-West, which are more rural in character.'

In Scotland the 1920s was a decade of emigration which was comparable only to the losses suffered in nineteenth-century Ireland, and to the more localised Highland clearance years of a century earlier. In places it achieved mythical dimensions. The largest Hebridean island, Lewis, contained 40 per cent of the population of Ross and Cromarty, the county which Andrew Froude had recorded as losing 12 per cent of its inhabitants. In April 1923, 260 people from Lewis, mostly young men from the rural croftlands of the island, responded to the Canadian government's persistent entreaties for immigrants and booked themselves aboard the SS *Metagama* from Stornoway to Ontario. Those 260 emigrants were just 1 per cent of the island's population. But they came from an important age group, they would be followed by many others, and they seemed to some to represent the end of hope.

On the Sunday before they left a local minister preached from Genesis 12: 'Now the Lord had said unto Abraham, Get thee out of thy country, and from thy kindred, and from thy father's house, unto a land that I will shew thee: And I will make of thee a great nation, and I will bless thee, and make thy name great; and thou shalt be a blessing: And I will bless them that bless thee, and curse him that curseth thee: and in thee shall all families of the earth be blessed.' Three dozen journalists and press photographers travelled to Lewis to watch the 'young men with sunburnt faces and new suits' arrive at Stornoway harbour like 'refugees fleeing before an advancing army'. A Canadian newspaper announced that 'These isles are now being emptied. Only the old are left behind.'

It was easy for none of them. For at least one it was his second, and final, emigration. Iain Morrison of Toronto would recall in the twenty-first century:

My father Norman Morrison ... came to Canada on his own in 1920 when he was seventeen. He worked here for a year or so and then returned to Stornoway.

His father John had sold his fishing boat to assist with Norman's payment of the necessary ocean passage.

Arriving at the old Union Station in Toronto and keen to get employment he went to the newsstand to buy a newspaper to see the 'Jobs Available' ads. Returning to where he had put down his only suitcase in the station hall he realized that someone had lifted it. This left him in a strange city with just the clothes he was wearing, his Sunday best, and no other belongings. Fortunately he had kept all his money in his pocket during his travels.

Seeing a 'wanted' ad for a construction labourer he rode the street car out to the west end of Toronto and found a queue of applicants forming at the job site. The job was manually excavating for a foundation for concrete supports for a railway bridge. Some of the applicants looked at the work being done which was pick-and-shovel work, decided not to apply and left the queue immediately. Soon Norman was at the head of the line. An earlier candidate was already down in one of the pits digging away steadily. After a while the man started to ease up, to take a rest and he was informed by the foreman that he would not qualify for the job.

By then there was a small line of determined men awaiting their opportunity. The foreman then waved Norman, still attired in his best clothes, to get in the pit and to start digging and shoveling the dirt out over the now quite high parapet. He knew that if he once lifted his head for any reason that the foreman would call him off the job. It had been clear from the start, that seeing Norman's smaller 5' 6" stature, the foreman did not expect him to go for very long ... However the end of the normal shift finally came and he was still going steadily. He was told to report for work the next day!

My father returned to Lewis and after learning the blacksmithing trade there he came back to Canada on the Metagama ... Apart from a period of WW2 Armed Service duty he spent the rest of his life here in Canada.

That epidemic of emigration would be very quickly arrested in the bulk of Scotland. Indeed it would be reversed in Shetland and in such north-eastern counties as Aberdeenshire by the discovery and exploitation of oil in the North Sea in the 1970s. But parishes in the north-western mainland and most of the Hebridean islands would continue to experience the most sustained population fall in the British Isles, not excluding Ireland. Their numbers of inhabitants inexorably declined during three centuries, every ten years between the 1841 census and that of 2011, by which time some, but not all, had begun to stabilise.

In the remainder of the United Kingdom the depression of the 1930s would end with yet another intercontinental war – a war which also caused the only cancellation of a national census since 1801.

In March 1938 the MP for Lambeth Norwood, Duncan Sandys, asked prime minister Neville Chamberlain in the House of Commons 'whether, in order to facilitate the immediate mobilisation of the services of the entire nation upon the outbreak of a war, it is his intention to introduce a system of universal national registration, the purpose of which would be to allocate in advance the duties, whether military or civilian, which each individual according to his or her age, sex, physique, and qualifications would, in the event of war, be called upon to perform?'

Chamberlain replied that 'A scheme for compulsory national registration in time of war, if the Government of the day should so decide, has been in existence for some years. Proposals for compulsory registration in peace time have also been considered, but on balance the advantages to be derived therefrom have been found to be outweighed by the difficulties and opposition which would have to be surmounted.'

Registrar General Sylvanus Percival Vivian had been working on plans for a national registration system since 1935. It was initially supposed to be included in the 1941 census, but was overtaken by events.

On 3 September 1939 Great Britain once again declared war on Germany following the latter's invasion of a smaller European country. Over the next two days a bill 'to make provision for the establishment of a National Register, for the issue of identity cards, and for purposes connected with the matters aforesaid' was rushed through the Houses of Parliament. Vivian's plans were promptly executed. Over 65,000 enumerators were quickly recruited to dash around the country gathering basic statistics of names, addresses, sexes, ages, marital conditions and occupations of the people.

There was no time to do anything more. In the House of Commons the representative of Newcastle upon Tyne

Central, Alfred Denville, suggested that there were in 1939 many qualified men in occupations into which they had been forced during the depression. Those men, suggested Denville, would willingly return to their former occupations at a time of national emergency.

There are many thousands of people in the entertainment industry who came out of certain industries and entered occupations in picture houses, theatres and music-halls of this country. I have in mind a personal friend who came to me the other day and said, 'I should like to offer my services.' I said to him jocularly, 'You are no good. You are a common or garden comedian and no good to anybody.' And his reply was, 'I am a first-rate draughtsman.'

Is such a man to put on his registration paper, 'comedian,' 'actor,' 'picture-house attendant,' 'cinematograph operator,' 'scenic artist' or 'wardrobe maker,' or anything of that sort, when he might put down a trade which might be of great benefit to the country at the present moment? I hope that the Minister will consider that it is very fair for the Committee to ask that every man and woman should be given the chance of offering their services to the country in any capacity whatever at the present time.

Sensibly enough, it was left to the comedian to declare himself suitable for draughtsmanship or other beneficial labour.

The national identity cards subsequently issued for the first and last time in British history were used not only for wartime security – to differentiate ordinary people on the street from German spies – but also for conscription and the distribution of rations. British involvement in the Second World War continued until 15 August 1945. During those six years censuses were taken of the nation's machine tools, tractors (in October 1940 there were 74,000 tractors in the United Kingdom, an increase of 44 per cent over the previous year) and public bomb shelters.

There would be no national census of the population until April 1951. The second war had been longer than the first and its carnage, particularly among civilians, even greater. But thanks largely to the fact that the country was governed by men still influenced by, and determined not to repeat, the horrors of 1914–18 Britain's military losses were smaller in both actual and relative terms. Just under 1 per cent of the population of the United Kingdom, 451,000 people, perished on land and at sea between 1939 and 1945. Registrar General George North commented of those deaths in his preliminary report of the 1951 census: 'though not large in relation to the total deaths of the period, their concentration among the younger adult male section of the population will have left a scar that will be visible for many years to come.' Almost 18 per cent of the British dead, 67,200 people, were civilians of both genders and all ages.

It also fell to Registrar General North to make the first official reference to what would become known as the great post-war baby boom. In the first full year of the war, 1940–1, almost uniquely in recorded history more people had died in England and Wales – 575,000 – than had been born – 569,000. That was only partly the result of war casualties and of soldiers and sailors serving abroad. It was chiefly because the birth rate in those dark months was one of the lowest registered in the twentieth century. As had been the case during the First World War, in 1940 British adults were particularly reluctant to bring new children into an uncertain world.

Following the end of the war in 1945 and the demobilisation of the troops, national fertility soared. In 1946–7 over 900,000 live births were recorded, resulting in nearly twice as many christenings as burials. The phenomenon was less marked in the next three years but at over 700,000 per annum births still outstripped deaths in healthy quantities: 'the feature to which will probably be assigned the greatest importance is the change of direction in the trend of births since the early years of the war', reported George North of the 1951 census.

> After having fallen more or less continuously for nearly 60 years the birth rate levelled itself out in the years immediately preceding the war and has since been subject to an increase as steep almost as the last stages of the fall.
> It is true of course that a number of the births following the cessation of the war will be regarded in the nature of postponements from the war period itself and theoretically transferable thereto in any satisfactory appreciation of the situation, but there can be no gainsaying the substantial recovery which has taken place . . .

That recovery was confirmed in 1961, of which year's census it was reported that 'the population of England and Wales has increased, since the last census in 1951, by 2,314 thousands. This is more than in any previous ten-year intercensal period since 1901–11 . . . this larger addition to the population is mainly attributable to a rise in the flow of births. In the intercensal period 1951–61 there were 7,121 thousand live births, rather more than in the period 1921–31, and a considerably larger flow of births (allowing for the different time interval) than in the twenty years 1931–51.'

The baby boomers born after the Great War were raised in an international depression and reached adulthood just in time to be plunged into another global conflict. Their successors, the boomers of the late 1940s, were allowed to grow old in a period of unprecedented peace and prosperity. Perhaps as a result, they would come to define the term.

Those baby boomers were needed especially in the blitzed capital of London, which had suffered a greater loss of population through evacuation, civilian deaths, the destruction by bombing of housing stock and post-war emigration than anywhere else in the United Kingdom. London's relative stability during the depression of the 1930s was more than cancelled out by its losses during the Second World War.

'After 1939,' reported Registrar General North in 1951, 'all orderly development [in London] ceased and the population became at once subject to the massive and alternating tides of evacuation and restoration which characterized the area during the war and which will long be a vivid memory to those who were in any way associated with them.

Based at first on anticipations of what the enemy might have in store they were later more rigorously conditioned by the actual results of the attacks in the diminishing numbers of dwellings fortunate enough to have escaped destruction and still capable of housing their returning occupants.

The ultimate result is that the total population in the Greater London area in 1951 is nearly 400,000 fewer (−4.4 per cent) than it was in 1939 and this despite such partial property restoration as has been possible by the restricted building operations of the post-war period.

Within the County of London alone, the present population of 3,348,336 is 16.6 per cent below its counterpart of 1939 and more than a million less than it was in 1931, a loss in the 20 years equivalent in magnitude to the entire population of Birmingham, our largest provincial town.

London was arguably at its lowest ebb since Boudica had almost razed the place. Stepney, Shoreditch, Poplar and the City of London had all lost more than half of their pre-war populations, and four adjacent boroughs contained between 40 and 50 per cent fewer people in 1951 than in 1931. The capital's renaissance in the following fifty years was both unpredictable and extraordinary.

15

Welcome Home

The British government attempted to replenish a small number of London's war losses from the colonies overseas. On the morning of 22 June 1948 a 'dirty white ship' sailed up the River Thames from the English Channel and tied up at Tilbury Docks. Her name was His Majesty's Naval Trawler *Empire Windrush* and she had made passage from Australia by way of Kingston in Jamaica.

At Kingston HMT *Empire Windrush* took on board almost 500 passengers, most of whom were Jamaicans exercising their right as subjects of the British crown to move from one part of King George VI's empire to another. A right which had always been taken for granted – British subjects were naturally exempted from the 1905 Aliens Act – it was reinforced by the British Nationality Act of 1948, which ratified the status of each inhabitant of every country within the new, post-imperial settlement of the British Commonwealth as a 'Commonwealth citizen'.

They were hardly the first. As recently as 1941, during the war, 345 West Indians had been persuaded to help the services and infrastructure of the vital port of Liverpool by going to live and work in Merseyside. Another 236 volunteers from the Caribbean to the British armed forces had been killed during the Second World War. 'Down in Kingston town, at a place they call Parade,' said Connie Mark of the Jamaican Auxiliary Territorial Service, 'they had two lists put up – a list of men reported missing and a list of men reported dead. And that list would go on and on – sometimes you'd go and you'd see the name of your cousin; you'd go back a few days later and see your friend's brother reported dead. So we damn well knew there was a war on.'

The immigrants believed that they were travelling not only to improve their own lives, but to help their bruised and battered mother country to reconstruct itself after the second great war of the first half of the twentieth century. They had been correctly informed that following the war's end there was a shortage of labour in such sections of the British economy as the London transport system and the newly established National Health Service. Some were ex-servicemen hoping to resume their careers in the armed forces. Up to the point of disembarkation they were given no reasons to doubt their welcome. As the *Empire Windrush* steamed towards England the London *Evening Standard* hired a light aircraft to carry a photographer and journalist over the Straits of Dover. As the plane sighted the *Windrush* and circled overhead, reported the *Standard*:

the passengers rushed to the side of the ship, but there was no waving or cheering.

Hands clinging tightly to the rails they stared in wonder as the airplane swept round and over them.

The airplane circled for 15 minutes, and gradually

apprehension turned to joy as the passengers realised they were receiving their first welcome to England. Brown and white hands waved so vigorously that one could imagine the cheers and smiles it was impossible to see or hear.

They were still waving as the airplane left for Croydon.

The *Standard*'s headline that evening, above a large photograph of the *Empire Windrush* in the Channel, was 'WELCOME HOME!'

Not everybody was so optimistic and hospitable. Six days before the *Empire Windrush* arrived the MP for Maldon, Tom Driberg, asked Arthur Creech Jones, Secretary of State for the Colonies, 'if he will inquire into the circumstances in which some 400 unemployed West Indians have sailed for this country in search of work; what provision he is making for the welfare of these men on their arrival here; and if he will issue a warning in the West Indies that, although some industries in Britain are undermanned, it is not easy for large numbers of unskilled or skilled immigrants to find suitable work here at once, and also initiate more vigorous efforts to deal with the considerable unemployment in the West Indies, especially among ex-Service men in Jamaica'.

'The West Indians in question,' replied Creech Jones, 'booked their passages privately. I am in consultation with my right hon Friend, the Minister of Labour and National Service, with regard to their welfare and employment on arrival. All of them were warned about the employment position before they sailed, and the situation in regard to employment in Britain has been made fully known to the people of the West Indies. It would appear, however, that the men concerned are prepared to take their chances of finding employment. The West Indian Governments are fully aware of the need to do everything possible to relieve the unemployment position.'

'May I ask my right hon Friend two questions?' persisted Driberg. 'First, has he arranged suitable accommodation, in hostels or otherwise, for these men, pending their employment, so that they will not merely drift down into the underworld; and, secondly, is he aware that the West Indian Governments have not done anything like enough – despite their awareness of the situation – to cope with the resettlement and employment of ex-Service men?'

'I cannot accept the last part of the supplementary question,' said Jones, 'and it would take far too long to explain the steps that have been taken by the West Indian Governments. As to the first part of the supplementary, this question of accommodating is very difficult and we are doing everything in our power to receive these men and find a place in which they can lodge.'

Oliver Stanley, the MP for Bristol West and a former Secretary of State for the Colonies, then wished to know if his successor would 'agree that the experience during the war was that unless these West Indian workers were carefully vetted before coming over here and their capabilities ascertained the experiment would be a complete failure, and will he make certain that if this is going to continue some organisation will be set up for the West Indians to ascertain beforehand if they are likely to be suitable for employment over here?'

'We recognise the need for some vetting,' replied Jones, 'but obviously we cannot interfere with the movement of British subjects. It is very unlikely that a similar event to this will occur again in the West Indies.'

Just three weeks after the passengers on the *Empire Windrush* set foot on Tilbury Docks, Peter Fryer reported in the Communist *Daily Worker* that '76 have gone to work in foundries, 15 on the railways, 15 as labourers, 15 as farm workers and 10 as electricians. The others have gone into a wide variety of jobs, including clerical work at the post office, coach building and plumbing.'

Despite the predictions of Arthur Creech Jones, the event did recur. West Indians continued to arrive in Britain throughout the late 1940s and 1950s. By the end of the latter decade, Peter Fryer estimated, 'there were in Britain about 125,000 West Indians who had come over since the end of the war.' The Welsh demographer Ceri Peach would write that 'the number of people in Britain born in the West Indies grew from 15,000 in 1951 to 172,000 in 1961'. Both estimates were more or less accurate. It was almost impossible to obtain precise statistics because even the early computers which by then were assisting census returns were not programmed to identify the exact birthplaces of citizens. Such a task would have required somebody in the General Register Office to go through every census form counting the number of people who had volunteered their place of birth as Antigua, Trinidad and Tobago, the Bahamas, Dominica, Grenada, Saint Kitts and Nevis, Saint Lucia, Saint Vincent and the Grenadines, Anguilla, the Virgin Islands, the Cayman Islands, Montserrat, the Turks and Caicos Islands, Jamaica or Barbados.

Even then, that clerk would have been unable to detect the colour of the citizens' skins, which was the main concern of those who affected to be concerned. That was chiefly because black British West Indians were the descendants of slaves. Unlike, for example, immigrants from Asia, most black West Indians consequently carried British family surnames (to further complicate matters, their children were often given such unusually patriotic Christian names as Winston) and so were indiscernible on the completed census forms from white West Indians, to whose return to the mother country nobody objected. Anybody able to study the census returns from 1971 to 2011 would have found living in London a broadcaster named Trevor McDonald, born in 1939 on the British Caribbean island of Trinidad. Without further, external information that student would have been unable to discover whether Mr McDonald was of direct British colonial descent or, as was in fact the case, from an Afro-Caribbean family. The census remained, for the moment, colour blind.

Many politicians and demographers, including Ceri Peach, thought that the census had neglected or underestimated the size of the West Indian immigrant community by as much as 20 or 30 per cent, losing in the process some 34,000 natives of the Caribbean who were living in the United Kingdom. Some were encouraged towards that conclusion by a statement in the 1951 census report that '9 per 1000 persons enumerated did not state their birthplace and 19 per thousand of the foreign born did not state their nationality'.

It is highly unlikely that such reticence had any effect on the enumeration of West Indians in Britain. They were identified by themselves, by the government and by tradition as being British or British Commonwealth citizens and therefore had nothing to hide. They were unlikely to regard themselves as 'foreign born'. Nine out of a thousand persons was a margin of error smaller than 1 per cent; nineteen out of a thousand less than 2 per cent. The Registrar General for England and Wales, a former under-secretary at the Health

Ministry named Michael Reed, addressed the controversy in his report of the 1961 national census.

By the middle of the twentieth century the General Register Office considered itself to be conducting a census which was accurate to a factor of more than 99 per cent. 'Even if the standard of enumeration,' conceded Reed, 'were high for the population in general, the quality of the enumeration may be lower for certain groups whose enumeration presents special difficulties. For example, the very mobile element in the population is likely to present such difficulties, as would the small part of the population with no fixed abode. It is not only difficult to enumerate such groups, but also practically impossible to make a check on the completeness of their enumeration.' Such white travelling people, wrote Reed pointedly, attracted at that time 'relatively little public attention'.

The same could not be said of Caribbean immigrants:

The surge of immigrants in the period preceding the 1961 Census, particularly the immigration of coloured people from certain Commonwealth countries, has focussed attention on a readily identifyable *[sic]* group in the population. This group is also one where, for a variety of reasons, there are likely to be difficulties in carrying out a complete enumeration. For example, in 1961, many may have found the whole notion of a census unfamiliar. There would also have been difficulties of language and comprehension of the census returns themselves. In addition, some people have felt that the fact that a disproportionate number of immigrants were probably living in crowded housing conditions would have tended also to lead to under-enumeration.

Reed's observation concerning overcrowded housing conditions was undoubtedly true. He was, as he probably suspected,
on less secure ground when raising 'difficulties of language'
and immigrant unfamiliarity with the notion of censuses.
They may have spoken patois, but all British West Indians
came from Anglophone islands, and in Jamaica, the largest
British Caribbean island, nine censuses had been taken at
irregular intervals between 1844 and 1960. By the summer of
1961 any Jamaican over the age of eighteen who lived either
in Jamaica or in Britain had already experienced at least two
censuses. He or she would not have presented an enumerator
with insurmountable difficulties of comprehension.

There was an informed estimate of 16,000 people of
West Indian birth living in the United Kingdom in 1951
and 174,000 in 1961. The Registrar General's conclusion
was that 'it seems quite probable that there was some
under-enumeration' caused by 'multi-occupied buildings
where enumeration tends to be difficult'. But that under-
enumeration had not failed to identify anything close to
34,000 people.

The total of West Indian-born British residents identified
in the census would peak at 304,000 in 1971, by which time
Jamaica and most of its neighbours were independent countries and immigration was curtailed. Those 304,000 people
were a huge proportion – almost 10 per cent – of the 3.3
million people estimated to live in the former British West
Indies in the 1960s. It was a relatively tiny proportion – 0.5
per cent – of the population of the United Kingdom, which
in 1971 was almost 60 million.

Most of the post-war new arrivals settled initially in London.
In 1961 the census recorded that the 70,500 'persons born in

colonies or protectorates in America' – rough longhand for the Caribbean possessions – living in London were chiefly concentrated in Hackney, Islington, Kensington, Lambeth, Paddington and Wandsworth. In none of those metropolitan boroughs did they exceed 6 per cent of the total population. That was not so many as the proportion of European Jews discovered to be living in Stepney during the alien panic in 1901, but it had a greater impact.

As Michael Reed had written, 'the immigration of coloured people . . . has focussed attention on a readily identifyable group'. The presence of tens and then hundreds of thousands of black people in London and elsewhere excited the insular xenophobia which had long been a feature of the indigenous British and turned it at times into outright racism. By the 1950s West Indians in London were not only subjected to discrimination from the public, from employers and from the police, while having to endure rack-renting and low wages; they were also the objects of regular physical assault, and even of murder, by young white males operating singly or in gangs and encouraged by such bodies as the League of Empire Loyalists, the White Defence League and the National Front.

Such violence was perceived by many politicians and much of the public not so much as a criminal matter to be prosecuted by due process of law, but as an understandable reaction by white Britons who considered the racial purity of their homeland to be threatened by another group of aliens. Their answer to such outrages as the riots in Notting Hill in 1958 was often not to blame or even to dissuade the white offenders, but to urge legislation against the innocent victims.

As a direct result the Conservative government of Harold

Macmillan passed in 1962 a Commonwealth Immigrants Act which henceforward permitted entry to Britain only to those people who possessed employment vouchers, which were issued by the government and limited in number. The Act was as clearly aimed at black people as the 1905 Aliens Act had been aimed at Jews – it was described by the leader of the Labour opposition, Hugh Gaitskell, as 'cruel and brutal anti-colour legislation'. The 1962 Act also echoed its predecessor of 1905 in its refusal to be informed by the sane and moderate statistics and conclusions offered by the national census returns and reports. It was followed in 1968 and 1971 by further immigration Acts which intended to close the borders to former imperial subjects of Asian descent.

In the end they proved to be Canutian measures. Thousands of Commonwealth citizens continued legitimately to emigrate to Britain. In the late 1960s they included a Pakistani couple called Amanullah and Nehrun Khan, both born in the British Raj. The Khans settled in a council flat in Tooting. Amanullah found work as a bus driver and Nehrun as a seamstress. In October 1970 Nehrun gave birth in Tooting's St George's Hospital to their fifth child, a boy named Sadiq, of whom more would be heard. The multiculturalism introduced to the United Kingdom by the passengers on the *Empire Windrush* in 1948, and by Jewish refugees from Tsarist oppression in the 1880s and 1890s, and before them by Irish people, French Huguenots and others would cause heated debate, no little unrest and further legislation in the late twentieth and early twenty-first centuries, but it would not end.

Despite misgivings among the resident population, and whatever the causes of those misgivings, the national census proved that the movement of peoples was irresistible. It could be dissuaded and even checked, but the impulse to seek greener fields was too great to abolish. Great Britain, and London in particular, had once gone out to claim the world. As a result, when its time came round the world claimed Britain, and especially London.

In 1991 questions aimed at identifying ethnicity were introduced to the census forms, which thereafter ceased to be colour blind. The census of 2011 showed London to be the second most multicultural city in the world after New York. Less than half, 45 per cent, of the 8,173,941 inhabitants of the metropolis were 'white British'. There were 12.1 per cent 'other white', chiefly from the United States, the former 'white dominions' and the continent of Europe. There were 2.2 per cent 'white Irish' and 0.1 per cent white gypsies. One-fifth of the population was of Asian descent, comprised chiefly of Indians, Pakistanis, Bangladeshis, Chinese and Arabs. ('The Commonwealth,' the Registrar General had reported following the 1951 census, 'which includes about one-quarter of the world's population, is three-quarters Asiatic.')

Black and mixed-race people made up 15.6 per cent of the population of London, 4.2 per cent of the capital's inhabitants in 2011 being of British Caribbean origin. In 2016 Sadiq Khan, the Muslim son of that Pakistani bus driver and seamstress who had raised him in Tooting, was elected mayor of London by a large majority. 'This is concrete evidence,' said Professor Tony Travers of the London School of Economics, 'that London is capable of putting race, religion and identity to one side.'

Less notice had been taken of the fact that Khan's

predecessor in the mayoral post, Alexander Boris de Pfeffel Johnson, had been born in Manhattan. As a result he held dual American and British citizenship. He also had a paternal grandfather of Turkish descent who was originally named Osman Kemal. Boris Johnson had as great-grandparents 'foreign' Jews and Muslims, as well as Christians.

What was more, the process was continuing apace. On the census day of 27 March 2011 no fewer than thirty-nine different foreign countries were represented in London by 20,000 of their citizens or more. They ranged from 20,637 Japanese-born residents of the United Kingdom's capital, through 27,288 Canadians, 30,880 Spaniards, 53,959 Australians, 62,050 Italians and 63,920 citizens of the United States to 87,467 Jamaicans, 129,807 Irish people, 158,300 Poles and 262,247 Indians. Living in London on that census day were 66,654 French-born people and 55,476 Germans. They were not all there to stay, but they were in short-term or long-term residence, and they were indicative of London's kaleidoscopic ethnic and cultural composition at any time in the early twenty-first century.

The city was not obviously suffering as a result. In the twenty-first century London generated over 20 per cent of the entire economic activity of the United Kingdom and was the world's most visited metropolis, as measured by international arrivals. It represented a notable transformation of the reduced and exhausted conurbation observed by George North with such great concern just sixty years earlier. A transcontinental imperial legacy still resisted by many was the economic and cultural saviour of a capital city which in John Rickman's lifetime had been considered by some to be disappearing from the face of the earth. There were still more people dying than being born in London, but the city's population was, as ever, at least stabilised by immigrants from Glastonbury, Gascony, Ghana and further afield.

In the 210 years between the censuses of 1801 and 2011 Britain had changed more dramatically than in the 700 years between the Domesday Book and the birth of John Rickman. But Rickman would not have been entirely mystified or disturbed by the twenty-first-century nation. It was not all as diverse as the 'world city' of London. In 2011 the whole of the United Kingdom was still 87 per cent 'white'. At Rickman's family seat in Hampshire the county was still dominated by the white Britons who comprised 96 per cent of its population and by Tory politicians who represented all but one of its eighteen House of Commons constituencies. The transformation of Hampshire's agricultural landscape had first become apparent in Rickman's lifetime and may even have been predictable to the former editor of *The Commercial and Agricultural Magazine.*

With the exception of the Highlands of Scotland, by 2011 the United Kingdom had been for over 100 years a relatively well-populated archipelago. In 1901, when sparsely populated Ireland was still included, its density was an average of 420 people per square mile. In 2011 it was 662 people per square mile. That was not significantly more crowded than other European states and was less busy than some. The Netherlands in the twenty-first century had a population density of 1019 people per square mile, Belgium 941 people per square mile. Germany had 583 people per square mile; Italy 522. Such statistics, particularly when applied to England alone, were nonetheless deployed throughout the twentieth and twenty-first centuries to present an image of an overcrowded country with little or no room for new-comers. But outside Ireland, it had been achieved without a Malthusian catastrophe.

That would all have pleased John Rickman, whose chief measure of a nation's well-being and security was the size of its population. As he wrote in 1821, 'If a commensu-rate increase of Food and of Raiment can be produced by Agriculture and by Manufacture, an accession of Consumers in the home market cannot but be beneficial to all parties; and the Increase of Population in such case may be deemed equally desirable in itself, and conducive to National strength and National prosperity.'

In the bustling streets of London Rickman would not have been at all surprised to hear French, Hindustani, Mandarin and Italian, as well as smatterings of Welsh and the seductive drawl of Irish accents beneath the cries of cockney stallkeepers. He had after all surveyed a trading and seafaring nation whose navies alone employed 100,000 foreigners. He would have been pleased to learn that his country had, with the help of allies, played a central role in winning two further major wars against aggression on the European continent. Having himself reached the grand age of sixty-eight, Rickman might have been satisfied to note that in 2011 most British men and even more women could expect to spend a little longer even than his own full time on earth.

John Rickman's curiosity would have been piqued by such twenty-first-century occupations as cosmetic surgeon, nanotechnologist and wind turbine technician. But, coming as he did from early industrial Britain, he may not have been surprised to discover that in post-industrial Britain 81 per cent of the working population fell into the broad category of service industries. In 2011 those services included the entire wholesale and retail trade, transportation, professional, scientific and technical vocations, education at all levels, public employees, the arts and entertainment, banking, hotels and restaurants.

That was not too different from the 'retail, trade and handicraft' category which in Rickman's nation of shop-keepers included grocers, carriers, chemists, innkeepers and dyers of materials, and employed a clear majority of British workers during the early decline of the peasantry and before the rise and fall of coal and steel.

Among those employed in the 'services' in 2011 were the people responsible for taking the national census. By 2011 the census, which for the first time that year could be completed online, was taken in England and Wales by the Office for National Statistics in Cardiff, by the General Register Office for Scotland in Edinburgh and by the Northern Ireland Statistics and Research Agency in Belfast. The census forms in those different countries asked an average of fifty questions. They were designed to discover the address, place of birth, religion, marital status, ability to speak English and self-perceived national identity of a 27-year-old Welsh-speaking Sikh metalworker living in Swansea. So far from John Rickman's handful of early nineteenth-century clerks with quill pens in the Cockpit, the Office for National Statistics employed 3302 people. The cost of the 2011 census for England and Wales alone was £482 million.

For that among other reasons, the British government established the 'Beyond 2011' programme, which was directed to examine cheaper and more efficient alternatives to a decennial census. Following 'an extensive programme of research and a three-month public consultation', it recommended in 2014 that a census should again be conducted in 2021. 'The National Statistician,' wrote Sir Andrew Dilnot, chair of the UK Statistics Authority, to the Cabinet Office, 'has concluded that the demand for a decennial census remains strong and that there is general support for the next census being conducted predominantly online (with help and support being provided to individuals who may not be willing or able to respond in this way).'

Those reasons for retaining a 216-year-old institution reflected an essay written by John Rickman in 1796 and revised and published in 1800. 'Immediately subsequent to the conviction of the importance of population,' Rickman had proposed in one of the most influential sentences written in the English language, 'naturally occurs the question, What is that population?'

Bibliography

Aaronovitch, David, *Party Animals: My Family and Other Communists* (London, 2016)

Abbot, Charles, *The Diary and Correspondence of Charles Abbot, Lord Colchester, Speaker of the House of Commons, 1802–1817* (London, 1861)

Austen, Jane, *Northanger Abbey* (London, 1817)

Bailey, Sydney, 'Parliament and the Prying Proclivities of the Registrar-General', *History Today* (April 1981), Vol. 31, Issue 4

Census Reports for England, Wales, Scotland, Ireland and Northern Ireland (London, Edinburgh, Dublin and Belfast, 1801–2011)

Glass, D. V., *Numbering the People* (Hants, 1973)

Goldblatt, David, *The Game of Our Lives: The Meaning and Making of English Football* (London, 2014)

Hansard, the Report of all Parliamentary Debates (London, 1800–2016)

Higgs, Edward, 'Unemployment', Online Historical Population Reports (2007)

Horlock, Rob, *I Remember When I was Young, 1920s–1960s* (Indiana, 2003)

Lilienfeld, D. E., 'Celebration: William Farr (1807–1883) – An Appreciation on the 200th Anniversary of his

Birth', *International Journal of Epidemiology* (2007), Vol. 36, Issue 5: 985–987

Malthus, Thomas, *An Essay on the Principle of Population* (London, 1798)

Morrison, Iain, 'Two Norman Morrisons Emigrate', Hebridean Connections (2014)

Nissel, Muriel, *People Count: A History of the General Register Office* (London, 1987)

Pankhurst, Emmeline, *My Own Story* (London, 1914)

Ranelagh, John O'Beirne, *A Short History of Ireland* (Cambridge, 2012)

Rickman, W. C., *Biographical Memoir of John Rickman, Esq., F. R. S., &c. &c.* (London, 1841)

Rose, George, *Diaries and Correspondence*, edited by Rev. L. V. Harcourt (London, 1860)

Siraut, M. C., Thacker, A. T. and Williamson, E., *A History of the County of Somerset: Volume 9, Glastonbury and Street* (London, 2006)

Smith, Alexander, *A Summer in Skye* (Edinburgh, 1865)

Stephens, Meic, *Linguistic Minorities in Western Europe* (Ceredigion, 1976)

Thompson, Flora, *Lark Rise to Candleford* (Oxford, 1945)

Williams, Orlo, *Lamb's Friend the Census-taker; Life and Letters of John Rickman* (Boston and New York, 1912)

Wilson, James, *A Voyage Round the Coasts of Scotland and the Isles* (Edinburgh, 1842)

Index

32, 75, 84; loss/destruction of Irish returns, 32–3, 65, 84; online completion of, 325, 326; questions asked on, 35–6, 50–1, 60, 67–9, 84, 96–7, 99, 166, 220, 321, 325
National Front, 319
National Health Service, 312
national registration system, 304–6
Netherlands, 67, 162, 323
New York, 70, 211, 212, 321
New Zealand, 241, 242, 252, 256, 257
Newburn, Northumberland, 3–4
Newcastle upon Tyne, 3, 4, 16, 70, 124
Nightingale, Florence, 91, 98
Norse empire, 182–3, 246
North, George, 307, 308, 309, 322
Northcote, Lady Agnes, 227–8
Northcote, Sir Stafford, 228
Northern Ireland, 185, 289, 290–2, 300
Northern Ireland Statistics and Research Agency in Belfast, 325
Notting Hill riots (1958), 319
Nuneham Courtenay, Oxfordshire, 43, 87
Nuremberg, Bavaria, 11

occupations: dictionary of, 110–11; extensive variety of, 101–6, 107, 110–11, 123, 146; George Graham on, 106–7; of immigrants (1901 census), 233–4; of imperial population, 251–2; 'job security' concept, 293; less respectable professions, 111–15; most and least healthy, 97–8; and new technologies, 108–9, 153–4; nineteenth-century Glastonbury, 141; 'out of work' category, 292–6; question on census form, 36, 50–1, 68–9, 84; service industries, 324–5; sport, 123–8; on St Kilda, 79–80; trade, manufacture or handicraft, 4, 5, 36, 41, 42, 43, 50, 52, 68–71, 72–3, 101–6, 325
O'Connor, Thomas Power 'Tay Pay', 88
Office for National Statistics in Cardiff, 325
Office of Population Censuses and Surveys (OPCS), 120
oil industry, 264, 304

Old Testament, 9–10
Ordnance Survey, 84
Orkney, 80, 162, 183, 301
Orridge, Frances, 175
Osborne Palace, Isle of Wight, 60
Overseers of the Poor, 15, 17, 29, 30, 34, 61, 68

Paddington, 43
Pankhurst, Emmeline, 116–18, 119–20
parts (districts), 133
Patch, Harry, 279–80
Patterson, Florence, 280
Pauncefoot, Emma, 286–7
Peach, Ceri, 315, 316
Pearse, Patrick, 268, 284
pension, state, 293
Pentelow, Rosina Elizabeth, 115
Perceval, Spencer, assassination of (1812), 58–9
Peterloo Massacre (1819), 66
Phipps, Edmund, 83, 84–6, 91
Pitt the Younger, William, 23, 25–6, 27, 29, 282
Place, Francis, 14
place names, 41–2, 162, 169, 191
Poland, 214, 226, 231, 232, 289
Poole, Dorset, 12
Poor Law Committee, 56, 59, 66
population acts, 49, 50, 270–1
Porson, Richard, 2, 3
Portsmouth, 67, 70
Portugal, 6, 31, 248
Potter, Thomas, census bill (1753), 15–17, 34
Preston North End F.C., 127, 128
Price, Helen, 276–7
Price, Richard, 18–19, 21–2, 33, 39, 40, 41
prisons, 99, 100, 136
Privy Council, 32
prizefighters, 124–5
prolific couples/mothers, 54–6
prostitution, 111–14
Prussia, kingdom of, 11, 214
Punch, 135

Quebec, 254, 255
Quetelet, Adolphe, 33
Quick, Saddleworth Moor, 41–2